NE능률 영어교과서

대한민국 고등학생 **10**명 중

4.7 명이 보는 교과서

영어 고등 교과서 점유율 1위

(7차, 2007 개정, 2009 개정, 2015 개정)

리딩튜터

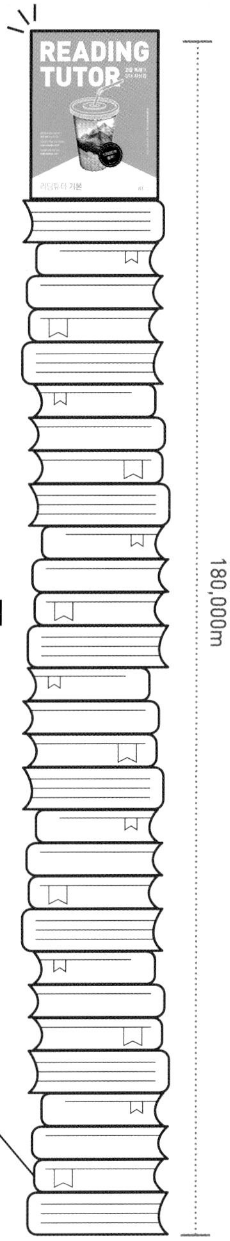

그동안 판매된
리딩튜터 1,800만 부
차곡차곡 쌓으면 18만 미터

에베레스트
20배 높이

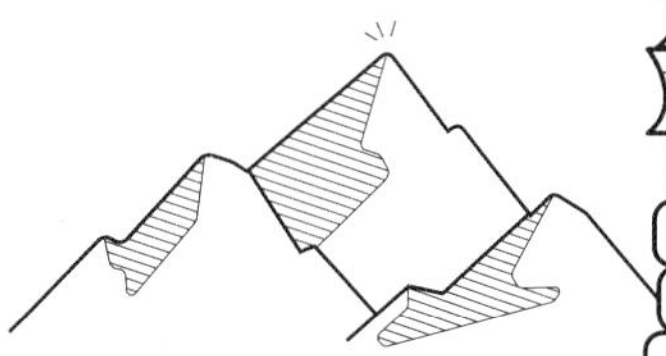

에베레스트 8,848m

능률보카

그동안 판매된
능률보카 1,000만 부

대한민국 박스오피스
천만명을 넘은 영화
단 27개

그래머존

그동안 판매된 400만 부의 그래머존을 비

1000km 서울-부

맞수 수능듣기 기본편

지은이	NE능률 영어교육연구소
선임연구원	전성호
연구원	선정아
영문교열	Olk Bryce Barrett, Nathaniel Galletta
디자인	송현아, 오솔길
맥편집	허문희
영업	한기영, 박인규, 이경구, 정철교, 김남준, 김남형, 이우현
마케팅	박혜선, 고유진, 남경진, 김상민

NE
NE능률이 미래를 그립니다.
교육에 대한 큰 꿈을 품고 시작한 NE능률
처음 품었던 그 꿈을 잊지 않고 40년이 넘는 시간 동안 한 길만을 걸어왔습니다.
이제 NE능률이 앞으로 나아가야 할 길을 그려봅니다.
'평범한 열 개의 제품보다 하나의 탁월한 제품'이라는
변치 않는 철학을 바탕으로 진정한 배움의 가치를 알리는
NE능률이 교육의 미래를 열어가겠습니다.

맞수

맞춤형 **수**능영어 단기특강 시리즈

수능듣기 기본편

STRUCTURE

❶ 유형 설명 및 해결 전략

각 유형에 대한 설명과 명쾌한 문제풀이 해법을 통해,
각 유형에 대해 정확히 파악할 수 있습니다.

❷ 기출 예제

각 유형별 해결 전략을 익힌 후, 이에 대한
기출 예제를 직접 풀어봄으로써, 문제 해결 감각을
기를 수 있습니다.

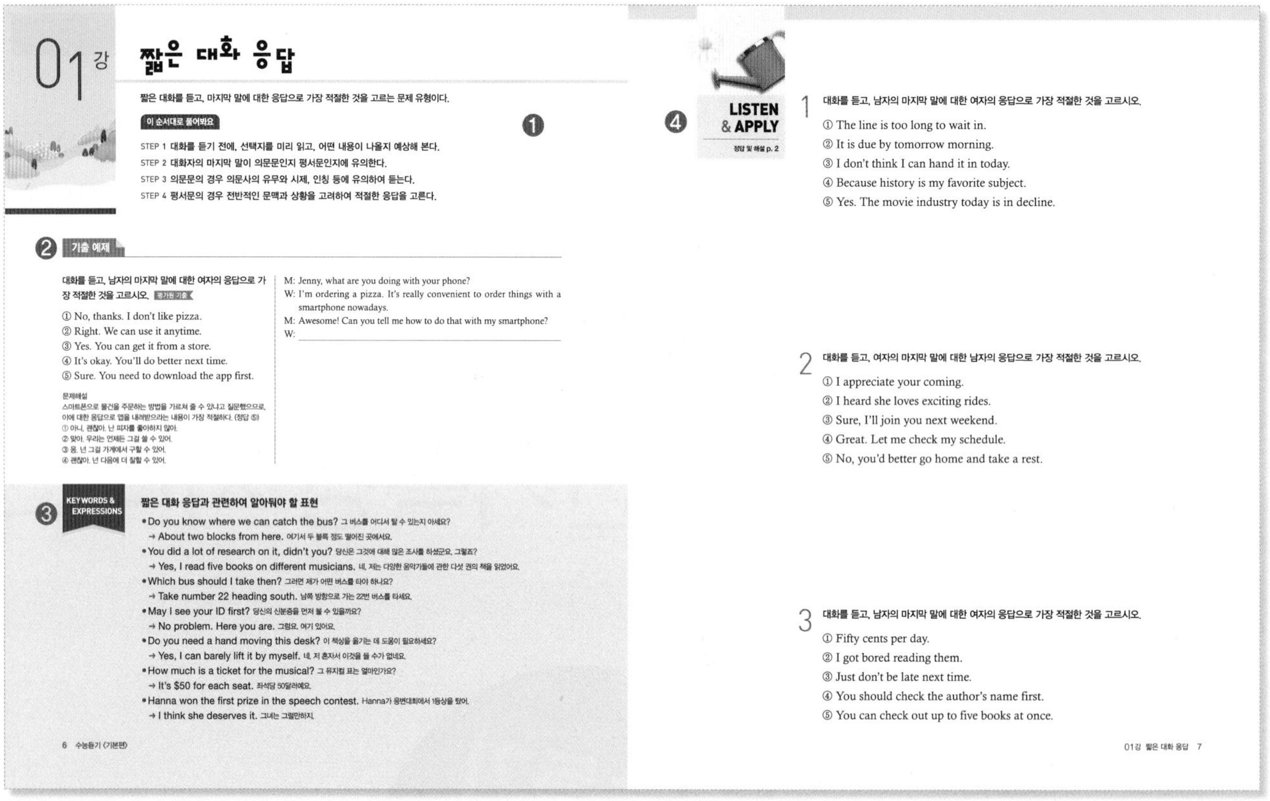

01강 짧은 대화 응답

짧은 대화를 듣고, 마지막 말에 대한 응답으로 가장 적절한 것을 고르는 문제 유형이다.

이 순서대로 풀어봐요 ❶

STEP 1 대화를 듣기 전에, 선택지를 미리 읽고, 어떤 내용이 나올지 예상해 본다.
STEP 2 대화자의 마지막 말이 의문문인지 평서문인지에 유의한다.
STEP 3 의문문의 경우 의문사의 유무와 시제, 인칭 등에 유의하여 듣는다.
STEP 4 평서문의 경우 전반적인 문맥과 상황을 고려하여 적절한 응답을 고른다.

❷ 기출 예제

대화를 듣고, 남자의 마지막 말에 대한 여자의 응답으로 가장 적절한 것을 고르시오. 평가원 기출

① No, thanks. I don't like pizza.
② Right. We can use it anytime.
③ Yes. You can get it from a store.
④ It's okay. You'll do better next time.
⑤ Sure. You need to download the app first.

문제해설
스마트폰으로 물건을 주문하는 방법을 가르쳐 줄 수 있냐고 질문했으므로, 이에 대한 응답으로 앱을 내려받으라는 내용이 가장 적절하다. (정답 ⑤)
① 아니, 괜찮아. 난 피자를 좋아하지 않아.
② 맞아. 우리는 언제든 그걸 쓸 수 있어.
③ 응. 넌 그걸 가게에서 구할 수 있어.
④ 괜찮아. 넌 다음에 더 잘할 수 있어.

M: Jenny, what are you doing with your phone?
W: I'm ordering a pizza. It's really convenient to order things with a smartphone nowadays.
M: Awesome! Can you tell me how to do that with my smartphone?
W: ______________________________

❸ KEYWORDS & EXPRESSIONS

짧은 대화 응답과 관련하여 알아둬야 할 표현

- Do you know where we can catch the bus? 그 버스를 어디서 탈 수 있는지 아세요?
  → About two blocks from here. 여기서 두 블록 정도 떨어진 곳에서요.
- You did a lot of research on it, didn't you? 당신은 그것에 대해 많은 조사를 하셨군요, 그렇죠?
  → Yes, I read five books on different musicians. 네, 저는 다양한 음악가들에 관한 다섯 권의 책을 읽었어요.
- Which bus should I take then? 그러면 제가 어떤 버스를 타야 하나요?
  → Take number 22 heading south. 남쪽 방향으로 가는 22번 버스를 타세요.
- May I see your ID first? 당신의 신분증을 먼저 볼 수 있을까요?
  → No problem. Here you are. 그럼요. 여기 있어요.
- Do you need a hand moving this desk? 이 책상을 옮기는 데 도움이 필요하세요?
  → Yes, I can barely lift it by myself. 네, 저 혼자서 이것을 들 수가 없네요.
- How much is a ticket for the musical? 그 뮤지컬 표는 얼마인가요?
  → It's $50 for each seat. 좌석당 50달러예요.
- Hanna won the first prize in the speech contest. Hanna가 웅변대회에서 1등상을 탔어.
  → I think she deserves it. 그녀는 그럴만하지.

6 수능듣기 〈기본편〉

❹ LISTEN & APPLY
정답 및 해설 p. 2

1 대화를 듣고, 남자의 마지막 말에 대한 여자의 응답으로 가장 적절한 것을 고르시오.
① The line is too long to wait in.
② It is due by tomorrow morning.
③ I don't think I can hand it in today.
④ Because history is my favorite subject.
⑤ Yes. The movie industry today is in decline.

2 대화를 듣고, 여자의 마지막 말에 대한 남자의 응답으로 가장 적절한 것을 고르시오.
① I appreciate your coming.
② I heard she loves exciting rides.
③ Sure, I'll join you next weekend.
④ Great. Let me check my schedule.
⑤ No, you'd better go home and take a rest.

3 대화를 듣고, 남자의 마지막 말에 대한 여자의 응답으로 가장 적절한 것을 고르시오.
① Fifty cents per day.
② I got bored reading them.
③ Just don't be late next time.
④ You should check the author's name first.
⑤ You can check out up to five books at once.

01강 짧은 대화 응답 7

❸ 주요 기출 어휘 및 표현

유형별로 정리된 주요 기출 어휘 및 표현을 익힌 후,
문제 해결에 있어 단서가 되는 어휘와 표현을 충분히
활용할 수 있습니다.

❹ LISTEN & APPLY

각 유형별 학습 전략을 실전 문제에 적용하여
실전 감각을 기를 수 있습니다.

NE Waffle

MP3 바로 듣기, 모바일 단어장 등 NE능률이 제공하는 부가자료를 빠르게 이용할 수 있는 통합 서비스입니다. 표지에 있는 QR코드를 스캔하여 한 번에 빠르게 필요한 자료를 이용하실 수 있습니다.

NE Waffle

MP3 & 단어장

❺

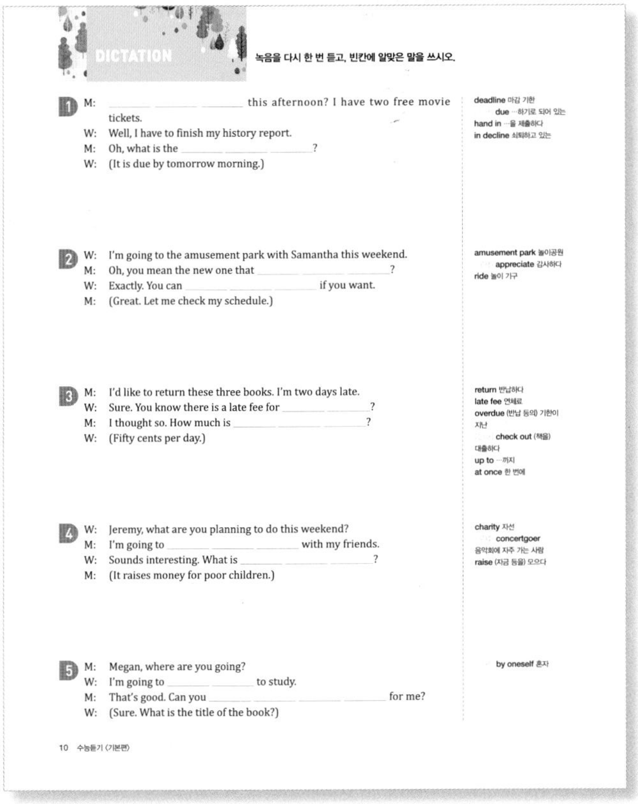

DICTATION 녹음을 다시 한 번 듣고, 빈칸에 알맞은 말을 쓰시오.

1
M: ______ ______ ______ this afternoon? I have two free movie tickets.
W: Well, I have to finish my history report.
M: Oh, what is the ______ ______ ______?
W: (It is due by tomorrow morning.)

deadline 마감 기한 / due …하기로 되어 있는 / hand in …을 제출하다 / in decline 쇠퇴하고 있는

2
W: I'm going to the amusement park with Samantha this weekend.
M: Oh, you mean the new one that ______ ______ ______?
W: Exactly. You can ______ ______ ______ if you want.
M: (Great. Let me check my schedule.)

amusement park 놀이공원 / appreciate 감사하다 / ride 놀이 기구

3
M: I'd like to return these three books. I'm two days late.
W: Sure. You know there is a late fee for ______ ______?
M: I thought so. How much is ______ ______ ______?
W: (Fifty cents per day.)

return 반납하다 / late fee 연체료 / overdue (반납 등의) 기한이 지난 / check out (책을) 대출하다 / up to …까지 / at once 한 번에

4
W: Jeremy, what are you planning to do this weekend?
M: I'm going to ______ ______ ______ with my friends.
W: Sounds interesting. What is ______ ______ ______?
M: (It raises money for poor children.)

charity 자선 / concertgoer 음악회에 자주 가는 사람 / raise (자금 등을) 모으다

5
M: Megan, where are you going?
W: I'm going to ______ ______ to study.
M: That's good. Can you ______ ______ ______ ______ for me?
W: (Sure. What is the title of the book?)

by oneself 혼자

10 수능듣기 〈기본편〉

❻

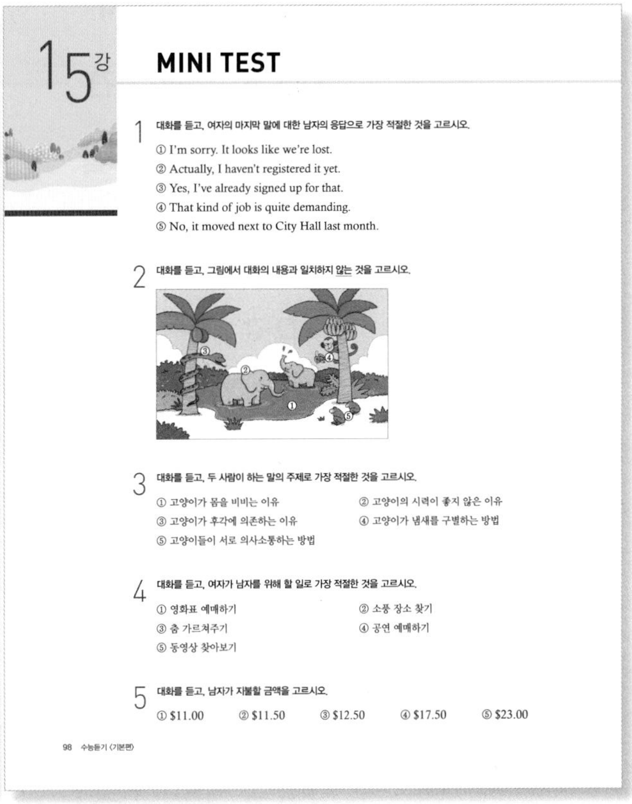

15강 MINI TEST

1 대화를 듣고, 여자의 마지막 말에 대한 남자의 응답으로 가장 적절한 것을 고르시오.
① I'm sorry. It looks like we're lost.
② Actually, I haven't registered it yet.
③ Yes, I've already signed up for that.
④ That kind of job is quite demanding.
⑤ No, it moved next to City Hall last month.

2 대화를 듣고, 그림에서 대화의 내용과 일치하지 않는 것을 고르시오.

3 대화를 듣고, 두 사람이 하는 말의 주제로 가장 적절한 것을 고르시오.
① 고양이가 몸을 비비는 이유 ② 고양이의 시력이 좋지 않은 이유
③ 고양이가 후각에 의존하는 이유 ④ 고양이가 냄새를 구별하는 방법
⑤ 고양이들이 서로 의사소통하는 방법

4 대화를 듣고, 여자가 남자를 위해 할 일로 가장 적절한 것을 고르시오.
① 영화표 예매하기 ② 소풍 장소 찾기
③ 춤 가르쳐주기 ④ 공연 예매하기
⑤ 동영상 찾아보기

5 대화를 듣고, 남자가 지불할 금액을 고르시오.
① $11.00 ② $11.50 ③ $12.50 ④ $17.50 ⑤ $23.00

98 수능듣기 〈기본편〉

❺ DICTATION (듣기 집중 훈련)

앞에서 풀어본 문제들을 다시 한 번 들어보면서 핵심 어휘와 주요 표현을 익힐 수 있습니다.

❻ MINI TEST

총 2회의 MINI TEST를 통해 14강에 걸쳐 학습한 내용을 최종적으로 점검해 볼 수 있습니다.

CONTENTS

CHAPTER
01

CHAPTER
02

CHAPTER **01**

유형 학습

01강 짧은 대화 응답

짧은 대화를 듣고, 마지막 말에 대한 응답으로 가장 적절한 것을 고르는 문제 유형이다.

이 순서대로 풀어봐요

STEP 1 대화를 듣기 전에, 선택지를 미리 읽고, 어떤 내용이 나올지 예상해 본다.
STEP 2 대화자의 마지막 말이 의문문인지 평서문인지에 유의한다.
STEP 3 의문문의 경우 의문사의 유무와 시제, 인칭 등에 유의하여 듣는다.
STEP 4 평서문의 경우 전반적인 문맥과 상황을 고려하여 적절한 응답을 고른다.

기출 예제

대화를 듣고, 남자의 마지막 말에 대한 여자의 응답으로 가장 적절한 것을 고르시오. 평가원 기출

① No, thanks. I don't like pizza.
② Right. We can use it anytime.
③ Yes. You can get it from a store.
④ It's okay. You'll do better next time.
⑤ Sure. You need to download the app first.

문제해설
스마트폰으로 물건을 주문하는 방법을 가르쳐 줄 수 있냐고 질문했으므로, 이에 대한 응답으로 앱을 내려받으라는 내용이 가장 적절하다. (정답 ⑤)
① 아니, 괜찮아. 난 피자를 좋아하지 않아.
② 맞아. 우리는 언제든 그걸 쓸 수 있어.
③ 응. 넌 그걸 가게에서 구할 수 있어.
④ 괜찮아. 넌 다음에 더 잘할 수 있어.

M: Jenny, what are you doing with your phone?
W: I'm ordering a pizza. It's really convenient to order things with a smartphone nowadays.
M: Awesome! Can you tell me how to do that with my smartphone?
W: ____________________

KEYWORDS & EXPRESSIONS

짧은 대화 응답과 관련하여 알아둬야 할 표현

- Do you know where we can catch the bus? 그 버스를 어디서 탈 수 있는지 아세요?
  → About two blocks from here. 여기서 두 블록 정도 떨어진 곳에서요.
- You did a lot of research on it, didn't you? 당신은 그것에 대해 많은 조사를 하셨군요, 그렇죠?
  → Yes, I read five books on different musicians. 네, 저는 다양한 음악가들에 관한 다섯 권의 책을 읽었어요.
- Which bus should I take then? 그러면 제가 어떤 버스를 타야 하나요?
  → Take number 22 heading south. 남쪽 방향으로 가는 22번 버스를 타세요.
- May I see your ID first? 당신의 신분증을 먼저 볼 수 있을까요?
  → No problem. Here you are. 그럼요. 여기 있어요.
- Do you need a hand moving this desk? 이 책상을 옮기는 데 도움이 필요하세요?
  → Yes, I can barely lift it by myself. 네, 저 혼자서 이것을 들 수가 없네요.
- How much is a ticket for the musical? 그 뮤지컬 표는 얼마인가요?
  → It's $50 for each seat. 좌석당 50달러예요.
- Hanna won the first prize in the speech contest. Hanna가 웅변대회에서 1등상을 탔어.
  → I think she deserves it. 그녀는 그럴만하지.

LISTEN & APPLY

정답 및 해설 p. 2

1 대화를 듣고, 남자의 마지막 말에 대한 여자의 응답으로 가장 적절한 것을 고르시오.

① The line is too long to wait in.
② It is due by tomorrow morning.
③ I don't think I can hand it in today.
④ Because history is my favorite subject.
⑤ Yes. The movie industry today is in decline.

2 대화를 듣고, 여자의 마지막 말에 대한 남자의 응답으로 가장 적절한 것을 고르시오.

① I appreciate your coming.
② I heard she loves exciting rides.
③ Sure, I'll join you next weekend.
④ Great. Let me check my schedule.
⑤ No, you'd better go home and take a rest.

3 대화를 듣고, 남자의 마지막 말에 대한 여자의 응답으로 가장 적절한 것을 고르시오.

① Fifty cents per day.
② I got bored reading them.
③ Just don't be late next time.
④ You should check the author's name first.
⑤ You can check out up to five books at once.

4 대화를 듣고, 여자의 마지막 말에 대한 남자의 응답으로 가장 적절한 것을 고르시오.

① Because I am a concertgoer.
② It raises money for poor children.
③ There will be K-pop stars performing.
④ Tickets are only $30 if you order them online.
⑤ To help my friends prepare for a school concert.

5 대화를 듣고, 남자의 마지막 말에 대한 여자의 응답으로 가장 적절한 것을 고르시오.

① I prefer to study by myself.
② Yes, I'd love to come with you.
③ Sure. What is the title of the book?
④ I'm sorry, but I don't have the book.
⑤ Do you want me to buy some books?

6 대화를 듣고, 여자의 마지막 말에 대한 남자의 응답으로 가장 적절한 것을 고르시오.

① No, thank you. I'm not thirsty.
② Sorry, but I don't have any coins.
③ You had better get it fixed right now.
④ You are not allowed to bring drinks in the hall.
⑤ You don't need to. There's another machine in the lobby.

7 대화를 듣고, 남자의 마지막 말에 대한 여자의 응답으로 가장 적절한 것을 고르시오.

① It is too hot in here.

② The rental deposit went up.

③ I'm sorry if I made you upset.

④ The color of the wall is too dark.

⑤ Because I don't want to miss the chance.

8 대화를 듣고, 여자의 마지막 말에 대한 남자의 응답으로 가장 적절한 것을 고르시오.

① There used to be a temple here.

② Right. It was a good experience for me.

③ How did you know about that program?

④ Maybe I can tell you about traditional Korean culture.

⑤ How about finding more information on the Internet?

9 대화를 듣고, 남자의 마지막 말에 대한 여자의 응답으로 가장 적절한 것을 고르시오.

① I'm sorry. I didn't make it.

② Tickets are already sold out.

③ Yes. We will be finished by 7:30.

④ Of course. We have plenty of time.

⑤ Sure. Maybe there will be another place nearby.

DICTATION 녹음을 다시 한 번 듣고, 빈칸에 알맞은 말을 쓰시오.

1
M: ________ ________ ________ this afternoon? I have two free movie tickets.
W: Well, I have to finish my history report.
M: Oh, what is the ________ ________ ________?
W: (It is due by tomorrow morning.)

deadline 마감 기한
| 문제 | due …하기로 되어 있는
hand in …을 제출하다
in decline 쇠퇴하고 있는

2
W: I'm going to the amusement park with Samantha this weekend.
M: Oh, you mean the new one that ________ ________ ________?
W: Exactly. You can ________ ________ ________ if you want.
M: (Great. Let me check my schedule.)

amusement park 놀이공원
| 문제 | appreciate 감사하다
ride 놀이 기구

3
M: I'd like to return these three books. I'm two days late.
W: Sure, Did you know there is a late fee for ________ ________?
M: Yes, I did. How much is ________ ________ ________?
W: (Fifty cents per day.)

return 반납하다
late fee 연체료
overdue (반납 등의) 기한이 지난
| 문제 | check out (책을) 대출하다
up to …까지
at once 한 번에

4
W: Jeremy, what are you planning to do this weekend?
M: I'm going to ________ ________ ________ with my friends.
W: Sounds interesting. What is ________ ________ ________?
M: (It raises money for poor children.)

charity 자선
| 문제 | concertgoer 음악회에 자주 가는 사람
raise (자금 등을) 모으다

5
M: Megan, where are you going?
W: I'm going to ________ ________ to study.
M: That's good. Can you ________ ________ ________ ________ for me?
W: (Sure. What is the title of the book?)

| 문제 | by oneself 혼자

6
W: Hey, do you know where ________ ________ ________ is?
M: It's at the end of the hall. But it's broken now.
W: Oh, no. Then ________ ________ ________ ________ the convenience store.
M: (You don't need to. There's another machine in the lobby.)

vending machine 자판기
convenience store 편의점
[문제] be allowed to-v …하는 것이 허용되다

7
M: How do you like our new apartment?
W: It looks ________ ________ ________, except for the living room.
M: What is wrong with it?
W: (The color of the wall is too dark.)

cozy 아늑한
[문제] deposit 보증금

8
W: ________ ________ ________ ________ something nice I can do with my friend from Canada?
M: I heard temple stay programs are ________ ________ ________.
W: That sounds great! But I don't know much about them.
M: (How about finding more information on the Internet?)

temple stay 템플 스테이(사찰 체험)
foreigner 외국인
[문제] traditional 전통적인

9
M: Look at this traffic! It's really bad.
W: ________ ________. Our movie starts in one hour.
M: Do you think we can ________ ________?
W: (Of course. We have plenty of time.)

traffic 교통량
make it 시간 맞춰 가다
[문제] sold out 표가 매진된
plenty of 많은
nearby 근처에

02강 그림 일치

대화를 듣고, 그림에서 대화의 내용과 일치하지 않는 것을 고르는 문제 유형이다.

이 순서대로 풀어봐요

STEP 1 대화를 듣기 전에, 그림에 나타난 사물의 특징 혹은 위치와 관련된 표현을 미리 생각해 본다.

STEP 2 그림에 나타난 사물의 번호 순서대로 대화가 진행되므로, 순서에 유의하여 대화를 듣는다.

STEP 3 주어진 사물과 연관된 내용을 집중하여 듣고, 대화의 내용과 다른 것을 고른다.

기출 예제

대화를 듣고, 그림에서 대화의 내용과 일치하지 않는 것을 고르시오. 수능 기출

문제해설

남자는 선물 상자가 두 개 있다고 했다. (정답 ④)

M: Hello, Ms. Miller. I'm Joshua's father.

W: Hi, Mr. Smith. Thanks for coming to our parent-teacher meeting.

M: It's nice to meet you. This room looks great. Wow! Look at the wall.

W: You know, Joshua loves the elephant between the lion and the panda.

M: Does he like the mobile hanging from the ceiling, too?

W: He does. The children made it together.

M: They did a wonderful job. That toy dinosaur next to the bookshelf looks good.

W: Oh, I put it there because the children have been learning about dinosaurs.

M: That sounds fun. There are two boxes under the Christmas tree. What are they for?

W: They're presents for the class. We've got some candies for the kids.

M: Aha. The Christmas tree is decorated so nicely. The star on top of the tree looks very pretty.

W: Thanks. The meeting will start soon. Let's go upstairs, Mr. Smith.

KEYWORDS & EXPRESSIONS

그림 일치와 관련하여 알아둬야 할 어휘와 표현

- **위치:** next to …의 옆에, in front of …의 앞에, across from …의 맞은편에, on the opposite side of …의 반대편에, in the middle of …의 가운데에, on top of …의 꼭대기에, between A and B A와 B 사이에
- **모양:** wide 폭이 넓은, narrow 폭이 좁은, round 둥근, square 정사각형(의), rectangular 직사각형의, oval 타원형(의), triangular 삼각형의, -shaped …모양의
- **무늬:** plain 무늬가 없는, striped 줄무늬의, checked / checkered 체크무늬의, plaid 격자[체크]무늬의, wavy 물결무늬의, polka-dotted 물방울무늬의, flower-patterned / floral 꽃무늬의
- **크기:** small 작은, big 큰, tiny 조그마한, huge 거대한
- I like the round frame with the flowers on the top. 저는 위에 꽃이 달린 둥근 액자가 좋아요.
- You must put the three small paintings on the wall. 당신은 세 개의 작은 그림을 벽에 걸어야 해요.
- Do you see the round mirror on the wall? 벽에 둥근 거울이 보이나요?
- I think the striped mat on the grass is too big. 잔디 위의 줄무늬 매트가 너무 큰 것 같아요.

LISTEN & APPLY

정답 및 해설 p. 3

1 대화를 듣고, 그림에서 대화의 내용과 일치하지 않는 것을 고르시오.

2 대화를 듣고, 그림에서 대화의 내용과 일치하지 않는 것을 고르시오.

3 대화를 듣고, 그림에서 대화의 내용과 일치하지 않는 것을 고르시오.

4 대화를 듣고, 그림에서 대화의 내용과 일치하지 않는 것을 고르시오.

5 대화를 듣고, 그림에서 대화의 내용과 일치하지 않는 것을 고르시오.

6 대화를 듣고, 그림에서 대화의 내용과 일치하지 않는 것을 고르시오.

7 대화를 듣고, 그림에서 대화의 내용과 일치하지 않는 것을 고르시오.

8 대화를 듣고, 그림에서 대화의 내용과 일치하지 않는 것을 고르시오.

DICTATION

녹음을 다시 한 번 듣고, 빈칸에 알맞은 말을 쓰시오.

1

W: How are the preparations for Peter Smith's book signing event going?
M: Oh, don't worry about it. I already finished all of the preparations.
W: Did you? Have you set out _________ _________ _________?
M: Yes, I put it in the front of the event hall.
W: Good. And did you put a flower arrangement on it? That will look nice.
M: Of course. And I placed some copies of his books on the desk, too. They _________ _________ _________ on it.
W: Oh, great. How about the chair?
M: I put a comfortable one behind the desk.
W: Perfect. Lastly, _________ _________ _________ some kind of banner on the wall?
M: Yes! I got one that says, "A Book Signing by Peter Smith."
W: Wow! Good job!

preparation 준비
set out …을 정리하다[진열하다]
flower arrangement 꽃꽂이
stack up …을 쌓다
comfortable 편안한
hang 걸다
banner 현수막

2

M: I think everything is almost ready for our garage sale.
W: Good. By the way, what is that on the garage door?
M: You mean the banner? I _________ _________ _________ and put it up this morning.
W: Oh, good.
M: And I put the table on the right side of the driveway.
W: I can see it. You made a price sign, too.
M: Right. All the clothes and hats on the table are $5 each.
W: What's on the left side of the driveway?
M: There's a box of books. I put some balloons on the box to _________ _________ _________.
W: That should work. Where did you get those old lamps _________ _________ _________ the books?
M: They belong to our neighbor, Mr. Fields. He asked me to sell them for him.
W: Oh, I see.

garage sale 중고 물품 세일
put up (간판 등을) 내걸다
driveway (도로에서 차고까지의) 진입로
attention 관심, 주의

3
W: Hi, Chris! Did you decorate your living room for Christmas?
M: Yes. I spent the whole weekend doing it. Do you want to see a photo of it?
W: Sure. [*Pause*] Wow, this is exactly how I want my house ________ ________ ________ for Christmas. Oh, you put the Christmas tree beside the fireplace.
M: Yes. It creates a cozy atmosphere, doesn't it?
W: It does! And you added ________ ________ ________ by putting this star-shaped decoration on top of the tree.
M: Yes, that's right. And my family and I just love enjoying the Christmas decorations while we rest on the couch next to the fireplace.
W: That sounds perfect. Oh, and these Christmas stockings ________ ________ the fireplace bring back my own childhood memories of Christmas. By the way, what is in these gift boxes?
M: Oh, there is chocolate in them. I put them on the table because the chocolate could melt if it were under the tree.
W: That's a good idea. The fireplace is quite close to the tree.

decorate 장식하다
fireplace 벽난로
atmosphere 분위기
finishing touch 마무리
decoration 장식, 장식품
couch 긴 의자, 소파
stocking 스타킹; *크리스마스 양말
bring back …을 기억나게 하다
melt 녹다

4
W: We finished redecorating the classroom, Mr. Kwon. What do you think?
M: It looks good. Oh! You put the round clock ________ ________ ________.
W: Yes, it's easier to see there. And look where we put the bulletin board.
M: You moved it to the left side of the wall, between the blackboard and the window.
W: That's right. And now the class schedule is ________ ________ ________ ________ of the blackboard.
M: I see. Good job!
W: We also opened the curtains to make the room brighter.
M: Good idea. But what happened to the fishbowl under the window?
W: It was ________ ________. We moved it and put a plant there instead.
M: Great. Everything is perfect. I can't wait until your classmates see it.

blackboard 칠판
bulletin board 게시판
fishbowl 어항
fragile 부서지기 쉬운

5

M: Look! I found a photo from our camping trip last summer.

W: Neat! I don't think I've seen that picture. Is that our tent on the left?

M: Yes, ________ ________ ________ is ours. Setting it up in the rain was tough.

W: I know! And if the rain hadn't stopped, that stream on the right might have flooded.

M: We couldn't have started that campfire either.

W: Look at all the wood ________ ________ ________. I can't believe how much we gathered.

M: Yeah, we didn't need it all. But I used some of it for cooking on that barbecue grill between the tent and the wood.

W: That's right. Oh, do you see those camping chairs in front of the tent? They were comfortable.

M: Right. Those were ________ ________ ________.

W: I want to go camping again.

neat 단정한; *훌륭한
set up …을 세우다[설치하다]
stream 개울
flood 범람하다
campfire 모닥불
gather 모으다
barbecue grill 바비큐용 그릴

6

W: Alan, did you decorate the classroom for Sujin's birthday?

M: Yes, everything is ready. It looks really good.

W: Did you hang the birthday banner I made?

M: Yes, it's ________ ________ ________ above the table.

W: How about flowers? You know Sujin loves flowers.

M: I didn't get any. But I put two flower-shaped balloons on the wall, to the right of the banner.

W: Oh, that's a cute idea. Where's the cake we bought?

M: It's on the table. And I ________ ________ ________ and put it under the table.

W: Great! We should get a camera so we can take pictures!

M: Don't worry. I ________ ________ and set it up on a tripod.

W: You thought of everything! This is going to be a great party!

wrap 포장하다, 싸다
tripod 삼각대

7
W: Hi, Billy! What are you doing?
M: Oh, Jenny! I was just looking at a picture of my home. I think ________ ________ ________.
W: I'm not surprised. You haven't been home for almost a year. Can I see the picture?
M: Sure. Here it is.
W: Oh, it's a two-story house. How gorgeous!
M: Thanks. It has ________ ________ ________.
W: I remember you told me that you like the view from those windows.
M: Right. Actually, I miss relaxing in the shade of this big tree the most. I planted it myself when I was young.
W: I see. Oh, there's a big square swimming pool in the yard!
M: Yeah. I ________ ________ ________ there with my brother. I also liked to lie on a chair under the umbrella.
W: I can imagine. Don't be so sad. You can go home this vacation.
M: I hope so.

homesick 향수병을 앓는
gorgeous 아주 멋진
shade 그늘
plant 심다
yard 마당

8
M: Have you finished the poster for our school's ________ ________?
W: Yes, I have. Here it is. What do you think?
M: I like it! The white background makes it easy to notice.
W: Thanks. And I wrote "RECYCLE" in big capital letters at the top.
M: The drawing in the middle is quite good. What is it?
W: It's the earth being held by ________ ________ ________ hands.
M: And there is one big tree growing in the center of the earth.
W: That's right. I also drew two clouds above the earth.
M: They look nice. But what does it say ________ ________ ________ ________ the poster?
W: "The World Is in Your Hands." It's the slogan of the campaign.

recycling campaign 재활용 캠페인
capital (나라의) 수도; *대문자
slogan 구호, 슬로건

03강

주제 · 의견

담화나 대화를 듣고, 화자가 말하고자 하는 주제나 의견 등을 파악하는 문제 유형이다.

이 순서대로 풀어봐요

STEP 1 **담화나 대화를 듣기 전에, 선택지를 미리 읽고 무엇에 관한 내용일지 예측해 본다.**
STEP 2 **특정한 세부 사항이 아닌 전반적인 내용을 통해 화자가 말하고자 하는 바를 추론한다.**
STEP 3 **정답을 고를 때는 너무 포괄적이거나 매우 지엽적인 선택지는 고르지 않도록 유의한다.**

기출 예제

대화를 듣고, 여자의 의견으로 가장 적절한 것을 고르시오.

교육청 기출

① 논리학은 일상생활과 밀접한 관계가 있다.
② 토론 활동은 논리적 사고력을 신장시킨다.
③ 모둠 활동을 통해 협동심을 기를 수 있다.
④ 토론 시 상대의 의견을 존중하는 것이 중요하다.
⑤ 강좌 선택 시 자신의 흥미와 수준을 고려해야 한다.

문제해설
토론의 장점을 말하며, 토론이 논리적 사고를 향상시키는 데 도움이 된다고 직접적으로 언급하고 있다. (정답 ②)

W: John, how are you doing in Mr. Anderson's social studies class?
M: Well, he said there will be many debates. I'm already stressed.
W: When I was in his class, I felt the same way, but I'm sure you'll find them very helpful.
M: In what way can debating be helpful?
W: Participating in debates will help improve your logical thinking.
M: I don't see how.
W: Debating teaches you to organize ideas logically to make your argument stronger.
M: I understand, but it still sounds difficult.
W: With more experience, you'll get better at it.
M: I see. I'll give it a try.

KEYWORDS & EXPRESSIONS

주제 · 의견과 관련하여 알아둬야 할 어휘와 표현

- **건강:** nonsmoking area 금연 구역, secondhand smoke 간접흡연, heart attack 심장마비, regular exercise 규칙적인 운동, medical checkup 건강 검진, diet 식이요법, vegetarian 채식주의자, fit 건강한
- **환경:** acid rain 산성비, air pollution 대기오염, contamination 오염, pollutant 오염물질, atmosphere 대기, greenhouse effect 온실 효과, public transportation 대중교통, endangered 멸종 위기의, recycle 재활용하다, conserve 보존하다
- **기아:** starvation 기아, famine 기근, international aid 국제적 지원, public opinion 여론, relief fund 구제 기금
- **기술:** technology 과학 기술, advance 진보, telecommunication 원거리 통신, automatic system 자동화 시스템, technical 기술의, wireless 무선의
- **구인:** qualification 자격, post / position 지위, confidence 자신(감), competent 유능한, require 요구하다, apply for …에 지원하다

- I think it should … . 저는 …해야 한다고 생각합니다.
- I want to remind … that ~ . …에게 ~을 상기시키고 싶습니다.
- The bottom line is … . 결론은 …입니다.
- What I'm trying to say is … . 제가 말하고자 하는 것은 …입니다.
- I firmly believe that … . 저는 …라고 굳게 믿습니다.
- In my opinion, you need to … . 제 의견으로는, 여러분은 …해야 합니다.
- I'm here today to ask for … . 저는 오늘 …을 요청하기 위해 이 자리에 나왔습니다.
- Please show your support by … . …함으로써 여러분의 성원을 보여 주십시오.

LISTEN & APPLY

정답 및 해설 p. 5

1 대화를 듣고, 두 사람이 하는 말의 주제로 가장 적절한 것을 고르시오.

① 좋은 일자리를 구하는 방법
② 단체 생활 시 규칙의 필요성
③ 룸메이트와의 갈등 해결 방법
④ 쾌적한 주거 환경을 유지하는 법
⑤ 친구 사이에서 솔직함의 중요성

2 대화를 듣고, 두 사람이 하는 말의 주제로 가장 적절한 것을 고르시오.

① 준비 운동의 필요성
② 과도한 운동의 위험성
③ 규칙적인 운동의 중요성
④ 효과적인 근력 운동 방법
⑤ 근육통을 완화시키는 방법

3 대화를 듣고, 두 사람이 하는 말의 주제로 가장 적절한 것을 고르시오.

① 온라인 쇼핑의 장단점
② 파워 블로거가 되는 방법
③ 휴대전화 구매 시 주의할 점
④ 인터넷 정보 맹신에 대한 경계
⑤ 기업들의 이색적인 온라인 홍보

4 대화를 듣고, 남자의 의견으로 가장 적절한 것을 고르시오.

① 야구 경기를 보는 것은 지루하다.
② 야구 경기는 혼자 보는 것이 낫다.
③ 야구 경기는 TV로 보는 것이 더 좋다.
④ 야구 경기장의 소음을 줄이는 방법을 고안해야 한다.
⑤ 야구 경기 중계는 스포츠 전문 아나운서들이 해야 한다.

5 대화를 듣고, 남자의 의견으로 가장 적절한 것을 고르시오.

① 트럭은 과적해선 안 된다.
② 트럭으로 벽돌을 나르면 안 된다.
③ 대부분의 사고는 과속으로 인한 것이다.
④ 최근 교통 체증이 더욱 심각해지고 있다.
⑤ 운전자들은 트럭을 지나칠 때 조심해야 한다.

6 다음을 듣고, 여자가 하는 말의 주제로 가장 적절한 것을 고르시오.

① 집을 장식하는 방법
② 사람들의 다양한 취미
③ 고가구 재활용의 중요성
④ 골동품을 구매하는 다양한 이유
⑤ 골동품을 저렴하게 구입할 수 있는 장소

7 대화를 듣고, 여자의 의견으로 가장 적절한 것을 고르시오.

① 그룹을 지어 공부하는 것이 최선의 학습 방법이다.
② 어휘를 암기하는 것은 잘못된 학습 방법이다.
③ 각자에게 맞는 공부 방법을 개발해야 한다.
④ 대부분의 사람들은 암기한 것을 금방 잊어버린다.
⑤ 매일 단어 몇 개씩 학습하는 것이 효과적이다.

8 다음을 듣고, 남자가 하는 말의 주제로 가장 적절한 것을 고르시오.

① 코르크의 다양한 용도
② 인공 코르크의 장단점
③ 플라스틱병의 유용성
④ 인공 코르크를 사용하는 이유
⑤ 품질 좋은 코르크를 고르는 방법

DICTATION

녹음을 다시 한 번 듣고, 빈칸에 알맞은 말을 쓰시오.

정답 및 해설 p. 7

1

[*Telephone rings.*]

M: Hello?
W: Hi, dad. It's Liz.
M: Hi, Liz. How's everything going?
W: Well, I wanted to ________ ________ ________ about something.
M: Is there a problem at your job?
W: It's not that. Actually, I'm not getting along well with my roommate.
M: I'm sorry to hear that. Have you been arguing with her?
W: Not exactly. She just doesn't help keep the apartment clean.
M: Oh, why don't you ________ ________ ________?
W: I did, but she still doesn't do them.
M: Then have you told her that she should ________ ________ ________?
W: No. I don't want to argue with her.
M: But she won't change her behavior if you don't talk to her.
W: I guess you're right. I will talk to her today.

get along with …와 잘 지내다
argue with …와 다투다
assign 할당하다, 배정하다
chore 가사, 일
considerate 사려 깊은
behavior 행동

2

W: Hi! You must be a new member here at Global Fitness.
M: That's right. How did you know?
W: I'm a trainer, so I know most of the members.
M: Oh, great! I want to ask you something. Actually, I ________ ________ ________ ________ for three hours. But I'm really sore after exercising.
W: Every day for three hours? Exercising too much can be dangerous.
M: I thought exercise was supposed to be painful.
W: That's not true. Excessive exercise can seriously ________ ________ ________.
M: Really?
W: Yes. You can easily hurt your spine or damage your joints.
M: Wow. I didn't know that.
W: And it can even cause muscle damage.
M: Thanks for letting me know. Can you give me some tips on ________ ________ ________ ________?
W: Sure. Please come this way.

work out 운동하다
sore 아픈
be supposed to-v …하기로 되어 있다
excessive 과도한
harm 해치다, 손상시키다
spine 척추
joint 관절
muscle 근육
effectively 효과적으로

3

M: What are you looking at?
W: I'm checking out some new cell phone models online.
M: Oh, are you planning on buying a new one?
W: Yes. This one looks pretty good.

review 비평, 제품 후기
post 올리다, 게시하다
positive 긍정적인
try out …을 테스트해 보다

M: I was just looking at the same one. It got excellent reviews.
W: Yes, but you can never be sure about reviews posted online.
M: What do you mean?
W: You have to ________ ________ ________ ________ on the Internet. Lots of companies these days are paying bloggers to post positive reviews.
M: Do you think so?
W: Yes. I heard on the news that it's becoming a big problem.
M: Then I guess we shouldn't always believe what we read on the Internet.
W: That's right. I'm going to ________ ________ ________ ________ at the store before I buy it.

4
W: Hi, Ted. Do you have any plans tomorrow?
M: Not yet. Why?
W: Rachel and I are going to the baseball game. ________ ________ ________ you'd like to join us.
M: Thanks, but I don't like going to the baseball stadium.
W: Oh, you don't like baseball? I didn't know that.
M: It's not that I don't like baseball. I just prefer watching it at home.
W: Oh, really? Isn't it more exciting to watch it at a baseball stadium?
M: I don't think so. The baseball stadium is so noisy that I cannot ________ ________ the game. Besides, if you watch the game on TV, you can get more information from the announcers.
W: You may be ________ ________, but I'd still rather go there in person.

baseball stadium 야구장
concentrate on …에 집중하다
would rather (차라리) …하겠다, …하고 싶다
in person 직접

5
M: I saw a truck get in an accident on the way to school today.
W: Did it ________ ________ the car in front of it?
M: No. It made a turn too quickly and tipped over.
W: Oh no! How did that happen?
M: It was carrying bricks. I think there were just too many.
W: Probably. Truck drivers sometimes try to carry too much at once. It's really dangerous.
M: Yes. The driver was lucky that ________ ________ ________ ________.
W: It would have been smarter to take half the bricks, and then go back and get the rest.
M: I agree. There were bricks all over the road. It caused a really ________ ________ ________.
W: That's too bad. I bet a lot of people were late for work.

crash into …와 충돌하다
make a turn 방향을 틀다
tip over 넘어지다, 쓰러지다
traffic jam 교통 체증
bet (…이) 틀림없다, 분명하다

6 W: In the past, it was considered strange to spend your money looking for old furniture to buy. These days, however, many people have begun to ________ ________ as a hobby or for home decorating. As a result, many antique shops have opened up in cities, but they are usually quite expensive. If you really want to find special antiques at ________ ________, you need to leave the city and check out shops in small towns. Another great place to look is at house sales. People are often simply trying to ________ ________ ________ unwanted old items, so they're happy to sell them for next to nothing. Remember the old saying: One person's trash is another person's treasure.

antique 골동품
decorating 장식
get rid of …을 없애다
unwanted 쓸모없는
for next to nothing 거저나 마찬가지로
old saying 옛말, 속담
treasure 보물

7 W: Hi, Mark. How did you do on the French quiz?
M: Terrible! It's impossible to memorize so many words.
W: I ________ ________ ________ ________ too, but then I started making flash cards.
M: Did that help?
W: It ________ ________ ________, as long as I learned only ten new words each day.
M: Only ten? I have been studying all of the words at once.
W: I think that is a mistake.
M: Why is that?
W: If you learn too many new words at once, you will forget most of them quickly.
M: So you make ten new flash cards every day?
W: That's right. Do you want to see ________ ________ ________ ________?
M: Sure. Let's make some together.

memorize 외우다, 암기하다
as long as …하는 한
at once 한꺼번에

8 M: If you've ever seen a bottle of wine opened, you know that they ________ ________ differently from soda and other drinks. Instead of caps, they have corks. Traditionally, corks are made from the wood of a special kind of tree. But these days, many corks ________ ________ ________ other materials, such as plastic. These artificial corks can effectively ________ ________ ________ ________ the bottle and don't change the taste of the wine. Also, they are cheaper for winemakers to use. However, there are some worries about the environmental effects of artificial corks, as they are not recyclable and remain in landfills for a long time.

seal 밀봉하다
cap 뚜껑
cork 코르크 (마개)
traditionally 전통적으로
material 재료, 물질
artificial 인공의
recyclable 재활용할 수 있는
remain 남다
landfill (쓰레기) 매립지

04강 유형(1) 할 일

대화를 듣고, 두 사람이 앞으로 할 일 혹은 상대방을 위해서 할 일을 고르는 문제 유형이다.

이 순서대로 풀어봐요

STEP 1 대화를 듣기 전, 지시문을 미리 읽고 할 일의 주체가 누구인지 파악한다.
STEP 2 대화의 뒷부분에 할 일에 대한 결정적인 단서가 많이 나오므로, 주의 깊게 듣는다.
STEP 3 정답과 관련된 단서는 여러 번 나오는 경우가 많으므로, 반복되는 어구를 잘 듣는다.
STEP 4 할 일을 결정하는 과정에서 오답이 되는 함정 요소가 많이 나오므로, 상대방의 반응에 유의하며 듣는다.

기출 예제 1

대화를 듣고, 여자가 남자를 위해 할 일로 가장 적절한 것을 고르시오. 평가원 기출

① 요리책 소개하기
② 조리사 추천하기
③ 요리 수업 신청하기
④ 조리 기구 준비하기
⑤ 요리 웹사이트 알려 주기

문제해설
누군가가 자신에게 요리법을 알려 주기를 바라는 남자를 위해 여자는 요리 웹사이트를 알려 주겠다고 했다. (정답 ⑤)

W: Hi, Jason. Is that a cookbook?
M: Yeah, this is a bestseller.
W: Oh, I didn't know you're interested in cooking.
M: Well, I want to start eating healthier food.
W: Great. Let me know if there are any good recipes in the book.
M: Sure, I will. [*Pause*] But these recipes don't look easy.
W: Just try cooking. You can learn from your mistakes.
M: I know, but I don't want to waste time experimenting.
W: Well, I heard that the local community center offers a cooking class. Why don't you check it out?
M: I already did. But it doesn't fit my schedule. I wish someone could just show me how to cook.
W: Then I can let you know about some useful cooking websites. You can visit those sites and watch online cooking videos.
M: Thanks. That would be a great help.

KEYWORDS & EXPRESSIONS

할 일과 관련하여 알아둬야 할 어휘와 표현

prepare 준비하다
assignment 숙제
miss 놓치다, 빠뜨리다
cultural 문화적인
exhibition 전시회
musical 뮤지컬
admission fee 입장료
make a reservation 예약하다
subway station 지하철역
traffic ticket 교통 위반 딱지
drop off (차로 …를) 내려주다
pick up (차로 …를) 마중 나가다
have lunch 점심을 먹다
go to the grocery store 식료품점에 가다
take care of …을 처리하다[돌보다]
take ... for a walk …을 산책시키다
be supposed to-v …하기로 되어 있다
do something different 색다른 것을 하다

〈할 일〉
- What should we do this weekend? 우리 이번 주말에 뭘 할까요?
- What do you want to do? 무엇을 하고 싶습니까?
- What do you have in mind? 생각해 둔 것이 있습니까?
- I suggest that we (should) ... . 우리 …하도록 합시다.
- Is there anything I can do for you? 제가 당신을 위해 할 수 있는 일이 있나요?

〈응답〉
- I'm available in the afternoon. 전 오후에 시간이 됩니다.
- That's a good idea. 그거 좋은 생각이네요.
- That'll be terrific. 그거 아주 좋겠네요.
- Sure. 물론이죠.
- Sorry, I can't. 죄송하지만, 저는 못 해요.

유형(2) 부탁

대화를 듣고, 화자가 상대방에게 부탁하는 일이 무엇인지 고르는 문제 유형이다.

이 순서대로 풀어봐요

STEP 1 대화를 듣기 전, 지시문을 미리 읽고 부탁하는 사람이 누구인지 파악한다.

STEP 2 선택지를 통해 화자가 부탁하려는 내용을 미리 추론해 본다.

STEP 3 부탁을 하는 사람의 상황 및 부탁을 받는 상대방의 반응 등을 잘 파악하며 듣는다.

기출 예제 2

대화를 듣고, 남자가 여자에게 부탁한 일로 가장 적절한 것을 고르시오. 수능 기출

① 발표 주제 정하기
② 식용 곤충 조사하기
③ 설문 조사 결과 분류하기
④ 사진 촬영하기
⑤ 유인물 배부하기

문제해설
과학 박람회에서 식용 곤충에 대해 발표하는 남자는 여자에게 청중들에게 유인물을 배부하는 일을 도와달라고 부탁하고 있다. (정답 ⑤)

W: Jim, are you doing a presentation for the science fair?
M: Yes. I'm really nervous because it's my first time presenting in public.
W: Don't worry. You'll do well. What's the topic?
M: Eating insects as food.
W: Sounds interesting. Why did you choose that?
M: Because it's a possible solution to future food problems.
W: So what are you going to do in your presentation?
M: I'll introduce some insect-based recipes and share my survey results on people's opinions about eating insects.
W: I can't wait to see it. I'll take some pictures for you since it's your first public presentation.
M: Thank you. But my brother Tom is going to take pictures.
W: Okay. Is there anything I can help you with?
M: Sure. Could you help with distributing hand-outs to the audience?
W: Yes, I'll do that.
M: Thank you.

KEYWORDS & EXPRESSIONS

부탁과 관련하여 알아둬야 할 어휘와 표현

recommend 추천하다 owe 빚지다 switch 바꾸다 advice 조언 assistance 도움 favor 부탁

〈부탁〉
- I wonder if you ... . …해 주실 수 있는지 궁금합니다.
- What would you like me to do? 제가 무엇을 해드리길 원하세요?
- I need some help with this. 전 이것에 대해 도움이 좀 필요해요.
- We need your advice on ... . 우리는 …에 관해 당신의 조언이 필요해요.
- Would you mind if I ...? / May[Can] I ...? 제가 …해도 될까요?
- Can[Could] you (please) ...? / Will[Would] you (please) ...? …해 주시겠어요?
- May I ask you a favor? / Can I ask you to do something for me? 부탁 좀 드려도 될까요?

〈응답〉
- With pleasure. 좋아요. 그러세요.
- If that's what you want, I'll ... . 그것이 당신이 원하시는 거라면, 제가 …할게요.

LISTEN & APPLY

정답 및 해설 p. 7

1 **대화를 듣고, 여자가 할 일로 가장 적절한 것을 고르시오.**

① 회의 참석하기
② 저녁 식사 장소 예약하기
③ 약속 일정 확인하기
④ 남편에게 전화하기
⑤ 자녀 데리러 가기

2 **대화를 듣고, 여자가 남자에게 부탁한 일로 가장 적절한 것을 고르시오**

① 약속 잡기
② 차트 설명하기
③ 환자들의 차트 찾기
④ 발표 자료 복사하기
⑤ 회의 준비하기

3 **대화를 듣고, 남자가 여자를 위해 할 일로 가장 적절한 것을 고르시오.**

① 요리법 알려주기
② 축구 경기 녹화하기
③ 손님 마중 나가기
④ 음식 주문하기
⑤ 음식 사다 주기

4 대화를 듣고, 남자가 여자에게 부탁한 일로 가장 적절한 것을 고르시오.

① 남자의 고양이를 같이 찾기
② 포스터 복사하기
③ 포스터 만들기
④ 남자의 고양이 사진 찍기
⑤ 포스터 붙이기

5 대화를 듣고, 남자가 여자를 위해 할 일로 가장 적절한 것을 고르시오.

① 발목을 확인하기
② 수업을 취소하기
③ 읽어야 할 것을 알려주기
④ 회의에 여자를 데려가기
⑤ 조교에게 전화하기

6 대화를 듣고, 여자가 남자에게 부탁한 일로 가장 적절한 것을 고르시오.

① 여자의 방을 재배치하기
② 여자의 방을 페인트칠하기
③ 가구 몇 개를 옮기는 것을 돕기
④ 여자의 엄마가 저녁을 요리하는 것을 돕기
⑤ 여자와 함께 브라우니 굽기

7 **대화를 듣고, 남자가 여자를 위해 할 일로 가장 적절한 것을 고르시오.**

① 아침에 깨워주기
② 버스 시간표 알아보기
③ 버스표 환불하기
④ 버스표 발급받기
⑤ 버스 좌석 변경하기

8 **대화를 듣고, 여자가 남자를 위해 할 일로 가장 적절한 것을 고르시오.**

① 책 반납하기
② 노트 필기 빌려주기
③ 책 내용 토론하기
④ 동아리 모임에 나가기
⑤ 점심 사주기

 녹음을 다시 한 번 듣고, 빈칸에 알맞은 말을 쓰시오. 정답 및 해설 p. 9

1

[*Cell phone rings.*]

W: This is Sally.

M: Hi, honey. It's me.

W: Oh, hi. Can I call you back later? I was about to go to a meeting.

M: Well, I'll make it quick. I just wanted to see if you had made a reservation for dinner.

W: A reservation? What's going on tonight?

M: Don't you ________ ________ to meet your parents?

W: I don't think so. I thought I rescheduled that for next week.

M: Oh, maybe I'm wrong.

W: I ________ ________ ________ in my daily planner. I'll take a look as soon as I can.

M: All right. Just call me on my cell phone and let me know.

W: Okay. If it is today, could you make sure to ________ ________ ________ ________ from the daycare center?

M: Of course.

be about to-v 막 …하려고 하다
make a reservation 예약하다
reschedule 일정을 변경하다
write down …을 적다[기록하다]
take a look 보다, 점검하다
make sure to-v 반드시 …하다
daycare center 어린이집

2

W: Dr. Adams, are you busy?

M: No, Dr. Green. In fact, I've just finished my morning appointments.

W: Great. Then, could you do something for me?

M: Sure. What is it?

W: Well, do you ________ ________ ________?

M: Yes. That's the chart showing the details of our cancer patients, right?

W: Right. But it only lists patients with names starting with A through M.

M: Ah. The other half of the list seems to be missing.

W: Yes. I'm going to need the ________ ________ for my presentation.

M: Would you like me to find it?

W: Yes, please. I can't do it now because I have to ________ ________ of some material for the meeting.

M: No problem. I'll do it right now.

appointment 일정, 약속
detail 《*pl.*》 상세한 설명
cancer 암
patient 환자
list 열거하다; 명단
missing 분실한
presentation 발표
make a copy 복사하다
material *자료; 물질

3

W: Dwayne, do you know ________ ________ ________ any Italian food?

M: Italian food? You know I'm not a very good cook.

W: I was just hoping that you might know a recipe.

M: If I did, I would share it with you. Unfortunately, I don't. Why do you ask?

W: My friends are coming over tonight to watch a soccer match. And I want to ________ ________ ________.

M: I see. So you want to make Italian food for them?

cook 요리하다; 요리사
recipe 요리법
order 주문하다
deliver 배달하다

W: It seemed like a good idea before, but maybe I should just order something.
M: The restaurant next to the library has great Italian food.
W: But I don't think they deliver.
M: Don't worry. I can drive and ________ ________ ________ ________.

4
W: Hey, Robert! Where are you running to?
M: Hi, Kelly. My cat ________ ________ from home.
W: Sorry to hear that. Have you looked around your house?
M: Yes, but I can't find her anywhere.
W: Oh, that's awful. Is there anything I can do?
M: Actually, I was going to make copies of these posters. I need some more.
W: Oh, you ________ ________ ________. Is that a picture of her?
M: Yes. And I put my address and phone number at the bottom.
W: Do you want me to help you copy them?
M: Well, would you take a few of these posters, instead? You can ________ ________ ________ in your neighborhood.
W: Okay. Hopefully someone will find your cat.
M: Thanks. I'd better get going now.

run away 도망치다
look around …을 둘러보다
awful 지독한, 끔찍한
address 주소
bottom 맨 아래
neighborhood 근처, 이웃

5
W: Hello, Professor Kent. Can I talk to you for a minute?
M: Sure. Come inside and ________ ________ ________.
W: Thank you. I wanted to talk about the class I missed last week.
M: Ah! I heard you had a small hiking accident.
W: Yes. I ________ ________ ________ pretty badly, but I'm okay now.
M: I'm glad to hear that. But we covered a lot of material in the class you missed.
W: That's why I'm here. Can you tell me what I need to read?
M: Well, I have a department meeting in a few minutes. But I'll phone my teaching assistant and have her help you.
W: Oh, thanks a lot. Where can I find her?
M: Just wait here. She'll ________ ________ in a few minutes.

ankle 발목
cover 덮다; *다루다
material 자료, 내용
assistant 조수, 보조원
come by 들르다

6
W: Brian, do you have any plans after school today?
M: Well, I have a few things to do. Why?
W: I was hoping you could ________ ________ ________ ________ with something.
M: Oh, really? I have to stop by a classmate's apartment right after school.
W: Are you free after that? I need ________ ________ ________ my bed and desk.

give … a hand …을 돕다
stop by …에 잠시 들르다
rearrange 재배열하다
reward 보답, 보상
brownie 브라우니

M: Oh, are you rearranging your room?
W: No. I painted it yesterday, but now I need to move everything back in.
M: I see. Well, I have to help my mother make dinner at six o'clock.
W: How about coming by around eight o'clock? It won't take long.
M: Sure, no problem.
W: Great. As a reward, I'll bake some of those brownies you like so much.
M: Really? Mmm... ________ ________ ________!

7 [*Telephone rings.*]
W: Um... Hello?
M: Ella? Are you still home?
W: Yes. What time is it?
M: It's ten o'clock. The bus to the mountain leaves in an hour. You should hurry up.
W: Oh, boy. I ________ ________ ________. I'll be right over.
M: I don't think you can get here in time. I should have gotten the tickets from you before.
W: Don't worry. If I hurry, I can ________ ________ ________ ________.
M: Hmm... Wait! Maybe I can get them from the ticket office.
W: That's a good idea. It will really ________ ________.
M: Tell me the ticket information, and I will write it down.
W: Okay. I bought them on May 20, and the numbers are from F20 to F27.
M: Okay. I'll go over to the office now.

oversleep 늦잠 자다
in time 제시간에

8 W: Hey, Nick. Is that Robert Ford's new novel?
M: Yes, it is. Are you reading it, too?
W: I finished it last week. I think it's brilliant.
M: I ________ ________ ________ ________ tonight. I have to return it to the library tomorrow morning.
W: So, what do you think of it?
M: Well... It's fascinating. But I'm not sure I completely ________ ________ ________.
W: Yes, the plot is quite complicated. I actually took notes while reading it.
M: I wish I had thought of that. I'm pretty confused.
W: Why don't we meet tomorrow? We can ________ ________ ________ ________ to help you understand it.
M: That'd be great. Are you free at twelve o'clock?
W: I have a club meeting until two o'clock, but I'm available then.
M: Great. Let's meet in the cafeteria.

brilliant 훌륭한, 멋진
plan on …할 예정이다
fascinating 매력적인, 대단히 흥미로운
completely 완전히, 완벽하게
plot (소설 등의) 줄거리
complicated 복잡한, 어려운
take notes 메모하다
confused 혼란스러운, 헷갈리는
available 시간[여유]이 있는
cafeteria 구내 식당

05강 지불할 금액

대화를 듣고, 남자나 여자가 지불할 금액을 고르는 문제 유형으로, 정답을 고르는 데 간단한 계산이 필요하다.

이 순서대로 풀어봐요

STEP 1 대화에서 언급되는 숫자나 금액을 메모하면서 듣는다.
STEP 2 혼동하기 쉬운 숫자의 발음에 주의한다.
STEP 3 대화 내용을 끝까지 유심히 듣고, 할인 및 개수의 변경 등과 같이 정답에 영향을 주는 정보를 파악한다.

기출 예제

대화를 듣고, 여자가 지불할 금액을 고르시오. 수능 기출

① $9 ② $16
③ $18 ④ $20
⑤ $27

문제해설
여자는 5달러짜리 조각 케이크 2조각($10)과, 한 잔에 5달러인 큰 커피 두 잔($10)을 주문했으므로 20달러를 지불해야 하지만, 10% 할인 쿠폰이 있으므로 18달러를 내면 된다. (정답 ③)

M: May I help you?
W: That cheese cake looks delicious! How much is it?
M: It's 30 dollars for the whole cake or 5 dollars per piece.
W: Okay. I'll take two pieces.
M: Would you like ice cream with your cake? It's two dollars per scoop.
W: No, thanks.
M: All right. Would you like anything to drink?
W: Yes, I'll have two medium coffees.
M: A medium coffee is 3 dollars and a large one is 6 dollars. But since you're buying cake, each large coffee costs just 5 dollars.
W: Great! Make them large then, please.
M: So, that's two pieces of cheese cake and two large coffees. Do you need anything else?
W: No, but I have a discount coupon. Can I use it now?
M: Let me see. [*Pause*] Sure. You get 10% off the total price.
W: Oh, great. Here's my credit card.

KEYWORDS & EXPRESSIONS

지불할 금액과 관련하여 알아둬야 할 어휘와 표현

- **금액:** charge (요금을) 청구하다, cost 비용이 들다, extra charge 추가 요금, on sale 할인 판매 중인, premium 할증금
- **단위:** 1 dollar = 100 cents, 1km = 1,000m = 100,000cm
- **배수:** a quarter 4분의 1, two thirds 3분의 2, a half / one half 2분의 1, double / twice / two times 2배, three times 3배, four times 4배
- How much will it cost? 그건 비용이 얼마나 들죠?
- How much did you spend? 당신은 돈을 얼마나 썼습니까?
- They are $7 each. 각각 7달러입니다.
- It's on sale now. 그것은 지금 할인 판매 중이에요.
- You can save 20% today. 당신은 오늘 20%를 할인받을 수 있습니다.
- Take 30% off the total price if you buy both items. 두 개를 모두 구입하면 전체 금액에서 30%가 할인됩니다.
- You can get 20% discount off the total with the coupon. 그 쿠폰으로 전체 금액에서 20%를 할인받을 수 있습니다.
- Here is the change for a $20 bill. 여기 20달러짜리 지폐에 대한 거스름돈입니다.

LISTEN & APPLY

정답 및 해설 p. 10

1 대화를 듣고, 여자가 지불할 금액을 고르시오.

① $60
② $75
③ $90
④ $105
⑤ $120

2 대화를 듣고, 남자가 지불할 금액을 고르시오.

① $10
② $15
③ $20
④ $30
⑤ $45

3 대화를 듣고, 여자가 지불할 금액을 고르시오.

① $55
② $70
③ $80
④ $90
⑤ $110

4 대화를 듣고, 남자가 지불할 금액을 고르시오.

① $14
② $18
③ $22
④ $24
⑤ $30

5 대화를 듣고, 여자가 지불할 금액을 고르시오.

① $45 ② $47
③ $50 ④ $54
⑤ $56

6 대화를 듣고, 남자가 지불할 금액을 고르시오.

① $36 ② $45
③ $48 ④ $55
⑤ $60

7 대화를 듣고, 여자가 지불할 금액을 고르시오.

① $27 ② $28
③ $30 ④ $36
⑤ $41

8 대화를 듣고, 남자가 지불할 금액을 고르시오.

① $120 ② $300
③ $360 ④ $380
⑤ $500

DICTATION

녹음을 다시 한 번 듣고, 빈칸에 알맞은 말을 쓰시오.

정답 및 해설 p. 11

1

W: Good afternoon. Do you still have front row seats available?
M: Yes, we do, ma'am.
W: Terrific. How much are they?
M: They're $40 for adults and $25 for children.
W: Okay, I'll take three— ________ ________ and one child.
M: Oh, I'm sorry. There are only two front row seats left.
W: Oh, no. What are the next best seats?
M: Balcony seats. They are $30 for adults and ________ ________ ________. They're quite good, too.
W: I suppose that will do, then. I just want to have a good view of the stage.
M: You'll have a great view from up there.
W: Good. I'd like ________ ________ in the balcony.

front row 앞줄
terrific 굉장한, 아주 멋진
balcony 발코니, 발코니석
suppose 생각하다, 추측하다
view 시야, 경치, 조망
stage 무대

2

W: Good morning, sir. How can I help you?
M: I was told that this hotel rents out scooters.
W: Yes, we do. It's really the best way to ________ ________ ________ of the city.
M: That's what I heard. How much is the rental fee?
W: If you're a guest of the hotel, it's $10 an hour.
M: Actually, I'm staying at a place down the street.
W: In that case, it'll be ________ ________ ________ more. How long do you want the scooter for?
M: Let's see… It's 11 a.m. right now.
W: Actually, sir, it's only ten.
M: Oh, I forgot to ________ ________ ________ ________ one hour. I just want the scooter until 1 p.m.
W: All right, sir. Just show me your ID, and I'll get you a scooter.

rent out …을 임대하다[빌려주다]
scooter 스쿠터
sight 명소, 관광지
rental fee 대여료
turn back (시계 등을) 늦추다, 되돌리다
ID 신분증(= identification)

3

[*Telephone rings.*]
M: Speedy Airport Shuttle. How can I help you?
W: Hi. My husband and I ________ ________ ________ to the airport tomorrow morning.
M: Okay. What time is your flight, and where are you located?
W: We're staying downtown, and our flight leaves at 9 a.m.
M: All right. It's $35 per person. Is it just the ________ ________ ________?
W: Yes. Is there any extra charge for our luggage?
M: Each person can bring one item of luggage for free. After that, it's ________ ________ ________.
W: I see. Well, that sounds reasonable.
M: How many bags will you be bringing?

ride 교통수단, 탈것
flight 비행편, 비행기
located (…에) 위치한
downtown 시내에
extra charge 추가 요금
luggage 수하물, 짐
for free 무료로
reasonable (가격이) 적당한, 비싸지 않은

W: My husband has one bag, and I have three.
M: All right. If you give me an address, I'll send someone to pick you up in the morning.
W: Great. Thanks.

4
W: Is everything okay over here?
M: Sure. The food was really delicious. You make the best meat loaf in the city.
W: I'll tell the chef you said so. Can I get you anything else?
M: No, ________ ________ ________. We need to get going.
W: All right. [*Pause*] Here it is. The total is $24.
M: Hmm. Are you sure that's correct? It seems a bit high.
W: Well, that's two meat loaf platters at $8 each and ________ ________ ________ apple pie at $4 each.
M: There must be a mistake. I had the meat loaf platter, but my wife just had a salad.
W: Oh, my gosh, that's right. My mistake. The salad was only $6.
M: No problem. ________ ________ ________.

meat loaf 미트로프 (다진 고기, 계란, 채소를 섞어 오븐에서 구운 것)
chef 요리사
check *계산서, 청구서; 수표
correct 옳은, 정확한
a bit 조금, 약간
platter 큰 접시; *모둠 요리
slice (얇게 썬) 조각

5
M: What can I do for you, ma'am?
W: Well, my watch stopped. I need to change the battery.
M: Okay, let me see. Is that all?
W: No, I want to ________ ________ ________, too. How much are these?
M: The gold ones are $40, and the silver ones are $30.
W: The gold ones are nice, but I already have one.
M: All right. So would you like ________ ________ ________?
W: Yes. So how much do I owe you?
M: It's $20 for a new battery and...
W: Oh, wait, I have a discount card. Do you accept it?
M: Sure. That will give you a 10% discount on the band, but not on ________ ________.
W: That's fine. Here you are.

owe 지불할 의무가 있다
discount 할인
accept 수락하다; *(신용카드를) 받아주다

6
[*Telephone rings.*]
W: Good morning. You've reached the Springfield Natural History Museum. How can I help you?
M: Hi, I would like to take my wife and two kids to visit the museum this week.
W: That's a great idea. We have ________ ________ ________ ________ and fun family activities.

educational 교육적인
exhibit 전시
activity 활동
admission fee 입장료

M: How much is the admission fee?
W: Well, the admission fee is $12 on weekdays. And it's $3 more ________ ________.
M: I see. That is quite expensive.
W: How old are your children?
M: My daughter is 11 years old, and my son is 8.
W: Well, actually children under 10 ________ ________ ________ ________ for free.
M: Oh, great. In that case, I think we will stop by this Sunday.

7 W: Excuse me. How much are these cushions?
M: The square ones are $10 each, and the round ones are $5.
W: That's not bad. I want to buy several for my couch.
M: Sure. The round ones ________ ________ ________ now. If you buy four, I'll give you a 10% discount.
W: Sounds great. I'll take four of them.
M: All right. Pick out any four you'd like.
W: Okay. [*Pause*] I like this square one, too. Could you ________ ________ ________ ________ on it as well?
M: I'm sorry, but those are already marked down to their lowest possible price.
W: Okay. I'll take it anyway. Do you have ________ ________ ________?
M: Sure. Your purchase is over $20, so delivery will be free.
W: Oh, great. Thanks.

couch 긴 의자, 소파
as well (…도) 또한, 역시
mark down 가격을 내리다
delivery 배달
purchase 구입

8 M: Hello. I want to buy a desk for my daughter. Could you recommend one?
W: Of course. This is our most popular model.
M: It is very nice. How much does it cost?
W: It is 300 dollars. Would you like to buy it?
M: That is a little too expensive. Can you ________ ________ ________?
W: Not for the desk. But the desk's matching bookshelf is currently 50% off.
M: What is the full price for the bookshelf?
W: It is 120 dollars.
M: Okay. I'll take both the desk and the bookshelf. Do I have to pay for the delivery?
W: Yes, it's 20 dollars. But if you spend more than 500 dollars, we offer ________ ________.
M: Well, I don't need anything else. I'll pay the delivery fee.
W: All right. Please ________ ________ your address here first.

recommend 추천하다
expensive 비싼
matching 어울리는
bookshelf 책장
shipping 배송
fill in (서류 등을) 채우다, 기입하다

06강 목적

담화를 듣고, 화자가 하는 말의 목적을 고르는 문제 유형이다.

이 순서대로 풀어봐요

STEP 1 담화를 듣기 전에 문제와 선택지를 미리 읽고, 어떤 내용이 나올지 예상해 본다.
STEP 2 주로 처음이나 마지막 부분에 단서가 드러나므로, 이에 주의하여 듣는다.
STEP 3 단서가 되는 표현이나 반복되는 어휘를 종합하여 정답을 찾는다.

기출 예제

다음을 듣고, 남자가 하는 말의 목적으로 가장 적절한 것을 고르시오. 수능 기출

① 교복 물려주기를 권장하려고
② 기부 행사 참여를 독려하려고
③ 생활용품 절약을 장려하려고
④ 학교 식당 공사를 안내하려고
⑤ 학부모 간담회 일정을 공지하려고

문제해설
기부 행사에 관한 내용으로 마지막 문장의 'I really encourage you to participate in this event(= month-long item donation event).'를 통해 기부 행사의 참여를 독려하고자 함을 알 수 있다. (정답 ②)

M: May I have your attention please? This is Principal Wilson. As you know, this Friday is the last day of our month-long item donation event. Thank you to those who have already participated. However, our involvement in the event has not met expectations yet, so we need to do more. The items we are still looking for are children's clothes, toys, school supplies, and books. If you have any of these items, please drop them off in the school cafeteria by Friday. Any donation, even just a single pencil, will be a great help. Don't forget that your small actions can make a big difference. I really encourage you to participate in this event. Thank you for listening.

KEYWORDS & EXPRESSIONS

목적과 관련하여 알아둬야 할 어휘와 표현

announce 알리다, 발표하다
book 예약하다
cancel 취소하다
celebrate 축하하다
warn 경고하다, 주의를 주다
criticize 비판하다
apologize 사과하다
entertain 즐겁게 해주다
attract (흥미 · 관심 등을) 끌다
aim 목표; 목표로 하다
goal 목표
for the purpose of …을 위해서
with the intention to-v …할 작정으로
intend to-v …할 작정이다
in order to-v …하기 위해서

- Be sure that … . …을 명심하세요.
- Please make sure that … . …을 확실하게 하세요.
- Can[May] I have your attention, please? 주목해 주시겠습니까?
- For further information, contact … . 더 많은 정보를 원하시면, …에 연락하십시오.
- I'm here to tell you about … . 여러분에게 …에 대해 말씀드리려고 이 자리에 나왔습니다.
- I would like to say a few words about … . …에 대해 몇 가지 말씀드리고자 합니다.
- I want to notify you that … . 여러분에게 …을 알려 드리고자 합니다.
- I'd like (you) to … . 저는 (당신이) …했으면 좋겠습니다.

LISTEN & APPLY

정답 및 해설 p. 12

1

다음을 듣고, 여자가 하는 말의 목적으로 가장 적절한 것을 고르시오.

① 해외여행을 권장하려고
② 새로 취항한 국제선을 홍보하려고
③ 각국의 다양한 문화를 소개하려고
④ 해외여행 시 유의할 점을 조언하려고
⑤ 여행사의 신규 직원들을 교육하려고

2

다음을 듣고, 남자가 하는 말의 목적으로 가장 적절한 것을 고르시오.

① 프로그램 종영을 공지하려고
② 수상한 배우들을 축하하려고
③ 새 TV 시트콤을 홍보하려고
④ 방송 스케줄 변경을 안내하려고
⑤ 인기 TV 프로그램 순위를 소개하려고

3

다음을 듣고, 여자가 하는 말의 목적으로 가장 적절한 것을 고르시오.

① 신규 회원을 환영하려고
② 새로운 대표를 선출하려고
③ 모임의 일정 변경을 알리려고
④ 회원들의 모임 참석을 독려하려고
⑤ 연말 파티에 관해 공지하려고

4

다음을 듣고, 남자가 하는 말의 목적으로 가장 적절한 것을 고르시오.

① 체중 감량 경험을 공유하려고
② 건강 프로그램 참가를 권유하려고
③ 천천히 식사하는 것의 이점을 알려주려고
④ 밤 늦게 먹는 습관의 위험성을 경고하려고
⑤ 포만감을 느끼게 도와주는 음식을 소개하려고

5 **다음을 듣고, 여자가 하는 말의 목적으로 가장 적절한 것을 고르시오.**

① 기획 상품을 홍보하려고
② 할인 판매를 공지하려고
③ 분실물 습득을 알리려고
④ 광고 내 오류를 사과하려고
⑤ 이벤트 당첨자를 발표하려고

6 **다음을 듣고, 남자가 하는 말의 목적으로 가장 적절한 것을 고르시오.**

① 수업을 취소하려고
② 학생들을 칭찬하려고
③ 현장 학습을 연기하려고
④ 안전 규칙을 재확인시키려고
⑤ 부모님에게 행사를 상기시키려고

7 **다음을 듣고, 여자가 하는 말의 목적으로 가장 적절한 것을 고르시오.**

① 아르바이트 자리를 제공하려고
② 교내 이메일 사용법을 알려주려고
③ 새로운 학교 주간지를 소개하려고
④ 학교에서 발행한 잡지 구독을 권유하려고
⑤ 위조된 이메일에 속지 않도록 경고하려고

8 **다음을 듣고, 남자가 하는 말의 목적으로 가장 적절한 것을 고르시오.**

① 승진자를 발표하려고
② 새 직원을 소개하려고
③ 직원의 퇴임을 알리려고
④ 신규 채용을 공고하려고
⑤ 직원의 공로에 대해 칭찬하려고

DICTATION

녹음을 다시 한 번 듣고, 빈칸에 알맞은 말을 쓰시오.

정답 및 해설 **p. 13**

1 W: It's very likely that many of you will ________ ________ for the first time this summer. Many airlines are offering big discounts to Europe, and travel agents are offering special packages designed to appeal to students. While it can be a great experience, visiting other countries isn't something to be taken lightly. Do your homework before you leave home—research the ________ ________ ________ of your destination. Also, choose a companion wisely. Make sure you are compatible and have the ________ ________ for your journey. Otherwise, what should be a very special time could turn out to be a disaster.

go abroad 외국에 가다
airline 항공 회사
travel agent 여행사, 여행업자
appeal to …의 관심을 끌다
research 연구하다, 조사하다
custom 관습, 풍습
destination 목적지, 도착지
companion 친구, 동반자
compatible 양립하는; *사이좋게 지내는
turn out 결국 …이 되다
disaster 재해, 재앙

2 M: For several years, *College Days* has been one of ________ ________ ________ sitcoms on this station. Viewers of all ages have enjoyed the adventures of the program's humorous main characters. This season, however, will be ________ ________ ________. It was a difficult decision, but we had to make it. Several of the main actors had already decided to leave the show in order to pursue their careers in Hollywood. Rather than try to replace them, we decided that ________ ________ ________ was the best thing to do. We will, however, continue to broadcast past episodes.

sitcom 시트콤
station 방송국
viewer 시청자
character 등장인물
pursue 추구하다
career 경력, 직업
replace 대체하다
broadcast 방송하다

3 W: Welcome to the last meeting of the Korean-American Women's Club this year. As you know, we'll be ________ ________ ________ over the Christmas and New Year holidays. Next year, as the result of several requests, there will be a change to our regular meeting day. Many of you have asked that we ________ ________ ________ from Monday to Wednesday evenings, and that has now been affirmed by vote. I'll also send an email to ________ ________ ________ that change. We'll be resuming our meetings in January with some new members joining us. Until next time, merry Christmas and happy New Year, everyone!

take a break 쉬다
as a result of …의 결과로서
request 요청, 요구
regular 정기적인
affirm 단언하다; *확정하다
vote 투표
remind A of B A에게 B를 상기시키다
resume 재개하다

4 M: Are you trying to lose weight or improve your health? Many people have removed junk food from their diets. Some have also stopped snacking at night before bed. But if you want to really _________ _________, I suggest that you also change how you eat. Focus on eating your food slowly and _________ _________ _________ completely before you swallow. It can take several minutes before our brains recognize that our stomachs are full. Eating slowly will give your brain time to process this information. So you will feel full before you overeat. By eating slowly and chewing our food carefully, we will also _________ _________ _________. It is much easier for our stomachs to absorb vitamins and nutrients from well-chewed food. So eat slower in order to enjoy a healthier lifestyle.

diet 식사, 음식
snack 간식; *간식을 먹다
make progress 진행하다, 전진하다
chew 씹다
mouthful 한 입, 한 모금
swallow 삼키다
recognize 인지하다
process 처리하다
digestion 소화
stomach 위
absorb 흡수하다
nutrient 영양소, 영양분

5 W: Attention, shoppers! Thank you for coming to Ferndale's to take advantage of our special holiday sale. It has just come to my attention, however, that there was _________ _________ _________ in our ad that appeared in the Saturday newspaper. In the ad, it says that all of our jackets are on sale at 40% off. Unfortunately, the word "leather" was left out of the ad. We sincerely _________ _________ _________. All of our other jackets are actually on sale at 10% off, which is still a wonderful bargain. And _________ _________ _________ that the rest of the information in the ad is correct. Enjoy your shopping!

take advantage of …을 이용하다
slight 약간의, 사소한
ad 광고(= advertisement)
appear 나타나다; *(신문에) 나다
leave A out of B B에서 A를 제외시키다
sincerely 진심으로
regret 후회하다; *유감으로 생각하다
bargain 싼 물건, 특가 상품
assured 보증된; *안심하여

6 M: May I have your attention, please? This is your principal, Dr. Gomez. As you know, our school's class field trips are scheduled for this Friday. However, according to the weather forecast, a _________ _________ _________ is expected Thursday night. For your safety, we considered canceling all of the trips. But we have decided to _________ _________ _________. Therefore, all the trips for first-year and second-year students will be held next Monday, while the third-year students' trips will be held next Tuesday. Please be sure to _________ _________ _________ with your parents.

principal 교장
field trip 수학 여행, 현장 학습
reschedule 일정을 변경하다
be sure to-v (명령문에서) 꼭[반드시] …해라

7 W: Good morning. Summer is approaching and many of you are looking for ways to make some money during your vacation. I have been told, however, that some of you have received emails from an address that seems to be from our school. The email says you can easily earn money by selling ________ ________ for the school this summer. But we've never sent this kind of email. Anytime you see the words "easy" and "money" together, you should ________ ________ ________. Please delete these emails ________ ________. If you want to find ways to make some money, you can drop by the Student Job Center after school. They'll help you find work.

approach 다가오다, 가까워지다
make money 돈을 벌다
subscription 구독
doubt 의심
delete 삭제하다
respond 응답하다, 반응하다
drop by …에 잠깐 들르다

8 M: Good morning. As you know, last month Harold Green retired from the company. He worked hard and was ________ ________ ________. I'd like to take this opportunity to thank him again. Last week, after considering many people for his position, we finally decided on ________ ________ ________ Harold. Starting today, Karen Johnson will be taking over as the manager of the customer service department. She previously worked in a similar position for ________ ________ ________ ________, and will bring many fresh ideas to our company. She'll be sitting at Harold's old desk, so stop by and say hello if you have a chance. Thanks for your time, and have a great day.

retire 퇴직하다, 은퇴하다
opportunity 기회
consider 고려하다
position 지위, 직책
replacement 후계자, 후임자
take over 인계받다
previously 이전에
competitor 경쟁자

07강 이유

대화를 듣고, 화자가 특정 행동을 하거나 감정을 갖게 된 이유를 고르는 문제 유형이다.

이 순서대로 풀어봐요

STEP 1 대화를 듣기 전에 지시문과 선택지를 미리 읽고, 어떤 내용이 나올지 예상해 본다.
STEP 2 화자가 처한 상황이 주된 단서가 되므로 대화의 흐름을 따라가며 단서를 찾는다.
STEP 3 대화 중에 언급된 표현을 오답으로 제시하는 경우가 많으므로 이에 주의한다.

기출 예제

대화를 듣고, 남자가 야구 경기를 보러 갈 수 없는 이유를 고르시오. 수능 기출

① 독감에 걸려서
② 비행기를 놓쳐서
③ 동생을 돌봐야 해서
④ 회의에 참석해야 해서
⑤ 입장권을 구할 수 없어서

문제해설
남자는 야구 경기 표를 두 장 가지고 있지만 고객과의 중요한 회의 때문에 시외로 출장을 가야 해서 야구 경기를 볼 수 없다고 했다. (정답 ④)

[*Telephone rings.*]
W: Hello?
M: Hey, Sarah. It's Alex. I have a question for you.
W: Sure. What's up?
M: Well, I've got two tickets to the National Baseball Championship next Friday, but unfortunately I can't go. Do you want them?
W: Yes, of course, but I thought the tickets were sold out.
M: They are. But my company buys tickets to every game in advance, and I was able to get some.
W: That's cool, but why can't you go?
M: I have to fly out of town for an important meeting with a client on that day, so I can't make it. Maybe you can take your brother with you.
W: Yeah, he'd love to go. But I feel sorry that you can't go to the game because of work.
M: Don't worry about it. Enjoy the game.

KEYWORDS & EXPRESSIONS

이유와 관련하여 알아둬야 할 어휘와 표현

reason / why / grounds / for what 근거, 이유
give rise to / bring about / cause / lead to 야기하다
understand / know 이해하다
mind / dislike 꺼리다, 싫어하다
motive 동기

- That's why I'm calling. 그것 때문에 전화드린 겁니다.
- I have something to tell you. 말씀드릴 게 있습니다.
- What's the matter[problem]? 무엇이 문제입니까?
- Is there anything wrong? 뭐가 잘못되었나요?
- What brings you here? 여기에는 왜 오셨습니까?
- What for? 무엇 때문에요? / How come? 어째서요? / What happened? 무슨 일이에요?
- I'd like to ask you a favor. 당신에게 부탁을 하나 드리고 싶어요.
- You know, I'm supposed to ... . 당신도 아시다시피, 제가 …하기로 되어 있어요.

LISTEN & APPLY

정답 및 해설 p. 13

1 **대화를 듣고, 여자가 강의를 수강할 수 없는 이유를 고르시오.**

① 1학년이 아니라서
② 성적이 너무 낮아서
③ 강의 시간이 맞지 않아서
④ 비슷한 강의를 들은 적이 있어서
⑤ 그 강의가 이번 학기에 제공되지 않아서

2 **대화를 듣고, 남자의 현수막이 철거된 이유를 고르시오.**

① 설치한 지 일주일이 지나서
② 지정된 장소에 설치되지 않아서
③ 댄스 클럽 현수막을 가려서
④ 학교 측의 승인을 받지 않아서
⑤ 직원이 다른 현수막과 혼동해서

3 **대화를 듣고, 여자가 회사에 지각하는 이유를 고르시오.**

① 아침마다 운동을 해서
② 자주 교통 정체에 걸려서
③ 알람 시계가 고장 나서
④ 밤늦게 게임을 하느라 늦잠을 자서
⑤ 새로운 집이 회사에서 멀어서

4 **대화를 듣고, 여자가 리조트 예약을 하지 않은 이유를 고르시오.**

① 호수 전망을 원해서
② 방들이 너무 비싸서
③ 수영장이 없어서
④ 이용 가능한 객실이 없어서
⑤ 셔틀버스를 운행하지 않아서

5 **대화를 듣고, 남자가 주문을 취소하려는 이유를 고르시오.**

① 상품의 수량을 잘못 기재해서
② 배송이 너무 지체되어서
③ 한정판을 구매하고 싶어서
④ 저렴한 상품을 구매하고 싶어서
⑤ 배송료를 지불해야 해서

6 **대화를 듣고, 남자가 약속을 지킬 수 없는 이유를 고르시오.**

① 길이 막혀서
② 다른 약속이 생겨서
③ 야근을 해야 해서
④ 시간을 착각해서
⑤ 감기에 걸려서

7 **대화를 듣고, 여자가 당황한 이유를 고르시오.**

① 회의 장소를 착각해서
② 중요한 메시지를 놓쳐서
③ 회의 중 큰 실수를 해서
④ 갑작스럽게 일정이 바뀌어서
⑤ 남자가 잘못된 정보를 알려줘서

8 **대화를 듣고, 남자가 햄버거를 많이 먹지 않는 이유를 고르시오.**

① 햄버거를 좋아하지 않아서
② 다이어트 중이라서
③ 저녁을 많이 먹으려고
④ 배가 아파서
⑤ 도시락을 갖고 와서

DICTATION

녹음을 다시 한 번 듣고, 빈칸에 알맞은 말을 쓰시오.

정답 및 해설 p. 15

1

M: Hi, Hannah. Can I help you with something?

W: Yes, Professor Smith. I want to ________ ________.

M: Do you want to take this class at a different time?

W: No, I want to switch from Business 101 to your Intro to Economics class. Is it too late?

M: No, it's not too late. Let me just ________ ________ ________.

W: Okay. My student ID number is 031-1178.

M: One second. [*Pause*] Oh, I'm sorry. You can't take that class after all.

W: Why not? Aren't my grades good enough?

M: That's not the issue. I thought ________ ________ ________ ________. That class is only being offered to first-year students.

W: Oh. What about next semester?

M: That would be fine. It will be open to all students next semester.

after all 어쨌든
issue 쟁점; *문제
freshman 신입생, 1학년생
semester 학기

2

W: Good morning. How can I help you?

M: Hi. I recently ________ ________ ________ ________ for the hiking club in front of the school library. But now it's gone.

W: I see. Did you get permission to put it up?

M: Yes. I came here and filled out the proper form.

W: Well, the school ________ ________ all banners after one week. Even the authorized ones.

M: But it was only up for three days!

W: Let me check our records. [*Pause*] Well, we took down the dance club's banner, but yours should still be up.

M: It's not. And the dance club's banner is still there.

W: A staff member must have confused the two banners. I'll ________ ________ ________ ________.

M: Thank you! That would be great.

put up …을 내붙이다[게시하다]
get permission 허락[허가]을 받다
proper 적절한, 알맞은
take down …을 내리다[철거하다]
authorized 허가를 얻은, 공인된

3

W: Sorry I'm late again.

M: You'd better be careful. The boss is going to get upset.

W: I know. It's becoming a real problem. I don't know what to do.

M: Is it ________ ________ ________? It's been pretty bad at rush hour lately.

W: No. I've been walking to work since I moved to a new apartment. I actually overslept.

M: Maybe you need a more ________ ________ ________.

W: No, it's nothing like that. I've just been playing games on my phone late at night.

M: That's not a good reason. You should just ________ ________ ________ and go to bed.

W: I know, but I can't stop!

rush hour 출퇴근 혼잡 시간대
reliable 신뢰할 수 있는

4 [*Telephone rings.*]

M: Thanks for calling the Lakeside Resort. How can I help you?

W: Hi. I'm calling to ________ ________ ________ for July 7.

M: All right. Unfortunately, the only ________ ________ on that day doesn't have a lake view.

W: That's fine. How much is it?

M: It's $170 per night.

W: That's a bit expensive. But I heard your rooms are nice, so I'll take it.

M: Great. Is there anything else I can help you with?

W: Yes. I'll need a reservation on your airport shuttle.

M: I'm sorry, but we no longer ________ ________ ________.

W: Oh. Please cancel the reservation then. Do you know any resorts that do offer one?

M: Yes, the Golden Resort. It's far from the lake, but it has a swimming pool.

make a reservation 예약하다
unfortunately 불행하게도, 유감스럽게도
no longer 더 이상 … 아닌

5 [*Telephone rings.*]

W: Thank you for calling Major Music Company. This is Hillary.

M: Hello. This is Felix Schwartz. I ordered a CD the other day. My order number is 321654.

W: [*Typing sound*] Hello, Mr. Schwartz. How may I help you?

M: I ordered the new album by the band Keane, but I'd like to ________ ________ ________.

W: Okay. Is there a problem?

M: No, but I ________ ________ ________ ________ autographed copy.

W: Actually, you can't get that on the Internet.

M: I know. I heard they will only be sold at the Birmingham Street shop. So I have to visit the store to buy one.

W: Okay. I can cancel your order, but ________ ________ ________ ________.

M: I see. I suppose I have no choice.

limited edition 한정판
autographed 사인[서명]이 있는

6 [*Telephone rings.*]

W: Hi, Brian. I was just about to head to the park to meet you.

M: Hi, Charlotte. I'm glad I caught you, then.

W: Oh? What's up? Are you ________ ________ ________?

M: No, but maybe we ought to reschedule our run for another time.

W: Oh. Do you need to ________ ________ again?

M: No. Actually, I got home from work about ten minutes ago.

W: Then what's wrong? Did something happen?

M: Everything is all right. But I feel sick. I must have ________ ________ ________.

be about to-v 막 …하려고 하다
head (…로) 가다, 향하다
stuck in traffic 교통이 막힌
work overtime 야근하다
catch a cold 감기에 걸리다

W: That's too bad. You should stay home and get some rest. I'll go without you.
M: Thanks, Charlotte. Enjoy your run.
W: Thank you, Brian. Take care.

7 M: You're back ________ ________ ________ ________. How was your meeting?
W: Something's not quite right, Mark. Didn't you tell me the conference starts at 2:00 p.m.?
M: Yes, I did. Is there something wrong?
W: Yes. I just came back from the conference room. Nobody was there.
M: Really? Did you go to conference room number two? You know, there are three conference rooms.
W: Yes, it was definitely room number two. Have you received any messages about ________ ________ ________?
M: No. Let me check the schedule again.
W: Please do. I don't want to miss this conference.
M: [*Pause*] Oh, I'm sorry. I made a mistake. The conference is supposed to be tomorrow afternoon.
W: Really? Well, I'm glad I'll be able to attend it. But please be careful not to ________ ________ ________ like this again.

conference 회의
definitely 틀림없이
delay 지연
cancellation 취소
be supposed to-v …하기로 되어 있다
attend 참석하다

8 M: What's wrong, Lisa?
W: I'm hungry, but I forgot my lunch money at home.
M: ________ ________ ________. I'm getting a hamburger for lunch. You can share it with me.
W: Are you sure?
M: Yes. Actually, you can have ________ ________ ________ if you want.
W: Thanks! Don't you like hamburgers?
M: Yes, I do. I could eat four. But I am trying not to eat so much.
W: Are you on a diet?
M: No. I'm having a huge dinner with my family tonight, so I want to eat a light lunch.
W: Oh, I see. You want to make sure you have room ________ ________ ________ for dinner.
M: Exactly! We're having my favorites—mashed potatoes and roast turkey.
W: A big home-cooked meal sounds great. I wish I were coming.
M: Sorry, this time it's just family. But you can come to dinner next weekend if you want.
W: Really? Thanks!

split 나누다
room 공간
mashed potato 으깬 감자
roast turkey 칠면조 구이

08강 관계 · 대화의 장소

대화를 듣고, 두 사람이 어떠한 관계인지 혹은 대화를 나누는 장소가 어디인지를 고르는 문제 유형이다.

이 순서대로 풀어봐요

STEP 1 대화를 듣기 전에 선택지를 미리 읽고, 대화의 내용을 추측해 본다.

STEP 2 대화의 주제가 두 사람의 관계 혹은 장소를 추측하는 데 중요한 단서가 되므로, 대화의 주제를 잘 파악한다.

STEP 3 특정 신분 · 직업 혹은 장소에서 자주 사용될 수 있는 어휘나 표현을 집중해서 듣는다. 단, 대화 중에 직접적으로 언급되는 직업이나 장소는 오답일 가능성이 높으므로 이에 유의한다.

기출 예제

대화를 듣고, 두 사람의 관계를 가장 잘 나타낸 것을 고르시오. 교육청 기출

① 호텔 직원 - 투숙객
② 매표소 직원 - 공원 방문객
③ 동물 사육사 - 관람객
④ 보험회사 직원 - 고객
⑤ 버스 기사 - 관광객

문제해설
공원 야생 동물 투어를 예약한 여자가 입장권을 찾으러 왔으며 남자가 이용권을 여자에게 건네며 이용 유의 사항을 말하는 것으로 보아, 매표소 직원과 공원 방문객 간의 대화임을 알 수 있다. (정답 ②)

M: Hello, how may I help you?
W: Hi. I reserved a wildlife tour in this park. I need to pick up the tickets.
M: Do you have the reservation number?
W: Yes. It's 32461, and I've already paid for the tour.
M: [*Typing sound*] You're Kate Smith, right?
W: Yes, I am.
M: You reserved a one-day tour for four people, right?
W: That's right. Two adults and two children.
M: Here are your passes. Please don't feed the animals.
W: Okay. Thank you.
M: Have a nice tour.

KEYWORDS & EXPRESSIONS

관계 · 대화의 장소와 관련하여 알아둬야 할 어휘와 표현

- **병원 · 약국:** dentist 치과 의사, physician 내과 의사, pharmacist 약사, patient 환자, dentist's office 치과, drugstore / pharmacy 약국, medicine 약, prescription 처방전, dose (약의) 1회 복용량, checkup 건강 검진, examine 진찰하다, first aid 응급 처치, sore 아픈, be in (the) hospital 입원 중이다, go see a doctor 진찰받으러 가다, be on operation 수술 중이다, take a pill 약을 복용하다
- **호텔:** manager 지배인, tourist 관광객, front desk 안내 데스크, single[double] room 1인실 [2인실], check-in[out] 체크인[체크아웃], three nights 3박
- **식당:** customer 손님, bill / check 계산서, dessert 후식, order 주문; 주문하다, go dutch 각자 지불하다, refill 다시 채워주다, treat 대접하다, 한턱내다
- **공항:** flight attendant 비행기 승무원, passenger 승객, passport 여권, boarding pass 탑승권, ticketing 티켓 구입, flight 항공편, customs 세관, baggage / luggage 수하물, 짐, land 착륙하다, take off 이륙하다, check in (짐을) 부치다, departure gate 출발 탑승구
- **도서관:** librarian 사서, overdue 반납 기한이 지난, due date 반납일, return a book 책을 반납하다, check out (책 등을) 대출하다
- **우체국:** mail carrier 집배원, postcard 엽서, stamp 우표, scale 저울, parcel / package 소포, packing 포장, registered mail 등기 우편, air mail 항공 우편, express mail 빠른 우편, surface mail 보통 우편, zip code 우편 번호, extra charge 추가 요금, fragile 깨지기 쉬운
- **은행:** cash 현금; 현금으로 바꾸다, loan 대출, interest 이자, interest rate 금리, 이율, withdraw 인출하다, make a deposit 예금하다, open an account 계좌를 개설하다

LISTEN & APPLY

정답 및 해설 p. 15

1 **대화를 듣고, 두 사람의 관계를 가장 잘 나타낸 것을 고르시오.**

① 의사 - 환자
② 의사 - 간호사
③ 약사 - 환자
④ 접수원 - 간호사
⑤ 접수원 - 환자

2 **대화를 듣고, 두 사람이 대화하고 있는 장소로 가장 적절한 곳을 고르시오.**

① 병원
② 수영장
③ 헬스클럽
④ 옷 가게
⑤ 스포츠용품점

3 **대화를 듣고, 두 사람의 관계를 가장 잘 나타낸 것을 고르시오.**

① 경찰관 - 운전자
② 택시 기사 - 승객
③ 버스 기사 - 승객
④ 운전 강사 - 수강생
⑤ 자동차 판매원 - 고객

4 **대화를 듣고, 두 사람의 관계를 가장 잘 나타낸 것을 고르시오.**

① 피부과 의사 - 환자
② 교수 - 연구원
③ 판매원 - 고객
④ 미용사 - 고객
⑤ 구급대원 - 부상자

5 대화를 듣고, 두 사람의 관계를 가장 잘 나타낸 것을 고르시오.

① 학생 – 교사
② 고객 – 판매원
③ 구매자 – 제조업자
④ 임원 – 프로그래머
⑤ 영업 부서 직원 – 기술 지원 부서 직원

6 대화를 듣고, 두 사람의 관계를 가장 잘 나타낸 것을 고르시오.

① 회사 사장 – 비서
② 식당 사장 – 종업원
③ 지배인 – 손님
④ 종업원 – 바리스타
⑤ 집주인 – 가사 도우미

7 대화를 듣고, 두 사람의 관계를 가장 잘 나타낸 것을 고르시오.

① 학생 – 학부모
② 학생 – 경비원
③ 교사 – 교장
④ 청소부 – 교사
⑤ 청소부 – 학생

8 대화를 듣고, 두 사람의 관계를 가장 잘 나타낸 것을 고르시오.

① 탐험가 – 작가
② 평론가 – 감독
③ 영화배우 – 감독
④ 프로듀서 – 매니저
⑤ 우주 비행사 – 기자

DICTATION

녹음을 다시 한 번 듣고, 빈칸에 알맞은 말을 쓰시오.

정답 및 해설 p. 17

1

W: Hello. What kind of problem are you having, sir?

M: I have a terrible ________ ________ ________ ________. I couldn't sleep at all last night.

W: I see. Have you visited us before?

M: Yes, I got a ________ ________ about two weeks ago.

W: Okay. Just fill out this form, please. Let me get your file.

M: Age? Blood type? Do I have to fill out all this information?

W: Yes. The doctor needs to know these things before he sees you.

M: Can't I just tell him when ________ ________ ________? You already have my file.

W: I'm sorry, but a basic information form must be completed with each visit.

M: Okay. [*Pause*] Here you are.

W: Thanks. Please wait here until the doctor calls you.

pain 통증, 고통
side 옆구리
general checkup 종합 검진
fill out …을 작성하다
form 양식
blood type 혈액형
examine 진찰하다
complete 완료하다; *기입하다, 작성하다

2

W: Oh my gosh! This place is so big. I don't know where to start.

M: Is this your first time here?

W: Yes. I just ________ ________ ________ a membership yesterday.

M: Well, you picked a good place. I've been coming here for years.

W: There are so many different kinds of machines. Which should I use?

M: It depends. Do you want to build up your muscles or just lose some weight?

W: I just want to ________ ________ ________ in general. I spend too much time sitting at a desk.

M: I know what you mean. You should talk to that woman over there.

W: You mean the one wearing the gray sweatshirt?

M: Yes. She works here. She could probably give you ________ ________ ________.

W: I'm sure she could.

sign up for …을 신청하다[등록하다]
machine 기구, 장치
build up (건강을) 증진시키다, (몸을) 단련하다
muscle 근육
lose weight 체중을 줄이다
in general 보통; *전반적으로
sweatshirt 운동복 상의

3

M: Now, ________ ________ ________ that bus pulling away from the bus stop.

W: Don't worry. I see it.

M: Good. Do you see those taxis parked along the street? Turn left after those.

W: Okay. [*Pause*] Oops, I forgot to check the side mirrors.

M: That's okay. It's good that you remembered afterwards. Now there's ________ ________ ________, so try going a little faster.

W: Okay. Is this fast enough?

M: Well, now you're going 65 kilometers per hour, and the speed limit here is 60. You're actually ________ ________ ________ ________.

W: Oh, sorry. I'll slow down.

pull away 움직이기 시작하다
park 주차하다
side mirror (자동차의) 사이드미러
afterwards 나중에
speed limit 제한 속도
break 깨다; *위반하다
slow down 속도를 늦추다
parking lot 주차장

M: You should be more careful next time. Okay, I think we're finished. Can you slow down and park in that parking lot, please?

W: Sure.

4

W: Hi. Can I help you find something?

M: Yes. My skin has gotten so rough these days.

W: Well, you need to care for your skin, especially in winter.

M: I guess so. My face feels ________ ________ ________. What do you recommend?

W: Hmm. Do you have any allergies?

M: No, I don't. I've never experienced this before.

W: It could just be dry skin, then. I recommend this product. Would you like to ________ ________ ________?

M: Sure. [*Pause*] Hmm... I like the scent. How much is it?

W: It's on sale for $20. Do you need body lotion as well?

M: No, just this.

W: If your condition doesn't improve, you should probably ________ ________ ________.

M: Okay. Thanks for your advice.

rough 거친
itchy 가려운
recommend 추천하다
allergy 알레르기
scent 향기, 냄새
condition 상태

5

W: Oh, there you are. What took you so long?

M: Sorry about that. One of the executives had a problem with his laptop.

W: That's okay. But I really need you to ________ ________ ________ as soon as possible.

M: All right. Well, you seem to be online right now.

W: Yes, but my email isn't working.

M: Oh, didn't you see the notice? We're updating the whole company's email system.

W: Oh, I didn't see it. I have to contact an important ________ ________ this afternoon.

M: Don't worry. It will be working again by two o'clock.

W: I hope so. If I don't offer a discount to him, he might decide to buy material from our rival instead.

M: This is just ________ ________ ________. There shouldn't be any problems.

W: Well, I'm glad to hear that.

executive 임원
laptop 노트북 컴퓨터
update 갱신하다
contact 연락을 취하다
overseas 해외의, 외국의
rival 경쟁 상대
routine 일상의, 정기적인

6

W: Thank you for ________ ________ ________, Steven. We were really busy today.

M: You're welcome. Is there anything else I should do?

W: No, but I just want to talk to you about tomorrow's schedule. Can you come in an hour early?

M: Sure. Is there a special event?

W: Well, we are expecting three large groups of businesspeople. They all

expect (오기로 되어 있는 대상을) 기다리다
rearrange 재배열하다

made lunch reservations for 11:30.

M: I see. But there aren't ________ ________ ________ for three groups.

W: Yes. So when you first arrive, rearrange the smaller tables so that everyone in the groups can sit together.

M: All right.

W: Also, one group wants us to ________ ________ ________ before they arrive, as they won't have much time to eat.

M: I'll make sure the drinks are ready.

W: All right. That's all for today. See you tomorrow.

7

M: Oh, I'm sorry, I didn't know you were in here.

W: Yes, I'm just working a little late tonight.

M: Would you like me to come back later?

W: No, that's okay. I'm almost finished ________ ________ ________.

M: All right. I'll just empty these trash cans now.

W: Okay. [*Pause*] May I ask you a question?

M: Sure. Is there something wrong?

W: No. I'm just wondering if my classroom ________ ________ than usual last week.

M: Last week? No... Your room is always one of the cleanest in the school.

W: Great. I was on vacation and wasn't sure if my students ________ ________ ________.

M: It was as clean as usual. It makes my job very easy.

W: I'm glad to hear it.

grade 채점하다
paper 과제물
empty 비우다
trash can 쓰레기통
messy 지저분한
be on vacation 휴가 중이다
clean up 청소하다
properly 적당히, 제대로
as usual 평소와 같이

8

[*Cell phone rings.*]

W: Hello?

M: Hello, Erica? This is David Smith. We met last year at Robert's Christmas party.

W: Yes, I remember. I really enjoyed your latest movie.

M: Thank you. I called because I'm beginning a new project and I think you would be perfect for ________ ________ ________.

W: What's the story about?

M: It's about Valentina Tereshkova, the first female astronaut to ________ ________ ________.

W: Oh, I've read about her! Her story is amazing. But why did you think of me for the role?

M: Well, you actually look a lot like her when she was young.

W: I see. Well, I'm interested, but I need to ask my agent if my schedule's open.

M: Okay, but I need your answer soon. We plan to ________ ________ next month.

W: Okay, I'll call him right now.

project 프로젝트
lead role 주인공 역할
female 여성인, 여성의
astronaut 우주 비행사
agent 에이전트, 대리인
film 촬영하다

09강

도표 정보 파악

다양한 종류의 도표를 보면서 대화를 듣고, 대화의 내용과 도표 내용의 일치 여부를 파악하는 문제 유형이다.

이 순서대로 풀어봐요

STEP 1 대화를 듣기 전에 도표를 미리 보고, 대화의 내용을 예상해 본다.

STEP 2 대화에서 언급되는 세부 사항들을 잘 듣고 선택지에서 오답을 지워나간다.

STEP 3 여러 개의 단서들을 종합하여 정답을 찾아야 하므로, 주요 정보를 메모하면서 듣는다.

기출 예제

다음 표를 보면서 대화를 듣고, 두 사람이 선택할 패키지 상품을 고르시오. 수능 기출

Attraction Packages at Grandlife Amusement Park

	Package	Price (per person)	3D Movie	Aquarium	Lunch Box
①	A	$20	*Amazing Sea*	×	×
②	B	$30	*Amazing Sea*	×	○
③	C	$35	*Amazing Sea*	○	×
④	D	$40	*Jungle Safari*	×	○
⑤	E	$55	*Jungle Safari*	○	○

문제해설

두 사람은 1인당 지출이 50달러를 넘지 않는 선에서, 3D 영화 〈Amazing Sea〉를 보기로 했으며, 수족관은 가지 않기로 했고, 점심 도시락은 선택하기로 했다. (정답 ②)

W: Honey. Here's a pamphlet for the attraction packages at Grandlife Amusement Park. Let's choose one of them.
M: Okay. How much do you think we should spend?
W: Well, I don't want to spend more than 50 dollars per person.
M: All right. For the 3D movie, would you rather watch *Amazing Sea* or *Jungle Safari*?
W: Either one sounds fine, but I'd prefer *Amazing Sea* because it would look really cool in 3D.
M: Good. Let's watch that movie then.
W: Okay. How about the aquarium? I've heard that there're some fantastic dolphins.
M: Well, if we're seeing a movie about the sea, I don't think we need to go to the aquarium, too.
W: Yeah, I agree. Should we include the lunch box option?
M: Sure. That way, we can save some time.
W: Then, that leaves this package.
M: Perfect! Let's choose that one.

KEYWORDS & EXPRESSIONS

도표 정보 파악과 관련하여 알아둬야 할 어휘와 표현

- **요금표:** bill 청구서, record 기록, warranty period 품질 보증 기간, on sale 할인[판매] 중인, run out of stock 품절되다, reasonable (가격이) 비싸지 않은, on installment 할부로
- **일정표:** anniversary 기념일, farewell party 송별회, competition 대회, submit / hand in 제출하다, cancel 취소하다, delay 미루다, participate in / take part in …에 참가하다, volunteer 자원봉사하다
- **수업 및 평가:** academic 학업의, tutor 가정교사, subject / course 과목, major 전공, session 수업 시간, project 과제, presentation 발표, evaluation 평가, organize 체계화하다, category 범주, credit 학점
- How much are you willing to pay? 얼마를 지불할 생각이십니까?
- I don't want to spend more than … . …이상의 돈을 쓰고 싶지 않습니다.
- Let me choose the cheaper one. 더 저렴한 것을 선택하겠습니다.
- How many bedrooms would you like? 몇 개의 방이 필요하십니까?
- Do you have a particular model in mind? 마음에 둔 특정한 디자인이 있나요?
- Would you like to pay in cash or by credit card? 현금으로 계산하시겠습니까, 카드로 하시겠습니까?

LISTEN & APPLY

정답 및 해설 p. 18

1 다음 표를 보면서 대화를 듣고, 여자가 신청한 수업을 고르시오.

Music Class Schedule

Time \ Day	Monday	Tuesday	Wednesday	Thursday	Friday
9:00 a.m.	① Film and Music (Williams)	Musical History (Anderson)	Film and Music (Williams)	Musical History (Cooper)	④ Film and Music (Miller)
2:00 p.m.	Musical History (Cooper)	② Composition (Anderson)	③ Composition (Bradley)	Composition (Bradley)	⑤ Musical History (Cooper)

2 다음 표를 보면서 대화를 듣고, 두 사람이 구입할 세탁기를 고르시오.

Washing Machine

	Model	Price	Capacity	Loading	Steam Wash
①	A	$500	7kg	Top	No
②	B	$600	7kg	Front	Yes
③	C	$700	10kg	Front	No
④	D	$800	10kg	Front	Yes
⑤	E	$850	15kg	Top	No

3 다음 표를 보면서 대화를 듣고, 두 사람이 볼 공연을 고르시오.

National Arts Center Performance Listings

	Play	Genre	Start Time	Running Time
①	*My Hero*	Comedy	8:00 p.m.	1.5 hours
②	*Room Numbers*	Comedy	6:30 p.m.	2 hours
③	*While You Were There*	Drama	7:00 p.m.	2.5 hours
④	*Secrets of Her*	Musical	3:30 p.m.	2 hours
⑤	*The Last Princess*	Drama	3:30 p.m.	2.5 hours

4 다음 표를 보면서 대화를 듣고, 여자의 멘토를 고르시오.

Student ID Number \ Department	Department of Humanities	Department of Engineering	Department of Science
01~10	David	Ashley	Justin
11~20	Rachel	Nathan	Martin
21~30	Jennifer	Austin	Chloe

① David
② Jennifer
③ Martin
④ Austin
⑤ Chloe

5 다음 표를 보면서 대화를 듣고, 두 사람이 신청할 활동을 고르시오.

Sunnyhill Resort Weekend Activity Schedule

	Activity	Times
①	Hiking Up Mt. Grand	7:00 a.m. – 9:30 a.m.
②	Soccer Tournament	10:00 a.m. – 12:00 p.m.
③	Local Art Show	2:00 p.m. – 3:30 p.m.
④	Snorkeling	2:00 p.m. – 3:30 p.m.
⑤	Fishing Trip	5:00 p.m. – 6:30 p.m.

6 다음 표를 보면서 대화를 듣고, 두 사람이 선택할 메뉴를 고르시오.

Green Chef Bistro

	Main Dish	Side Dish	Drink	Price
①	Deluxe Burger	French Fries	Soft Drink	$20
②	Seafood Platter	Fresh Salad	Coffee	$30
③	Chicken Delight	X	X	$15
④	Gourmet Steak	French Fries	X	$30
⑤	Grilled Fish	Fresh Salad	X	$40

7 다음 표를 보면서 대화를 듣고, 남자가 선택할 일자리를 고르시오.

Help Wanted Ads

	Job	Hours	Location	Payment
①	Pet Sitter	6:00 p.m. - 10:00 p.m.	Downtown	$16/hour
②	Waiter	7:00 a.m. - 1:00 p.m.	Uptown	$15/hour
③	Waiter	3:30 p.m. - 8:30 p.m.	Downtown	$20/hour
④	Librarian	2:00 p.m. - 8:00 p.m.	Uptown	$20/hour
⑤	Pet Sitter	5:00 p.m. - 11:00 p.m.	Uptown	$15/hour

8 다음 표를 보면서 대화를 듣고, 여자가 선택할 집을 고르시오.

Newtown Real Estate Listings

	Rooms	Rent per Month	Part of Town	Near Subway
①	2	$500	East	No
②	3	$600	East	Yes
③	3	$600	West	No
④	3	$700	West	No
⑤	6	$1,000	West	Yes

DICTATION

녹음을 다시 한 번 듣고, 빈칸에 알맞은 말을 쓰시오.

1

M: Did you ________ ________ ________ a music class yet, Lisa?
W: Yes, I did. It was hard to choose one.
M: Did you take a class with Professor Miller, like I suggested?
W: No, he's only teaching one class this semester, and it was full.
M: That's too bad. What class did you decide on, then?
W: Well, I was interested in Film and Music, but I needed ________ ________ ________.
M: Oh, is Film and Music only offered in the morning?
W: Yes, and I've already taken Musical History.
M: I remember. We were in Professor Cooper's class together.
W: Right, and ________ ________ ________ on Tuesdays and Thursdays, I didn't have much choice.
M: Yes, there's only one class you can take. But, I heard that most students really enjoy it.
W: Do they? That's good to know.

sign up for (수업 등을) 신청하다
suggest 제안하다
semester 학기
full 가득 찬, 만원의
decide on …로 결정하다
be interested in …에 관심이 있다
| 문제 | **composition** 작곡(법)

2

M: Which washing machine should we buy?
W: Well, we really ________ ________ ________ spend more than $800.
M: That's true. What about the size? I think capacity is the important factor for us to consider.
W: Since we're a family of three, a 7-kilogram machine should be good.
M: I think that would be too small for us. I prefer the bigger one.
W: All right. Let's buy a bigger one then.
M: What do you think about top-loading machines?
W: They are very inconvenient. I ________ ________ ________ have a machine that is front-loading.
M: I agree. Front-loading machines are easier to use.
W: What do you think about having a steam wash feature? I don't think they are necessary.
M: Really? I disagree. A steam wash helps ________ ________ ________.
W: Okay. I guess that leaves us with only one option.

can't afford to-v …할 여유가 없다
capacity 용량
top-loading 위쪽으로 세탁물을 넣는
remove 제거하다
stain 얼룩

정답 및 해설 p. 19

3

M: What would you like to do this Saturday?
W: We haven't seen a performance in a while. Are there any good shows ________ ________ ________?
M: Let's have a look. Oh, I heard this musical is really exciting.
W: To be honest, I'm not interested in musicals.
M: Okay. Well, it looks like we still ________ ________ ________.
W: Why don't we have lunch together and then go see this show at 3:30?
M: I'm having lunch with my cousin on Saturday. How about having dinner together and then going to a play?
W: All right. But I don't want to ________ ________ ________ ________.
M: If we see this one, we'll be out of the theater before nine o'clock.
W: That sounds perfect!

performance 공연
to be honest 솔직히 말하자면
| 문제 | **genre** 장르
running time 상영 시간

4

M: Hi. You're a freshman, aren't you? This chart will tell you ________ ________ ________ ________.
W: Yes, I am. But what's a mentor?
M: Mentors are older students who volunteer to help freshmen during their first year.
W: Oh, really? How does the chart work?
M: First you need to check your department. I ________ ________ ________, which is in the Department of Humanities.
W: Oh, I see.
M: Next, you check the first two numbers of your student ID. Mine are zero and one. And there's my mentor's name.
W: Let me try. My major is computer science, and my ID number starts with a two and a one.
M: Computer science? That's the Department of Science, right?
W: Actually, computer science is part of the Department of Engineering.
M: Oh, really? In that case, here's ________ ________ ________ ________ ________.
W: Cool! Thanks for your help.

mentor 멘토, 조언자
volunteer 자원하다
department (대학의) 학부, 과
major in …을 전공하다
philosophy 철학
humanities 인문학
computer science 컴퓨터 공학
engineering 공학

5

W: Oh, look at this activity schedule. Let's choose something.

M: Sure. I heard the hiking is nice. Mt. Grand is beautiful ________ ________ ________ ________.

W: That's fine, but I don't like getting up early on the weekends.

M: All right. Do you think you'll be up ________ ________ ________ the next activity?

W: Yes, but I don't like soccer.

M: Okay. What's this art show?

W: They take us to a village where local artists sell their work.

M: That could be interesting. It would certainly be better than snorkeling.

W: Why? Are you afraid of ________ ________ ________ ________?

M: Yes, I am. And I'm not interested in fishing.

W: Neither am I. So let's sign up for this one.

M: Sounds good.

activity 활동
in time for …에 시간 맞춰
local 현지의, 지역의
snorkeling 스노클링(스노클을 쓰고 잠수를 하는 스포츠)

6

W: Wow, this restaurant looks really nice!

M: It sure does. And I've heard that ________ ________ ________ ________.

W: I can't wait to try it!

M: Let's take a look at the menu. How about getting hamburgers?

W: No, I don't really like hamburgers. But the other main dishes all look good.

M: Yes, then let's decide on a side dish and a drink first.

W: Well, I don't need a drink. Water is fine.

M: Okay, but we should ________ ________ ________ ________. I'm sure they're delicious.

W: Good idea. There are two options. I can't decide!

M: Then why don't you just get the cheaper one?

W: Well, the more expensive option ________ ________ ________.

M: All right. Order that one!

main dish 주[메인] 요리
side dish 곁들임 요리

7

W: Hey, Steve. What are you reading?

M: Oh, I'm just looking at these classified ads. I want to find a part-time job this semester.

W: Have you found anything that you would like to do?

M: Well, I wouldn't mind being a pet sitter or waiter, but being a librarian would probably ________ ________ ________.

W: Yeah, that does sound boring. What time do you have classes this semester?

M: I have classes every day, but I'm always finished by 3:00 p.m.

W: All right. And you probably don't want to work uptown, do you?

M: No, it's ________ ________ ________.

W: Then you have two options.

M: This one pays more per hour. I'll ________ ________ ________ ________ right now.

classified ad 모집 광고
pet sitter 애완견 돌보는 사람
librarian (도서관) 사서
uptown 도심을 벗어나, 시 외곽으로
pay 보수를 주다

8

[*Telephone rings.*]

M: Hello. You've reached Newtown Real Estate. How can I help you?

W: Hi. I'm interested in renting a house in the Newtown area.

M: Great. There are several locations that are currently ________ ________ ________.

W: That's good news. I'm looking for a place for six college students.

M: All right. Does each of you need your own room?

W: No, three rooms would be enough.

M: I see. And what's ________ ________?

W: We don't want to spend more than $700.

M: Okay. Do you have a preference for the east side or the west side of town?

W: Something on the west side would be better.

M: Do you need to be near a subway station?

W: All of us ________ ________ ________ ________ ________, so that doesn't matter. But we do care about the price—the cheaper, the better.

M: Then I think I have the perfect place for you.

real estate 부동산 (중개업)
rent 빌리다, 임대하다
currently 현재
budget 예산
preference 선호
matter 중요하다

10강 내용 일치

담화를 듣고, 담화의 내용과 일치하지 않는 내용을 고르는 문제 유형이다. 안내문이나 광고문 같은 실용적인 내용 또는 학술적인 내용이 담화의 소재로 사용된다.

이 순서대로 풀어봐요

STEP 1 담화를 듣기 전에, 선택지를 미리 읽고, 담화의 내용을 예상해 본다.

STEP 2 대개 선택지 순서대로 내용이 전개되므로, 담화를 들으면서 오답을 하나씩 지워나간다.

STEP 3 담화에서 언급된 일부 어휘나 표현만을 활용한 오답에 유의한다.

기출 예제

Global in Action에 관한 다음 내용을 듣고, 일치하지 <u>않는</u> 것을 고르시오. 평가원 기출

① 비영리 기관이다.
② 전직 테니스 선수가 설립했다.
③ 1,000명 이상의 회원이 있다.
④ 집 짓는 일을 도와준다.
⑤ 재정적 기부를 받지 않는다.

문제해설
재정적 기부도 언제나 환영한다(we always welcome financial contributions)고 했다. (정답 ⑤)

W: Hello, I am Janet Danish of Global in Action. As you know, more and more people now want to do something meaningful. But a lot of them don't know what to do. So I'd like to introduce Global in Action. Global in Action is a nonprofit organization which aims to help people in developing countries. It was founded by Sarah Hatch, a former tennis player, in 2000. Global in Action has more than 1,000 members all over the nation. Every year, we send our members to many countries like Laos or Cambodia for volunteer work. We help build houses, dig wells, teach children, and do various other things to improve the community. If you're not sure how to spend your vacation, consider joining us. I'm sure you'll have one of the most valuable experiences of your life. If you don't have time, we always welcome financial contributions. For more information, please call us at 1-800-555-2134. Thank you.

KEYWORDS & EXPRESSIONS

내용 일치와 관련하여 알아둬야 할 어휘와 표현

deadline 마감 일자	destination 목적지	admission fee 입장료
application 지원(서)	accommodation 숙소	hand in / submit 제출하다
scholarship 장학금	graduation 졸업	apply for …에 지원하다
announcement 공지, 발표	submission 제출	organization 기관
contribution 기여, 기부	be allowed to-v …하는 것이 허용되다	sign up for / register / enroll …에 등록하다

- Please remember that food is not allowed in the zoo. 동물원에는 음식물이 허용되지 않는 것을 명심하십시오.
- The admission fee is $30, which includes meals and transportation.
  입장료는 식대와 교통비를 포함해서 30달러입니다.
- Welcome to the City Bus Tour of Rome, taking you through the most romantic city in the world!
  여러분을 세계에서 가장 낭만적인 도시로 안내해 줄 로마 시내버스 관광에 오신 것을 환영합니다!
- Attention, all visitors! Please follow the visitation guidelines for our patients.
  주목해 주십시오, 방문객 여러분! 저희 환자들을 위해 방문 지침을 따라 주십시오.
- To sign up for our membership, call 606-777-3879 weekdays during business hour.
  회원 가입을 하시려면, 주중 영업시간 중 606-777-3879번으로 전화 주십시오.

LISTEN & APPLY

정답 및 해설 p. 20

1 essay contest에 관한 다음 내용을 듣고, 일치하지 않는 것을 고르시오.

① 백일장 주제는 가족이다.
② 우승 상품은 뷔페 상품권이다.
③ 이메일을 통해 제출해야 한다.
④ 제출 기한은 5월 5일까지이다.
⑤ 참가자는 하나의 작품만 제출할 수 있다.

2 미술 전시회에 관한 다음 내용을 듣고, 일치하지 않는 것을 고르시오.

① 학생들이 만든 작품들이 전시된다.
② 모든 전시품들은 구입 가능하다.
③ 수익금은 보육원 아이들을 돕는 데 사용된다.
④ 기금 마련을 위해 다과를 판매한다.
⑤ 오후 8시 30분에 종료된다.

3 Sea Poison tree에 관한 다음 내용을 듣고, 일치하지 않는 것을 고르시오.

① 열대 해변 지역에 서식한다.
② 새로 난 잎사귀는 노란색이다.
③ 꽃은 밤에 피어난다.
④ 열매는 물에 뜬다.
⑤ 모든 부분에 독을 가지고 있다.

4 Sunnyvale 만화 동아리에 관한 다음 내용을 듣고, 일치하지 않는 것을 고르시오.

① 매주 목요일 한 번 학교에서 모인다.
② Williams 선생님이 동아리를 지도한다.
③ 미술 기법을 배울 수 있다.
④ 한 달에 한 번 만화 영화를 상영한다.
⑤ 웹사이트를 통해 추가 정보를 얻을 수 있다.

5 The Edgar Washington Show에 관한 다음 내용을 듣고, 일치하지 않는 것을 고르시오.

① 사회자는 코미디언이다.

② 첫 회에는 가수와 배우가 게스트로 출연한다.

③ 방청객과의 게임이 준비되어 있다.

④ 게스트는 TV에서 최초로 신곡을 부를 예정이다.

⑤ 채널 50에서 오후에 방송된다.

6 과학 박물관에 관한 다음 내용을 듣고, 일치하지 않는 것을 고르시오.

① 과학 교육의 대중화를 위해 설립되었다.

② 전시품들은 쌍방향적 요소를 지니고 있다.

③ 투어 소요 시간은 45분이다.

④ 내부에서 카메라 촬영이 금지되어 있다.

⑤ 기념품점 방문이 투어의 마지막 순서이다.

7 음료 시음회에 관한 다음 내용을 듣고, 일치하지 않는 것을 고르시오.

① 소화 불량에 도움이 되는 음료 시음회이다.

② 회의실에서 진행된다.

③ 시음 후 설문지를 작성해야 한다.

④ 모든 참가자는 음료 할인 쿠폰을 받을 수 있다.

⑤ 참가 신청은 회사 웹사이트를 통해 할 수 있다.

8 Open Campus Day에 관한 다음 내용을 듣고, 일치하지 않는 것을 고르시오.

① 고등학교 학생들을 위한 날이다.

② 모든 학생들은 각자 가이드를 배정받게 된다.

③ 학생들은 점심시간 전에 질문을 할 수 있다.

④ 학생들은 교수진들과 그룹별로 이야기할 수 있다.

⑤ 마지막 행사로 합창 공연이 예정되어 있다.

DICTATION

녹음을 다시 한 번 듣고, 빈칸에 알맞은 말을 쓰시오.

정답 및 해설 p. 21

1 M: Good evening to all of our listeners. I have a special announcement to make. As you know, next month is Family Appreciation Month, so we have decided to _______ _______ _______ _______ to celebrate. Write us an essay about your family and what they mean to you, and we will select a winner to read his or her story _______ _______ _______ on May 5. The winner will also receive a gift certificate to Fresh Garden Buffet. Please email your essay to familycontest@wkcp.org. The deadline is April 15, and we will not consider any late submissions. Also, _______ _______ _______ is allowed per person. If you have any questions about the contest, call us at 555-9786.

appreciation 감사
celebrate 축하하다, 기념하다
on the air 방송 중에
gift certificate 상품권

2 W: Good evening, and welcome to the Sejong High School student art show. All of the artwork on display tonight was created _______ _______ at our school. Please feel free to wander around the school's halls and admire it. All of the art is also _______ _______, and prices are marked on the back of each piece. The money that we raise tonight will be used to purchase _______ _______ for children at the local orphanage. Also, to my left, a variety of _______ _______ and refreshments for you to enjoy have been provided. The show will run until 8:30 p.m. Enjoy yourself, and let me know if you have any questions.

artwork 미술품
on display 전시된, 진열된
feel free to-v 마음대로 …하다
wander 돌아다니다
admire 감탄하다; *감상하다
mark (…에) 표시하다
piece 조각; *작품
purchase 사다
art supply 미술용품
orphanage 보육원
refreshment 《*pl.*》 다과

3 W: The Sea Poison tree is a large tree that grows on tropical coasts of the Indian Ocean and the western Pacific Ocean. Its leaves are a beautiful bronze color, and they have pink veins. _______ _______ _______ _______, they turn a yellowish color. The tree's flowers are closed during the day, but at night they open and attract nectar-feeding bats and large moths. The fruits of the tree are lantern-shaped and _______ _______ _______. In fact, it can survive for up to two years while drifting on the sea. Every part of the tree contains a poison called saponin. Nevertheless, the leaves have traditionally been used in the Philippines to _______ _______ and joint and muscle pain.

tropical 열대의
coast 해안
Indian Ocean 인도양
Pacific Ocean 태평양
bronze 구릿빛의
vein (식물의) 잎맥
attract 끌어들이다
nectar 꿀
feed 먹이로 하다
moth 나방
float 뜨다
drift 떠다니다
stomachache 복통
joint 관절

4 M: Good morning Sunnyvale High School students. Do you enjoy reading comic books or watching cartoons? Do you love to draw and ________ ________ interesting stories? If so, I would like to invite you to join the new Sunnyvale Cartoon Club. We will meet in the school's art room every Thursday afternoon. Mrs. Williams will be supervising the club. She will be ________ ________ ________ ________ about different artistic techniques. Everyone is welcome at this club, even if you have no experience drawing cartoons. We will also hold a monthly cartoon party. On the last Friday of each month, our club will watch our favorite cartoons in the school's auditorium. ________ ________ ________ the Sunnyvale Cartoon Club today. Please visit the art room by this Thursday for more information.

cartoon 만화, 만화 영화
supervise 감독하다, 지도하다
give a presentation 발표하다
artistic 미술적인
hold 개최하다, 열다
auditorium 강당
sign up for …에 가입하다

5 M: Do you want to find a new talk show to watch? Then you should try *The Edgar Washington Show*, a new TV show hosted by comedian Edgar Washington. ________ ________ ________ the first episode, when Edgar speaks to singer John Green. John shares stories about his personal struggle to become ________ ________ ________. Then Edgar asks John about his marriage and children with actress Laura Samson. You'll never guess what John says about being a famous father. Afterward, Edgar and John play a game with the studio audience. One lucky audience member could win backstage tickets to John's upcoming concert! Plus, John sings ________ ________ ________ ________ for the first time on television. *The Edgar Washington Show* can be seen daily at 4:00 p.m. right here on Channel 50.

host (TV · 라디오 프로를) 진행하다
tune in 청취하다, 시청하다
struggle 분투
successful 성공적인
marriage 결혼
audience 청중, 관중
backstage 무대 뒤(의)
upcoming 곧 다가오는
brand new 완전 새것인

6 W: Hello everyone. My name is Samantha Walters, and I will be guiding you through the museum today. The Springfield Science Museum was founded by Professor Albert Schwartz. His goal was to make science education more ________ ________ ________ ________. That is why our three main exhibits each have interactive components. Today's tour will last for 45 minutes, and then all visitors will be ________ ________ ________ these unique displays. Please note that cameras are allowed, but food and drinks ________ ________ ________ inside of the museum's exhibition halls. Feel free to ask questions during the tour. And we ask that all guests exit through the gift shop at the front of the museum.

found 설립하다
accessible 접근 가능한; *이해하기 쉬운
exhibit 전시(회), 전시품
interactive 쌍방향적인
component 요소
last 지속되다
display 전시(품)
allow 허용하다, 허락하다
permit 허락하다

7 M: This is a special announcement for all employees. There will be an event this Friday for testing a new health drink from Best Beverage. The drink is intended to help office workers who ________ ________ ________. At 3:00 p.m., representatives from Best Beverage will be in our meeting room to ________ ________ ________ ________ of their new drink. After participants try the drink, they will be asked to fill out a short questionnaire. And all participants will ________ ________ ________ for a free drink from Best Beverage. If you would like to participate in the event, please sign up on the company website before Friday.

announcement 알림, 공지
intended (…을 위해) 만들어진
suffer from …을 앓다
indigestion 소화 불량
representative 대표자, 영업사원
participant 참가자
questionnaire 설문지
participate in …에 참가하다

8 W: Good morning. I'd like to welcome all the high school students to Open Campus Day. After this welcome speech, you will each be ________ ________ ________ ________ as a personal guide. He or she will take you around and show you all the features of our university. After two hours, we'll meet back here for lunch, at which time you'll be able to ask any questions you might have. After lunch, a number of our professors will be available to talk to you ________ ________ about our various departments and majors. Finally, to end the day, our university's singing club will perform for you ________ ________ ________. I hope it will be an enjoyable day for everyone.

welcome speech 환영사
assign 맡기다, 배정하다
feature 특색, 특징
available 시간[여유]이 있는
perform 공연하다
farewell 작별 (인사)

11강 언급 내용

대화를 듣고, 대화 속의 인물이 언급하거나 언급하지 않은 것을 고르는 문제 유형이다.

이 순서대로 풀어봐요

STEP 1 지시문과 선택지를 미리 읽고, 어떤 내용이 나올지 추측해 본다.
STEP 2 언급하지 않은 것을 고르는 문제의 경우, 대화를 들으면서 오답을 하나씩 지워나간다.
STEP 3 언급한 것을 고르는 문제의 경우, 세부 내용을 집중해서 들으며 정답을 찾는다.

기출 예제

대화를 듣고, 슬라이드 자료에 관해 두 사람이 언급하지 않은 것을 고르시오. 평가원 기출

① 디자인 ② 글자 크기
③ 음향 효과 ④ 사진
⑤ 도표

문제해설
남자는 슬라이드의 디자인은 마음에 들고, 글자 크기는 지금 그대로가 좋으며, 음향 효과는 넣지 않는 게 좋을 것 같다고 했다. 그리고 도표는 너무 많이 넣지 않는 게 좋겠다고 조언했지만, 사진에 대해서는 언급하지 않았다. (정답 ④)

W: Daniel, do you have a minute?
M: Yeah, what's up?
W: I'm working on my presentation for tomorrow. I'd like to get your opinion on my slides.
M: What's your presentation about?
W: It's about marketing strategies for a new product.
M: Okay, let me look at the slides. Hmm... They look great! I like the design. It's simple but eye-catching.
W: Thanks! Do you think I should increase the font size?
M: No, the font size looks okay as it is.
W: What do you think about adding sound effects to the slides?
M: Well, I don't think it's necessary. It could distract people from the main content.
W: I see. Do you think it's good to include charts to convey the information more effectively?
M: Yeah, but too many of them won't help.
W: Hmm... I think you're right.

KEYWORDS & EXPRESSIONS

언급 내용과 관련하여 알아둬야 할 표현

〈시간〉
- When was this organization founded? 이 기구는 언제 설립되었습니까?
- How long did it take to rebuild this building? 이 건물을 다시 짓는 데 얼마나 걸렸죠?

〈장소〉
- Where is Microsoft's headquarters located? 마이크로소프트사의 본사는 어디에 있나요?
- Our restaurant is located in the center of the city. 저희 식당은 시내 중심에 있습니다.

〈가격〉
- How much will it cost to fix the computer? 컴퓨터를 고치는 데 비용이 얼마나 들까요?
- You need to pay $3 a month to get more information. 더 많은 정보를 얻기 위해서는 한 달에 3달러를 내야 합니다.

〈수량〉
- How many people are participating in this event? 이 행사에 얼마나 많은 사람들이 참가하고 있죠?
- How much vitamin C should we take in a day? 하루에 비타민 C를 얼마나 섭취해야 하나요?

〈이유〉
- Could you tell me why you were absent from work today? 오늘 왜 결근했는지 말해 주시겠어요?
- There was an outage due to a mechanical problem. 기술적인 문제 때문에 정전이 있었습니다.

〈문제점〉
- There seems to be something wrong with the battery. 배터리에 문제가 있는 것 같네요.
- There's a little problem with this system. 이 시스템에 약간의 문제가 있습니다.

LISTEN & APPLY

정답 및 해설 p. 22

1 **대화를 듣고, 박물관에 관해 두 사람이 언급하지 않은 것을 고르시오.**

① 운영 시간
② 입장료
③ 설립 시기
④ 소장품 수
⑤ 방문객 수

2 **대화를 듣고, Fenway Park에 관해 언급되지 않은 것을 고르시오.**

① 용도
② 특징
③ 건축 연도
④ 수용 인원
⑤ 한 해 관중 수

3 **대화를 듣고, 복원된 문화재에 관해 두 사람이 언급하지 않은 것을 고르시오.**

① 복원 기간
② 복원 비용
③ 훼손된 이유
④ 최초 준공 시기
⑤ 한 해 관광 수입

4 **대화를 듣고, 남자의 유학에 관해 두 사람이 언급하지 않은 것을 고르시오.**

① 유학 비용
② 체류 국가
③ 유학 기간
④ 배울 과목
⑤ 거주지

5 대화를 듣고, 운전 학원에 관해 두 사람이 언급하지 않은 것을 고르시오.

① 수업 시간
② 휴무일
③ 수강료
④ 주행 코스
⑤ 환불 정책

6 대화를 듣고, 기말고사 과제에 관해 두 사람이 언급하지 않은 것을 고르시오.

① 참여 인원
② 과제 주제
③ 과제 분량
④ 제출 기한
⑤ 참고 자료

7 대화를 듣고, 파티 준비에 관해 두 사람이 언급하지 않은 것을 고르시오.

① 집안 장식
② 케이크 주문
③ 간식 준비
④ 생일 선물 구입
⑤ 초대장 작성

8 대화를 듣고, Da Vinci Salon에 관해 언급되지 않은 것을 고르시오.

① 분위기
② 영업 시간
③ 가격
④ 미용사의 실력
⑤ 위치

DICTATION

녹음을 다시 한 번 듣고, 빈칸에 알맞은 말을 쓰시오.

정답 및 해설 p. 23

1

M: Excuse me, I'd like to ask a few questions about this museum.
W: All right. What would you like to know?
M: Can you tell me what the museum's hours are?
W: Sure. We're open from 10 a.m. to 6 p.m. from Tuesday to Thursday, and from 10 a.m. to 9 p.m. from Friday to Sunday.
M: I see. How much does it ________ ________ ________ ________?
W: It is $15 for a one-day pass.
M: That seems expensive!
W: Maybe, but the museum has about 35,000 pieces of art. We ________ ________ ________ our excellent collections.
M: Really? Do many people visit the museum?
W: Yes. In fact, we have more than three million visitors every year.
M: Oh, in that case, I really want ________ ________ ________ ________ ________.
W: That's an excellent idea. Please enjoy your visit.

collection 소장품
take a look around 주위를 둘러보다

2

M: I'm so excited to see Fenway Park in Boston!
W: I think you'll love it.
M: Actually, I've always wanted to see it. It's such a famous baseball stadium.
W: It's been used for other sports, too.
M: Really? I didn't know that.
W: It's true. Fenway Park has hosted ________ ________ ________, football games, and even ice hockey games!
M: Wow, I can't imagine that.
W: By the way, do you know what its most famous feature is?
M: You mean the ________ ________ ________ ________?
W: Yes. It's called the Green Monster. It's green and much taller than the average wall, so it got that nickname.
M: I see. When was the stadium built?
W: It was built in 1912, and ________ ________ ________ more than 37,000 people.
M: Wow. You know everything about the stadium!
W: Of course. I'm a big fan of the Boston Red Sox!

stadium 경기장
host 주최하다
match 경기
field 들판; *경기장
average 평균의; *보통의
nickname 별명
hold 수용하다

3

W: Are you one of the construction workers who has been working on this building?
M: Yes. It has been a difficult project.
W: How long have you been ________ ________ ________ ________?
M: I joined the team one year ago, but the project has taken two years.
W: It must be a very expensive project.
M: Yes, it is. It has cost almost $10 million ________ ________ ________ ________.

construction worker 공사현장 인부
restore 복원하다
destroy 파괴하다
shame 수치심; *애석한 일
originally 원래

W: That is expensive. Was there a lot of damage?
M: Yes. The building was almost destroyed by the fire.
W: That would have been a shame.
M: Yes, it would have. The building ________ ________ ________ almost 500 years ago. There will be thousands of visitors when it opens again.
W: I hope so. Thank you for your time.
M: You're welcome.

4 W: Hey, Ted! I heard you are going to study in France soon.
M: Yes. I'll leave for Paris next month and stay there for two years.
W: Congratulations! So, what are you going to study there?
M: Mostly French. But I guess I could also ________ ________ ________ ________.
W: Good for you. You've always wanted to learn the French style of baking.
M: That's right. And I can practice what I learn at home after the class.
W: At home? You'll have an oven ________ ________ ________ ________?
M: No, actually I won't live in a dorm room. I'll live with a host family. They said I can use their kitchen.
W: Oh, great! That was nice of them.
M: I feel very lucky to have found them.
W: It sounds like ________ ________ ________ ________ well. I hope you have a good time there.
M: Thanks. I will miss you very much.

Congratulations! 축하해!
dorm 기숙사(= dormitory)
host family (외국인 방문객을 받아들이는) 민박 가정
work out (계획 등이) 잘되어 가다

5 M: Welcome to Amazing Driving School! Would you like to know more about our classes?
W: Yes. When do you offer classes?
M: We have classes every day from 6 a.m. to 8 p.m. ________ ________ ________. We're closed every Monday.
W: Oh, I see. How much do the classes cost?
M: Our classes are 300,000 won for 10 hours of instruction.
W: I see. Where is your driving course?
M: We have a special driving course near our offices.
W: Would I have a chance to practice on the streets?
M: Yes, we ________ ________ ________ ________ on the city streets.
W: That sounds great. I think I'd like to enroll.
M: I'm glad to hear that. I'm sure it will be ________ ________ ________.
W: Thank you. I hope so.

instruction 설명; *가르침, 지도
enroll (…에) 등록하다
worth one's while …할 가치가[보람이] 있는

6 M: Hey, Rachel. I didn't see you in class today. Are you all right?
W: Hey, Evan! Yes, I was just sick this morning. But I'm okay now. Did Mr. Kim mention anything about the final project?

mention 언급하다, 말하다
topic 주제
invention 발명(품)

M: Yes. It's going to be a group project for groups of three. You'll be in a group with Sam and me.
W: Okay. __________ __________ __________ __________?
M: We have to research an invention. We chose the clock. Then we have to write a paper about it.
W: That sounds fun.
M: Yes, but it's __________ __________ __________ __________.
W: Two weeks? We'd better get busy right away. Where can we find information?
M: Well, we can look online, but we should also look at some books.
W: Good idea. I'll __________ __________ __________.

due (…하기로) 예정된
get busy 일을 시작하다

7
W: You know that Mike's birthday is in two weeks, right?
M: Oh, right! Have you started planning his party?
W: Well, he just __________ __________ __________ __________ to invite. So, now we can start planning.
M: I see. I will decorate the house. What kind of decorations should we have?
W: Mike loves balloons. We'll need a lot of balloons.
M: Okay. I can get the balloons. Have you __________ __________ __________?
W: Not yet, but I will do that soon. I'm also planning to make some snacks.
M: That's a good idea. You can make some cookies, and I'll get some candy.
W: Thanks. Then we just need to __________ __________ __________.
M: Okay. Did you get some invitation cards?
W: Yes. If you write in them, I'll seal the envelopes.
M: Sure.

invite 초대하다
invitation 초대(장)
seal (봉투를) 봉하다
envelope 봉투

8
M: Valerie, your haircut looks fantastic. You look like a movie star.
W: Thanks, Abe. I got it cut at the Da Vinci Salon.
M: I've never heard of it. Is it new?
W: No, it's not. It is the same salon I've gone to since I was little.
M: Really? Why do you keep going to the same place?
W: The atmosphere is __________ __________ __________.
M: It sounds nice. How about the price?
W: The price is reasonable, too. And my hairstylist is brilliant.
M: It sounds like the __________ __________ __________ __________.
W: But there is one problem. It's in the Land Department Store two towns away.
M: Oh, that's quite far from here. It must be burdensome if you get your hair cut often.
W: Luckily, I only go __________ __________ __________ __________.
M: Then I guess it's not so bad.

atmosphere 분위기
peaceful 평화로운
relaxing 편안한, 느긋한
reasonable (가격이) 적정한, 너무 비싸지 않은
brilliant 뛰어난, 우수한
burdensome 부담스러운, 힘든

12강 긴 대화 응답

긴 대화를 듣고, 남자나 여자의 마지막 말에 대한 응답으로 가장 적절한 것을 고르는 문제 유형이다.

이 순서대로 풀어봐요

STEP 1 대화를 듣기 전에 선택지를 미리 읽고, 어떤 내용이 나올지 예상해 본다.

STEP 2 응답자가 남자인지 여자인지 미리 확인하여, 응답자가 어떤 입장인지 유의해서 듣는다.

STEP 3 전반적인 대화의 내용을 파악하면서 상대방의 마지막 말을 주의 깊게 듣는다.

기출 예제

대화를 듣고, 남자의 마지막 말에 대한 여자의 응답으로 가장 적절한 것을 고르시오. 평가원 기출

Woman: ____________________

① Okay. I'll go find another one soon.
② Never mind. I'll give you my advice.
③ But didn't you already contact him last year?
④ I'm sure you'll do a great job at the program.
⑤ Then can you send them to me by text message?

문제해설

여자가 원하는 강사의 연락처를 남자가 가지고 있다고 했으므로 그것을 보내달라는 응답이 와야 자연스럽다. (정답 ⑤)

① 알았어요. 가서 곧 다른 걸 찾아볼게요.
② 신경 쓰지 마세요. 당신에게 조언을 좀 해줄게요.
③ 그런데 당신은 작년에 이미 그에게 연락하지 않았나요?
④ 당신은 그 프로그램에서 잘 해낼 거라고 확신해요.

M: Hey, Susan. How's your new position?
W: Very busy. I'm preparing the employee training program.
M: I understand. That was my job last year.
W: Did you also have so many things to prepare at that time?
M: Sure, I did.
W: I just wonder how you handled all those things alone.
M: Yeah, it was tough. But the hardest part was getting a qualified instructor. Did you find someone?
W: I'm trying, but not yet. Well, do you think it'll be okay if we hire the same person as last year?
M: Why not? He did a great job.
W: Good to hear that. Do you still have the instructor's contact information?
M: Yes. I have his phone number and email address.
W: ____________________

KEYWORDS & EXPRESSIONS

긴 대화 응답과 관련하여 알아둬야 할 표현

- One person's trash may be another's treasure. 누군가의 쓰레기가 다른 사람에겐 보물이 될 수도 있어.
  → You're right. I'd like to take these clothes to the store. 네 말이 맞아. 이 옷들을 상점으로 가지고 가야겠다.
- But the store closes at 8:00 p.m. Oh, it's already seven o'clock. 그런데 상점이 오후 8시에 문을 닫아. 아, 벌써 7시네.
  → I'd better go right now to buy new shoes. 새 신발을 사러 지금 당장 가야겠어.
- I think it will take time to find what we're looking for. 우리가 찾는 걸 발견하는 데 시간이 걸릴 것 같아.
  → Don't worry. Just ask a librarian for help. 걱정하지 마. 그냥 사서에게 도와달라고 하면 돼.
- Somebody spilled juice all over the bench. It's all sticky. 누군가가 벤치에 온통 주스를 흘렸네. 전부 끈적거려.
  → They should have wiped it up before they left. 그들은 떠나기 전에 그걸 닦았어야 했어.
- It just skipped this floor. Do we have to wait again? 그것은 방금 전에 이 층을 지나가 버렸어요. 또 기다려야 할까요?
  → Forget the elevator. Let's take the stairs. 엘리베이터는 잊어요. 계단으로 가죠.
- Do you have time to help me pack for moving tomorrow? 내일 내가 이삿짐 싸는 걸 도와줄 시간 있니?
  → I'm sorry. I need to study for my history exam. 미안해. 역사 시험을 대비해서 공부를 해야 해.

LISTEN & APPLY

정답 및 해설 p. 24

1 대화를 듣고, 남자의 마지막 말에 대한 여자의 응답으로 가장 적절한 것을 고르시오.

Woman: ______________________________

① Oh, I have a map of the downtown area.
② We should have taken a bus.
③ Forget your troubles and take a nap instead.
④ Then let's switch seats. I'll drive while you relax.
⑤ Don't worry. The traffic is very light on this road today.

2 대화를 듣고, 여자의 마지막 말에 대한 남자의 응답으로 가장 적절한 것을 고르시오.

Man: ______________________________

① Well, I've learned my lesson.
② That's why I prefer dogs to cats.
③ I really like playing with my cats.
④ I can't understand why it did that.
⑤ You can go to Lisa's house anytime.

3 대화를 듣고, 남자의 마지막 말에 대한 여자의 응답으로 가장 적절한 것을 고르시오.

Woman: ______________________________

① I hope to do some volunteer work.
② I forgot to tell you about the fundraiser.
③ But in this case, quantity comes before quality.
④ Don't worry. You have plenty of time to finish.
⑤ Let's take a break and make the rest of them this evening.

4 대화를 듣고, 여자의 마지막 말에 대한 남자의 응답으로 가장 적절한 것을 고르시오.

Man: ______________________________

① How was your trip to Spain?
② I'd like to move out like you.
③ Everyone has their own taste.
④ Why don't you clean your house?
⑤ As you know, we both like fancy ornaments.

5 대화를 듣고, 남자의 마지막 말에 대한 여자의 응답으로 가장 적절한 것을 고르시오.

Woman: ______________________________

① I don't think you should ignore him.
② It's important to be on time to meetings.
③ You should stop criticizing other people.
④ I don't understand why you yelled at me.
⑤ You know, two wrongs don't make a right.

6 대화를 듣고, 여자의 마지막 말에 대한 남자의 응답으로 가장 적절한 것을 고르시오.

Man: ______________________________

① I enjoyed that romantic movie.
② That's the best movie in my life.
③ I told you I don't want to see a movie.
④ It's a historical drama, not a documentary.
⑤ Maybe we should go to the movies another time.

7 대화를 듣고, 남자의 마지막 말에 대한 여자의 응답으로 가장 적절한 것을 고르시오.

Woman: ______________________________

① Please don't worry about me.
② You'd better prepare for the report.
③ Just study extra hard for the final exam.
④ I should have hurried up to finish it on time.
⑤ Why don't you ask your teacher for more time?

8 대화를 듣고, 여자의 마지막 말에 대한 남자의 응답으로 가장 적절한 것을 고르시오.

Man: ______________________________

① Don't worry. It's working just fine now.
② You need to be more careful with my cat.
③ Didn't I tell you not to touch any of my stuff?
④ I should have told you about that before I left.
⑤ I promise I'll buy you a new one when I get back.

DICTATION

녹음을 다시 한 번 듣고, 빈칸에 알맞은 말을 쓰시오.

정답 및 해설 p. 26

1

M: Oh, no! Why is ________ ________ ________ ________ with traffic?
W: I don't know. It's not like this usually.
M: Can you check the traffic information on my smartphone? It's updated in real time.
W: Okay. But how do I do that?
M: There is an icon on the second page. Just touch it and ________ ________ ________.
W: I got it. [*Pause*] Oh, the traffic is heavy all the way to Fifth Avenue.
M: Really? Is there a route that is less busy?
W: No. All the roads on the map ________ ________.
M: You mean we have to sit in traffic until we reach Fifth Avenue? I'm so tired.
W: (Then let's switch seats. I'll drive while you relax.)

jammed 빽빽이 찬, 몹시 붐비는
in real time 실시간으로
refresh (최신 정보로) 재생하다, 새로고침하다
route 길, 경로
blocked 막힌, 봉쇄된
| 문제 | **take a nap** 낮잠 자다
switch 바꾸다
light (교통량이) 많지 않은

2

W: Kevin, what happened? How did you get that ________ ________?
M: Oh, it's nothing, Mom. I was just playing with Lisa's cat.
W: Oh, my goodness. Why did it scratch you?
M: I don't know. I was just playing with it and it suddenly scratched me.
W: Does Lisa's cat usually scratch people?
M: No. It's usually ________ ________ ________.
W: You must have done something wrong.
M: Well, I guess I was teasing it a little bit.
W: What do you mean by "teasing"?
M: Well, I was trying to get it to dance on two feet.
W: That's terrible! You should never ________ ________ ________ like that.
M: (Well, I've learned my lesson.)

awful 심한, 지독한
scratch 긁힌 자국; 할퀴다
suddenly 갑자기
sweet 귀여운, 사랑스러운
tease 괴롭히다, 놀리다
terrible 끔찍한
| 문제 | **lesson** 교훈
prefer A to B B보다 A를 선호하다

3

M: Wow, I didn't know making posters was such hard work.
W: I know. ________ ________ ________ to help.
M: No problem. I'm glad to help you out.
W: Good. This fundraiser will raise a lot of money for our school.
M: Yes. I've finished four already.
W: Four? That's all? But you've been working for two hours.
M: Yes, but I want them to look nice. Look at this one.
W: It looks great. But we need these posters by noon so we can ________ ________ ________.
M: That's only an hour away. How many do you need?
W: Eight. You're going to have to make four more in an hour.
M: I ________ ________ ________ ________. They won't look good.
W: (But in this case, quantity comes before quality.)

help out …을 도와주다
fundraiser 기금 모금자; *모금 행사
raise (돈을) 모으다
put up …을 게시하다
| 문제 | **quantity** 양, 수량
quality 질, 품질
plenty of 많은
take a break 휴식하다
rest 나머지

4
W: Thank you for inviting me over. I brought a cake that I baked today.
M: Wow, it looks delicious. Thank you.
W: Can I take a look around your new house?
M: Sure. Please follow me. I'll give you a tour.
W: What an ________ ________! What is it?
M: Oh, I brought it back from Spain. It is supposed to bring its owner good luck.
W: Wow. You really have ________ ________ ________ ________ here.
M: I love keeping interesting things in my home.
W: Well, it's very different from my house.
M: Yes. Your house is always so ________ ________ ________.
W: Yeah, I don't like having a lot of stuff in my house.
M: (Everyone has their own taste.)

invite over …를 집으로 초대하다
sculpture 조각(품)
owner 소유자
good luck 행운
neat 단정한, 깔끔한
stuff 물건
| 문제 | move out 이사 가다
taste 취향
fancy 화려한
ornament 장식(품)

5
M: I really don't want to go to work tomorrow.
W: Why not? I thought you were enjoying your new job.
M: I am. The work is great, but on Mondays we have ________ ________ ________.
W: What's so bad about having a meeting?
M: It's one of my coworkers. He just sits there and ________ ________.
W: Oh, there's someone like that at every meeting. Just ignore him.
M: I tried that at first. But last week, I couldn't take it any longer.
W: Uh-oh. What happened?
M: Oh, I ________ ________ ________, and then he yelled at me. The situation was pretty bad.
W: (You know, two wrongs don't make a right.)

coworker 동료
criticize 비판하다, 비난하다
ignore 무시하다
take it 견디다, 참다
yell 소리치다
situation 상황
| 문제 | on time 제시간에

6
M: Would you like to watch a horror movie with me tonight?
W: Oh, I hate horror movies. I ________ ________ after watching them. What else is playing?
M: Let's see. There are three other movies at the theater.
W: Are they showing that new romantic comedy from France?
M: Not yet. It'll ________ ________ tomorrow. What about a Japanese movie instead?
W: I don't usually like Japanese movies. Oh, I want to watch this one!
M: *Terry's Story*? It doesn't start until 10:15 p.m.
W: Oh, that's too late for me.

horror movie 공포 영화
nightmare 악몽
play 상영하다
show 상영하다
release 발매하다; *개봉하다
documentary 다큐멘터리
| 문제 | historical 역사의, 역사와 관련된

M: Hmm... The only thing left is a documentary.

W: You know, documentaries are __________ __________.

M: (Maybe we should go to the movies another time.)

7

M: Hi, Heather.

W: Hi, Clark. What's wrong? You look really down.

M: I sure am. I just __________ __________ __________ __________ to my history teacher.

W: Wasn't it due yesterday?

M: Yes. That's why I'm worried. You know, my history teacher is notorious for being __________ __________ __________.

W: But I know you pulled out all the stops on the report. I'm sure the teacher will be satisfied with it.

M: Even if the report is perfect, I won't get higher than a B because it's late.

W: Well, you've always done well in class. I'm sure your final grade will be fine.

M: I don't know. I really need an A in that class, and there's only the __________ __________ __________.

W: (Just study extra hard for the final exam.)

down 기운 없는, 의기소침한
hand in 제출하다
notorious 악명 높은
strict 엄격한
grader 채점자
pull out all the stops 온갖 노력을 다하다
be satisfied with …에 만족하다
final 최종의
grade 성적
final exam 기말고사
문제 extra 여분으로; *특별히

8

[*Cell phone rings.*]

M: Hello. This is Mike.

W: Hi, Mike. It's Wendy.

M: Hi, Wendy. Is everything going okay with my apartment?

W: Well, I'm __________ __________ __________ and playing with your cat like you asked.

M: Great. You didn't forget to bring in the mail, did you?

W: No, it's all on the kitchen counter. But...

M: Uh-oh. Did something happen?

W: Well, I was spending time with your cat, and I decided to turn on the TV.

M: Oh, I see.

W: But it suddenly __________ __________ __________ __________! I don't know what I did. I'm sorry.

M: No, no. There's been something wrong with that TV for a while.

W: Oh, really? I thought I __________ __________ __________!

M: (I should have told you about that before I left.)

water (식물에) 물을 주다
bring in 가져오다, 들여오다
mail 우편물
kitchen counter 부엌 조리대
turn on …을 켜다
flash 번쩍거리다
go off (불 · 전기 등이) 나가다
for a while 잠시, 얼마 동안
break 고장 내다

13강 상황에 적절한 말

특정 상황에 대한 담화를 듣고, 그 상황에서 해당 인물이 할 말로 가장 적절한 것을 고르는 문제 유형이다.

이 순서대로 풀어봐요

STEP 1 대화를 듣기 전에, 지시문을 미리 읽고, 누가 누구에게 하는 말인지 파악한다.

STEP 2 전체적인 상황 속에서 해당 인물이 처한 입장을 파악한다.

STEP 3 앞부분은 전반적인 상황 설명이고, 주로 뒷부분에 구체적인 힌트가 제시되므로, 마지막 부분에 특히 유의한다.

기출 예제

다음 상황 설명을 듣고, Peter가 Sandra에게 할 말로 가장 적절한 것을 고르시오. 수능 기출

Peter: Sandra, ______________________

① I think you need to take a break for a while.
② I recommend you return your book soon.
③ I'd suggest changing where you study.
④ you'd better review what you learned.
⑤ you should've slept more last night.

문제해설
Sandra가 도서관에서 집중할 수 없는 상태이므로, Peter가 Sandra에게 할 말로 ③번이 가장 적절하다. (정답 ③)
① 넌 좀 쉬어야 할 것 같아.
② 책을 곧 반납하는 걸 권해.
④ 네가 배운 걸 복습하는 게 좋겠다.
⑤ 넌 어젯밤에 더 잤어야 했는데.

M: Peter and Sandra are classmates. They've been in the library over the weekend reading for their literature class. Sandra is unable to concentrate and is feeling exhausted. However, she has noticed that Peter seems to be focused and full of energy. In fact, Peter has a secret for maintaining his focus. Whenever he is losing his concentration, he gathers his belongings and moves to another place. To him, a new environment feels like a new beginning. A different desk, chair, and view help him to feel refreshed and ready to continue for another hour or two. When Sandra asks Peter about how she can stop herself from losing concentration, he wants to advise her to switch study spaces. In this situation, what would Peter most likely say to Sandra?

KEYWORDS & EXPRESSIONS

상황에 적절한 말과 관련하여 알아둬야 할 표현

〈부탁할 때〉
- Could you be a substitute for me? 제 일을 대신해 줄 수 있습니까?
- Could I borrow your cell phone? 당신의 휴대전화를 빌릴 수 있을까요?

〈감사 인사할 때〉
- Madam, your kindness will not be forgotten. 부인, 당신의 호의는 잊지 않을게요.
- Thank you for your kind words. 당신의 친절한 말씀에 감사드립니다.

〈칭찬할 때〉
- I'm proud of you. You set an excellent example. 당신이 자랑스럽습니다. 당신은 훌륭한 본보기가 되었어요.
- You are the best! 당신이 최고예요!
- Good job. / Well done. 잘했어요.

〈도움을 줄 때〉
- I'm glad that I can do it for you. 당신을 위해 이 일을 할 수 있어서 기뻐요.
- I'll be happy to help you with any problems. 무슨 문제가 있으면 제가 기꺼이 도와 드릴게요.
- Cheer up! You'll do better next time. 기운 내요! 다음번엔 더 잘할 수 있을 거예요.

〈격려할 때〉
- We can make it. 우리는 해낼 수 있어요.
- Everything will be fine. 모든 일이 잘될 거예요.

〈충고할 때〉
- If I were you, I wouldn't go there. 제가 당신이라면, 그곳에 가지 않겠어요.
- I think you need to get your priorities straight. 당신의 우선순위를 제대로 정해야 할 것 같아요.

〈거절할 때〉
- Sounds good, but it's too late for a last-minute change. 괜찮긴 한데, 마지막 순간에 바꾸기에는 너무 늦었어요.

LISTEN & APPLY

정답 및 해설 p. 26

1 다음 상황 설명을 듣고, Trevor가 Jacob에게 할 말로 가장 적절한 것을 고르시오.

Trevor: ____________________

① Please don't bother me.
② Sorry for breaking your printer.
③ Can you show me how to use the printer?
④ Is it okay if we share everything?
⑤ You'd better get your own computer.

2 다음 상황 설명을 듣고, Lucy가 Jerry에게 할 말로 가장 적절한 것을 고르시오.

Lucy: ____________________

① This is your lost kitten, isn't it?
② I'm afraid my kitten hurt its leg.
③ Call me if you see my kitten, please.
④ Please try to be quieter in the morning.
⑤ Can you take care of my kitten for a few days?

3 다음 상황 설명을 듣고, Ben이 직원에게 할 말로 가장 적절한 것을 고르시오.

Ben: ____________________

① I have a 10% off coupon here.
② This is not what I ordered.
③ Could you warm the bagel for me?
④ It's much cheaper here than I expected.
⑤ I think you overcharged me by mistake.

4 다음 상황 설명을 듣고, Vincent가 남자에게 할 말로 가장 적절한 것을 고르시오.

Vincent: ____________________

① Do you have a similar pair of jeans in a larger size?
② Sorry, but I think you took my cell phone by mistake.
③ I think you dropped something in the changing room.
④ Excuse me, but have you seen my cell phone anywhere?
⑤ I'm finished with the changing room, so you can use it now.

5 다음 상황 설명을 듣고, Gail이 이웃에게 할 말로 가장 적절한 것을 고르시오.

Gail: ______________________________

① I prefer to stay at home in this weather.
② That's okay. I wake up early in the morning.
③ There is an affordable health club near here.
④ Well, I'd rather jog alone than with someone else.
⑤ I'm sorry, I didn't realize my exercising was bothering you.

6 다음 상황 설명을 듣고, 선생님이 Brandy에게 할 말로 가장 적절한 것을 고르시오.

Teacher: ______________________________

① I'm very proud of the progress you've made.
② You should not be afraid of making mistakes.
③ How about learning some foreign languages?
④ Please don't talk to your friends while I'm teaching.
⑤ It is important to complete all of your work on time.

7 다음 상황 설명을 듣고, Amy가 아버지에게 할 말로 가장 적절한 것을 고르시오.

Amy: ______________________________

① Why didn't you help me look for a job?
② I can't afford to come visit you right now.
③ I'm considering moving to the city to find a job.
④ I don't want to stay here because I miss my family.
⑤ My major would help me to find a well-paying job.

8 다음 상황 설명을 듣고, Andrew가 Melissa에게 할 말로 가장 적절한 것을 고르시오.

Andrew: ______________________________

① You should look for a new job.
② I really wish you'd consider my advice.
③ The work is really not that hard to get done.
④ You don't have to complete all of your projects.
⑤ Don't give up. You will get used to working here soon.

DICTATION

녹음을 다시 한 번 듣고, 빈칸에 알맞은 말을 쓰시오.

정답 및 해설 p. 28

1 M: Trevor and Jacob live together. To save money, they ________ ________ ________. For example, they both use Trevor's television and coffee maker. And they also share Jacob's computer. Because it is a model that Trevor is unfamiliar with, however, he doesn't know ________ ________ ________ the printer. The first time he needed to print something, Jacob did it for him. The next time, Trevor asked how to use it, but Jacob said it would be easier if he just did it for him. These days, Trevor has many things to print, and he's afraid he's annoying Jacob ________ ________ ________. In this situation, what would Trevor most likely say to Jacob?

Trevor: (Can you show me how to use the printer?)

save 저축하다; *절약하다
share 함께하다, 같이 쓰다
unfamiliar 익숙지 않은, 생소한
annoy 성가시게 하다, 귀찮게 하다
request 부탁, 요구
| 문제 | **bother** 귀찮게 하다
had better …하는 편이 낫다

2 W: Lucy lives in an apartment downtown. One morning, she was awakened by the sound of ________ ________ ________ ________. At first she tried to ignore it, but she finally got up and looked out her window to see what was happening. She saw a small kitten that seemed to have ________ ________ ________. She thought it might be her neighbor Jerry's cat and remembered seeing a poster for a lost kitten in the apartment lobby the day before. She went downstairs and got the kitten. Then she ________ ________ to Jerry's apartment. In this situation, what would Lucy most likely say to Jerry?

Lucy: (This is your lost kitten, isn't it?)

awaken (잠에서) 깨우다
kitten 새끼 고양이
hurt 다치게 하다
lost 잃은, 분실한
downstairs 아래층으로

3 M: Ben likes to have coffee and a bagel for breakfast. One day, he stops by his favorite coffee shop on his way to work. When he greets the clerk, he notices that she is ________ ________ ________. He orders a latte and a plain cream cheese bagel as usual. When he is ready to pay, she says the bill is $12. But since he is a ________ ________ of the shop, he knows it should be $10. He asks her if the prices ________ ________ ________, but she says no. In this situation, what would Ben most likely say to the clerk?

Ben: (I think you overcharged me by mistake.)

on one's way to …로 가는 길에
greet 인사하다
clerk (가게의) 점원
notice 알아차리다
as usual 평소처럼
regular customer 단골 손님
| 문제 | **overcharge** 많이 청구하다
by mistake 잘못하여, 실수로

4 W: One day, Vincent is shopping for new pants in a department store. He finds a pair of jeans that he ________ ________ ________ ________. However, someone is already in the changing room, so he has to wait. After the man leaves, Vincent goes in. But while he's trying on the jeans, he notices a cell phone ________ ________ ________ ________. When he is finished, he picks up the cell phone and goes looking for the man. After a few minutes, he sees him ________ ________ ________ at the cash register. In this situation, what would Vincent most likely say to the man?

Vincent: (I think you dropped something in the changing room.)

changing room 탈의실
lie 놓여 있다
in line 줄을 서서
cash register 계산대

5 M: Gail lives in an apartment building in the city. Because she was gaining weight, she decided to ________ ________ ________. She started jogging through the park every morning. However, last week the weather turned very cold. So Gail decided to ________ ________ ________ in front of the television. One afternoon, Gail found a note on her door from her downstairs neighbor asking her to please stop making ________ ________ ________ early in the morning. Gail decided to go talk to him. In this situation, what would Gail most likely say to her neighbor?

Gail: (I'm sorry, I didn't realize my exercising was bothering you.)

gain weight 체중이 늘다
get in shape 좋은 몸매를 유지하다
in place 제자리에
[문제] affordable (가격이) 알맞은
would rather A than B B하기 보다는 차라리 A하겠다

6 W: Brandy is taking a Chinese class. She is a good student who always hands in her assignments on time. But her teacher has noticed that she ________ ________ in class. Whenever she does speak and says something wrong, she ________ ________. Because of this, she only gives simple answers to his questions, using words she's comfortable with. Her teacher is worried that Brandy's speaking ability will ________ ________ unless she changes her ways, so he asks her to stay after class. In this situation, what would Brandy's teacher most likely say to her?

Teacher: (You should not be afraid of making mistakes.)

assignment 숙제
ashamed 부끄러운, 창피한
comfortable 편안한; *편하게 생각하는
[문제] progress 진보, 발전
foreign language 외국어
complete 완료하다, 끝마치다

7 M: After graduating university, Amy had a hard time ________ ________ ________. One day, her friend moved away from her hometown to try to find work in a bigger city. Later, she called Amy and said she finally found a well-paying job at a big company. Amy envies her friend and is thinking of ________ ________ ________ ________ because there are more job opportunities there than in her hometown. Amy ________ ________ ________ with her father about this. That evening, when her father came back, Amy asked him if she could talk to him about something. In this situation, what would Amy most likely say to her father?

Amy: (I'm considering moving to the city to find a job.)

graduate 졸업하다
move away 떠나다, 이사하다
hometown 고향
well-paying 보수가 좋은
envy 부러워하다, 질투하다
job opportunity 취업 기회
| 문제 | **afford to-v** …할 여유가 되다
consider 숙고하다, 고려하다

8 W: Andrew has been working at the same company for three years. When he first started working for the company, he ________ ________ ________ the amount of work he had to complete. He was always working on several projects at the same time. After a few months, however, Andrew ________ ________ his new responsibilities and began to appreciate the company's supportive work environment. Recently, a new employee named Melissa began working at the company. One day, Melissa began crying and told Andrew that she doesn't know if she can keep up with the company's demanding workload. Andrew wanted to ________ ________ ________ and encourage her. In this situation, what would Andrew most likely say to Melissa?

Andrew: (Don't give up. You will get used to working here soon.)

overwhelmed with …에 압도된, 벅찬
amount 양
complete 완료하다, 완수하다
adjust 적응하다
responsibility 책임, 책무
appreciate 고마워하다
supportive 지지하는
keep up with …을 따라가다, 뒤처지지 않다
demanding 부담스러운, 어려운
workload 업무량, 작업량
encourage 북돋우다
| 문제 | **look for** …을 찾다
give up 포기하다
get used to …에 익숙해지다

14강 세트 문항

담화나 대화를 두 번씩 듣고, 주제나 목적을 묻는 문제와 세부 사항을 묻는 문제를 연달아 푸는 유형이다.

이 순서대로 풀어봐요

STEP 1 발화를 듣기 전에 지시문과 선택지를 미리 읽고, 담화 혹은 대화의 내용을 예상해 본다.

STEP 2 주제나 목적을 묻는 문제의 경우, 전반적인 내용을 바탕으로 정답을 추론하되, 처음이나 마지막에 단서가 제공되는 경우가 많으므로 이에 유의하며 듣는다.

STEP 3 세부 사항을 묻는 문제의 경우, 문제에서 요구하는 구체적인 내용에 집중하면서 선택지를 지워나간다.

기출 예제

[1~2] 다음을 듣고, 물음에 답하시오. 평가원 기출

1. 남자가 하는 말의 주제로 가장 적절한 것은?

① how to become organized
② the importance of donation
③ factors that affect personality
④ why we should collect things
⑤ problems of throwing things away

2. 언급된 물건이 아닌 것은?

① papers ② clock ③ toys
④ lamp ⑤ flower vase

문제해설

1. 자신에게 필요하지 않은 것들을 없애버림으로써 주변의 물건들을 정돈하는 방법에 대해서 설명하는 글이다. (정답 ①)
① 정돈하는 법
② 기부의 중요성
③ 성격에 영향을 미치는 요소들
④ 우리는 왜 물건을 모아야 하는가
⑤ 물건을 버리는 데 대한 문제점들
2. 불필요한 것들을 정리하는 사례로 시계에 대해서는 언급하지 않았다. (정답 ②)
① 종이 ③ 장난감 ④ 램프 ⑤ 꽃병

M: Are you trying to be a tidy person? It's really difficult to get organized, isn't it? A simple way to get organized is to remove unnecessary things around you. For example, when you're facing a desk covered with papers, throw away the unnecessary ones. If you have old toys that your children don't use any more, it is a good idea to donate them to charity. Have you kept a broken lamp for more than six months? Is it fixed? If not, just get rid of it. The same goes for that flower vase in your living room. If it hasn't had flowers for months, give it away. I'm not saying you should throw away everything. You might want to keep some items for old memories. But you should choose those items carefully. So, why don't you look around and see if there's anything you don't need? By removing these unnecessary things, you can keep your stuff organized.

KEYWORDS & EXPRESSIONS

세트 문항과 관련하여 알아둬야 할 표현

- Ladies and gentlemen, please fasten your seat belts. 신사 숙녀 여러분, 안전벨트를 착용하십시오.
- Before you go climbing, check all of your equipment. 등산하러 가기 전에, 여러분의 모든 장비들을 점검하십시오.
- I think the new highway should pass through our town. 저는 새 고속도로가 우리 마을을 통과해야 한다고 생각합니다.
- We need your cooperation for our annual event next month.
우리는 다음 달에 있을 연례행사에 당신의 협조가 필요합니다.
- This is one of the ways you can think outside the box.
이것은 당신이 고정관념에서 벗어나 창의적으로 생각할 수 있는 방법들 중 하나입니다.

LISTEN & APPLY

정답 및 해설 p. 28

[1-2] 다음을 듣고, 물음에 답하시오.

1 여자가 하는 말의 주제로 가장 적절한 것은?

① benefits of volunteering
② tips for lowering your electricity bill
③ how to get involved in the community
④ various ways to help the environment
⑤ roles of local environmental organizations

2 언급된 활동이 아닌 것은?

① saving water
② saving electricity
③ making posters
④ picking up trash
⑤ participating in campaigns

[3-4] 다음을 듣고, 물음에 답하시오.

3 남자가 하는 말의 주제로 가장 적절한 것은?

① the main functions of the heart
② factors that affect your heart rate
③ how to maintain a healthy heart
④ ways to slow down your heart rate
⑤ the importance of checking heart conditions

4 언급된 원인이 아닌 것은?

① exercise
② body position
③ temperature
④ emotions
⑤ medications

[5-6] 다음을 듣고, 물음에 답하시오.

5 남자가 하는 말의 주제로 가장 적절한 것은?

① the history of traditional medicine
② how to boost the immune system
③ the use of natural remedies for illnesses
④ the dangers of prescription medications
⑤ what to consider when choosing a doctor

6 언급된 것이 아닌 것은?

① cinnamon
② clove oil
③ elderberry syrup
④ honey
⑤ ginger

[7-8] 다음을 듣고, 물음에 답하시오.

7 여자가 하는 말의 주제로 가장 적절한 것은?

① food taboos around the world
② how religion affects people's diets
③ how to understand unique traditions
④ the healthiest foods in various countries
⑤ some of the world's most interesting dishes

8 언급된 음식이 아닌 것은?

① fish eggs
② beef
③ chicken
④ coconut milk
⑤ pork

[9-10] 다음을 듣고, 물음에 답하시오.

9 남자가 하는 말의 목적으로 가장 적절한 것은?

① to promote a new campground
② to ask customers to provide feedback
③ to check out preparations
④ to introduce a variety of camping activities
⑤ to inform precautions for safe camping

10 언급된 점검 대상이 아닌 것은?

① tables
② firewood
③ charcoal grills
④ food
⑤ tents

DICTATION

녹음을 다시 한 번 듣고, 빈칸에 알맞은 말을 쓰시오.

1-2 W: Good afternoon, everyone. My name is Emily and I am from the environmental group One Green Earth. We believe that a clean, healthy environment is important to our community, so I would like to talk to you for a few minutes about some ways that you can ________ ________ ________ in the world. First, remember to save water by only using what you need. Also, you can save electricity by always ________ ________ ________ ________ when you leave your home and by unplugging any appliances that are not being used. If you want to do something with others, joining an environmental group like One Green Earth can be a good choice. Groups like ours usually have events during which volunteers can ________ ________ ________ from the street or plant trees in the forest. They often recruit volunteers to help out with their awareness campaigns, too. These are all great ways to help support a greener community! Thank you for listening.

environmental group 환경보호 단체
community 지역 사회
electricity 전기
unplug 플러그를 뽑다
appliance 가전제품
recruit 모집하다
awareness 인식, 지각
support 지원하다, 후원하다
| 문제 | **benefit** 이익, 이점
lower 낮추다
get involved in …에 관여하다
organization 조직, 단체

3-4 M: Good morning, class. Today I will be talking to you about one of the body's most important organs—the heart. Did you know that the position of your body has ________ ________ ________ on your heart rate? If you go from a sitting position to a standing one, your pulse may actually go up slightly. However, it usually returns to normal after a few minutes. In very warm weather, your heart actually pumps a little more blood than it normally would, so your pulse may increase when ________ ________ ________ ________, but only by about five to ten beats per minute. Your heart rate is significantly affected by your emotions, so if you are stressed or anxious it will increase. It can also be affected by certain medications. For example, medications that block adrenaline will also ________ ________ ________ ________.

organ 장기, 기관
minor 작은
pulse 맥박
slightly 약간, 조금
pump 퍼 올리다, 퍼내다
temperature 기온
beat 박동
significantly 상당히, 크게
affect 영향을 미치다
medication 약물
adrenaline 아드레날린
| 문제 | **function** 기능
factor 요소
maintain 유지하다
heart condition 심장 질환

5-6 M: Welcome everyone to the wellness center's monthly meeting. When ill, we commonly visit a doctor and receive medications from the pharmacy. While these medicines are certainly effective, they often have ________ ________ ________. So I would like you to consider choosing some natural remedies to treat common illnesses. For example, cinnamon has been shown to help diabetics lower their blood sugar levels. And clove oil has long been used to soothe sore teeth. Many people find

pharmacy 약국
medicine 약(물); 의학
side effect 부작용
natural remedy 민간요법
treat 다루다, 처리하다
diabetic 당뇨병의; *당뇨병 환자
blood sugar level 혈당 수치
soothe 진정시키다, 누그러뜨리다

that elderberry syrup is as effective at relieving headaches as aspirin. And dried or fresh ginger is a great way to cure nausea. These natural remedies are ________ ________ on our bodies than prescription medications. Many have been used safely and effectively for hundreds of years. The next time that you are ________ ________ ________ ________, check to see if there is a natural alternative that you could try instead.

relieve 덜어주다, 완화하다
nausea 메스꺼움, 구역질
prescription 처방, 처방된 약
alternative 대안
| 문제 | immune system 면역체계

7-8 W: Everywhere you go, you will find unique traditions, and some of the most interesting have to do with food. Many countries have surprising laws and ________ ________ about what people can eat. For example, when an older woman in a tribe in Papua New Guinea becomes pregnant, she is ________ ________ ________ ________ fish eggs. In India, because the majority of the population is Hindu, eating beef is generally taboo. Cows are sacred animals in Hinduism, and thus should not be killed. In Jamaica, people believe that a child who eats chicken before learning to speak will never be able to do so. In Nigeria, it is thought that a child who drinks coconut milk will grow up to be unintelligent. You might find some of these traditions odd, but every culture has something that outsiders will find ________ ________ ________.

have to do with …와 관련 있다
limitation 제약, 제한
tribe 부족
pregnant 임신한
majority 대다수
population 인구
Hindu 힌두교인
taboo 금기
sacred 신성한
Hinduism 힌두교
unintelligent 우둔한
odd 이상한
outsider 외부인, 국외자
| 문제 | religion 종교

9-10 M: Good morning. We have a big group coming tonight, so I want to make sure that ________ ________ ________ ________. Remember, if our visitors have an enjoyable experience, they will tell their friends about how much fun they had at Luxury Campgrounds. And if their friends want to come, then we'll have more business in the future. So to ensure that our visitors have ________ ________ ________ ________ tonight, I would like you to check the following. Make sure that the tables and chairs are set up before the guests arrive at 4:00. Also, prepare plenty of firewood and neatly stack it next to the campfire area. Make sure the charcoal grills are cleaned and that there is plenty of charcoal to use. Finally, and most importantly, the tents must be completely set up before the guests get here. So ________ ________ ________ each of these things right away. I want our guests to give Luxury Campgrounds an excellent review.

enjoyable 즐거운
campground 캠프장, 야영지
ensure 확실하게 하다
set up …을 세우다[설치하다]
firewood 장작
neatly 깔끔하게
stack 쌓다
charcoal 숯
double check 재확인하다
| 문제 | promote 홍보하다
preparation 준비(사항)

Check What You've Learned So Far

CHAPTER 02

MINI TEST

15강

MINI TEST

1 대화를 듣고, 여자의 마지막 말에 대한 남자의 응답으로 가장 적절한 것을 고르시오.

① I'm sorry. It looks like we're lost.
② Actually, I haven't registered it yet.
③ Yes, I've already signed up for that.
④ That kind of job is quite demanding.
⑤ No, it moved next to City Hall last month.

2 대화를 듣고, 그림에서 대화의 내용과 일치하지 않는 것을 고르시오.

3 대화를 듣고, 두 사람이 하는 말의 주제로 가장 적절한 것을 고르시오.

① 고양이가 몸을 비비는 이유
② 고양이의 시력이 좋지 않은 이유
③ 고양이가 후각에 의존하는 이유
④ 고양이가 냄새를 구별하는 방법
⑤ 고양이들이 서로 의사소통하는 방법

4 대화를 듣고, 여자가 남자를 위해 할 일로 가장 적절한 것을 고르시오.

① 영화표 예매하기
② 소풍 장소 찾기
③ 춤 가르쳐주기
④ 공연 예매하기
⑤ 동영상 찾아보기

5 대화를 듣고, 남자가 지불할 금액을 고르시오.

① $11.00 ② $11.50 ③ $12.50 ④ $17.50 ⑤ $23.00

정답 및 해설 p. 30

6 대화를 듣고, 남자가 여자에게 부탁한 일로 가장 적절한 것을 고르시오.

① 남자의 개를 돌보아 달라고
② 병원 식당에 전화하라고
③ 과일을 좀 사라고
④ 피자를 갖다 달라고
⑤ 책을 도서관에 반납하라고

7 대화를 듣고, 밴드에 관해 두 사람이 언급하지 않은 것을 고르시오.

① 밴드 이름
② 발매 앨범 수
③ 해체 이유
④ 공연 계획
⑤ 수상 경력

8 직원 채용에 관한 다음 내용을 듣고, 일치하지 않는 것을 고르시오.

① 편집 경력이 필수 요건이다.
② 교정 시험을 봐야 한다.
③ 풍부한 문법 지식이 필요하다.
④ 연봉은 36,000달러이다.
⑤ 서류는 이메일로 제출해야 한다.

9 다음 비행기 일정표를 보면서 대화를 듣고, 여자가 비행할 요일을 고르시오.

European Air: Daily Flights from Seattle to Madrid

	Day	Departs	Arrives	Stops	Available Seats
①	Monday	10:00 p.m.	11:10 a.m.	nonstop	Business / Economy
②	Tuesday	11:00 p.m.	11:50 a.m.	nonstop	Business only
③	Wednesday	6:25 p.m.	1:40 p.m.	one	Economy only
④	Thursday	1:30 p.m.	6:40 a.m.	one	Business / Economy
⑤	Friday	4:20 p.m.	2:55 p.m.	two	Business / Economy

10 대화를 듣고, 여자의 마지막 말에 대한 남자의 응답으로 가장 적절한 것을 고르시오.

Man: ______________________________

① That's why I decided to go alone.
② I'm so happy that you can join me.
③ I should have checked it before leaving.
④ Don't worry. I won't make the same mistakes.
⑤ I don't know exactly when I'll come back home.

16강

MINI TEST

1 대화를 듣고, 남자의 마지막 말에 대한 여자의 응답으로 가장 적절한 것을 고르시오.

① Unfortunately, I am running late.
② No, I don't take dance classes anymore.
③ Yes, she has been my teacher for three years.
④ Actually, I would prefer to take an afternoon class.
⑤ Well, our class was moved to the morning just for today.

2 다음을 듣고, 남자가 하는 말의 목적으로 가장 적절한 것을 고르시오.

① 명절 선물을 광고하려고
② 재정에 맞는 소비를 당부하려고
③ 휴가철 쇼핑을 권장하려고
④ 신용카드 발급 절차를 설명하려고
⑤ 새로 문을 연 쇼핑몰을 소개하려고

3 대화를 듣고, 두 사람의 관계를 가장 잘 나타낸 것을 고르시오.

① 의사 – 환자
② 의사 – 페인트공
③ 관리인 – 청소부
④ 관리인 – 페인트공
⑤ 건물주 – 부동산 중개인

4 대화를 듣고, 여자가 남자에게 부탁한 일로 가장 적절한 것을 고르시오.

① 만화책 읽어주기
② 아기 돌보기
③ 장난감 돌려주기
④ 물건 조심히 다루기
⑤ 동생에게 책 빌려주기

5 대화를 듣고, 여자가 지불한 금액을 고르시오.

① $135 ② $180 ③ $220 ④ $240 ⑤ $270

6 대화를 듣고, 수강할 과목에 관해 두 사람이 언급하지 않은 것을 고르시오.

① 신청 기한
② 담당 교수
③ 최대 수강 인원
④ 수업 요일
⑤ 학점

7 Hamarton Marathon에 관한 다음 내용을 듣고, 일치하지 않는 것을 고르시오.

① 세 가지 종류의 레이스가 있다.
② 등록비에는 티셔츠 값이 포함된다.
③ 16세 이상만 참가할 수 있다.
④ 각 레이스 별 출발점이 서로 다르다.
⑤ 마라톤 후 공연이 있을 예정이다.

8 다음 상황 설명을 듣고, Susan의 어머니가 Susan에게 할 말로 가장 적절한 것을 고르시오.

Susan's mother: Susan, ____________________

① if you're not careful, you might lose everything.
② prepare for the worst so you won't be disappointed.
③ it can't be avoided. Just leave the matter as it is.
④ the best is yet to come. Just enjoy what you have now.
⑤ I'm sorry all your efforts didn't pay off. You'll do better next time.

[9-10] 다음을 듣고, 물음에 답하시오.

9 남자가 하는 말의 주제로 가장 적절한 것은?

① types of leadership at work
② methods for capturing people's attention
③ how to communicate effectively to a group
④ the best way to display visual information
⑤ common mistakes made during presentations

10 언급된 전략이 아닌 것은?

① using body language ② delivering a clear message ③ sticking to the topic
④ displaying visual aids ⑤ asking questions

MEMO

MEMO

지은이

NE능률 영어교육연구소

NE능률 영어교육연구소는 혁신적이며 효율적인 영어 교재를 개발하고
영어 학습의 질을 한 단계 높이고자 노력하는 NE능률의 연구조직입니다.

맞수 수능듣기 〈기본편〉

펴 낸 이	주민홍
펴 낸 곳	서울특별시 마포구 월드컵북로 396(상암동) 누리꿈스퀘어 비즈니스타워 10층 ㈜NE능률 (우편번호 03925)
펴 낸 날	2020년 10월 5일 개정판 제1쇄 2021년 8월 15일 제2쇄
전 화	02 2014 7114
팩 스	02 3142 0356
홈페이지	www.neungyule.com
등록번호	제1-68호
I S B N	979-11-253-3478-1
정 가	10,000원

NE 능률

고객센터

교재 내용 문의 : contact.nebooks.co.kr (별도의 가입 절차 없이 작성 가능)
제품 구매, 교환, 불량, 반품 문의 : 02-2014-7114
☎ 전화문의는 본사 업무시간 중에만 가능합니다.

NE능률 교재 MAP

수능

아래 교재 MAP을 참고하여 본인의 현재 혹은 목표 수준에 따라 교재를 선택하세요.
NE능률 교재들과 함께 영어실력을 쑥쑥~ 올려보세요!
MP3 등 교재 부가 학습 서비스 및 자세한 교재 정보는 www.nebooks.co.kr 에서 확인하세요.

초1-2

초3

초3-4

초4-5

초5-6

초6-예비중

중1

중1-2

중2-3

- 첫 번째 수능 영어 기초편

중3

- 첫 번째 수능 영어 유형편
- 첫 번째 수능 영어 실전편

예비고-고1

- 기강잡고 독해 잡는 필수 문법
- 기강잡고 기초 잡는 유형 독해
- The 상승 직독직해편
- 올클 수능 어법 start
- 얇고 빠른 미니 모의고사 10+2회 입문

고1

- 빠바 기초세우기
- 능률기본영어
- The 상승 문법독해편
- 수능만만 기본 영어듣기 20회
- 수능만만 기본 영어듣기 35+5회
- 수능만만 기본 문법·어법·어휘
- 수능만만 기본 영어독해
- 맞수 수능듣기 기본편
- 맞수 수능문법어법 기본편
- 맞수 구문독해 기본편
- 맞수 수능유형 기본편
- 수능유형 PICK 독해 기본
- 수능유형 PICK 듣기 기본
- 수능 구문 빅데이터 기본편
- 얇고 빠른 미니 모의고사 10+2회 기본

고1-2

- 빠바 구문독해
- The 상승 구문편
- 맞수 수능듣기 실전편
- 맞수 수능문법어법 실전편
- 맞수 구문독해 실전편
- 맞수 수능유형 실전편
- 맞수 빈칸추론
- 특급 독해 유형별 모의고사
- 수능유형 PICK 독해 실력
- 수능 구문 빅데이터 수능빈출편
- 얇고 빠른 미니 모의고사 10+2회 실전

고2-3, 수능 실전

- 빠바 유형독해
- 빠바 종합실전편
- The 상승 수능유형편
- 수능만만 어법어휘 모의고사 345제
- 수능만만 영어듣기 모의고사 20회
- 수능만만 영어듣기 모의고사 35회
- 수능만만 영어독해 모의고사 20회
- 특급 빈칸추론
- 특급 어법
- 특급 듣기 실전 모의고사
- 특급 수능·EBS 기출 VOCA
- 올클 수능 어법 완성
- 능률 EBS 수능특강 변형 문제 영어(상), (하)
- 능률 EBS 수능특강 변형 문제 영어독해연습(상), (하)
- 능률 EBS 수능완성 변형 문제 영어

수능, 학평 기출

- 다빈출코드 영어영역 고1독해
- 다빈출코드 영어영역 고2독해
- 다빈출코드 영어영역 고3독해
- 다빈출코드 영어영역 듣기
- 다빈출코드 영어영역 어법·어휘
- 다빈출코드 수학영역 수학 I
- 다빈출코드 수학영역 수학 II
- 다빈출코드 수학영역 미적분
- 다빈출코드 수학영역 확률과 통계

수능 이상/ 토플 80-89· 텝스 600-699점

수능 이상/ 토플 90-99· 텝스 700-799점

수능 이상/ 토플 100· 텝스 800점 이상

맞수

맞춤형 수능영어
단기특강 시리즈

수능듣기
기본편

정답 및 해설

NE 능률

맞수

맞춤형 **수**능영어
단기특강 시리즈

수능듣기
기본편

정답 및 해설

01강 짧은 대화 응답

기출예제

p. 6

남: Jenny, 전화기로 무엇을 하고 있니?
여: 피자를 주문하고 있어. 요즘에는 스마트폰으로 물건을 주문하는 것이 정말 편리해.
남: 아주 멋지네! 내 스마트폰으로 그것을 하는 방법을 나에게 알려 줄 수 있니?
여: 물론이지. 너는 먼저 앱을 내려받아야 해.

LISTEN & APPLY

pp. 7-9

1 ② 2 ④ 3 ① 4 ② 5 ③
6 ⑤ 7 ④ 8 ⑤ 9 ④

1 정답 ②

남: 오늘 오후에 시간 있니? 공짜 영화 표가 두 장 있거든.
여: 음, 나는 역사 보고서를 끝내야만 해.
남: 아, 그것의 마감일이 언제인데?
여: 내일 아침까지 끝내야 해.

문제해설 | 보고서 마감일을 묻는 남자의 질문에 대한 여자의 응답으로는 ②번이 가장 적절하다.
① 기다리기에는 줄이 너무 길어.
③ 난 그것을 오늘 제출하지 못할 것 같아.
④ 역사가 내가 가장 좋아하는 과목이기 때문이야.
⑤ 응. 오늘날 영화 산업은 쇠퇴하고 있어.

2 정답 ④

여: 난 이번 주말에 Samantha와 함께 놀이공원에 갈 거야.
남: 오, 지난달에 문을 연 데를 말하는 거니?
여: 맞아. 원한다면 우리와 같이 가도 돼.
남: 좋아. 내 일정을 확인해 볼게.

문제해설 | 원하면 놀이공원에 같이 가도 된다고 하는 여자의 말에 대한 남자의 응답으로는 ④번이 가장 적절하다.
① 와 줘서 고마워.
② 그녀가 신나는 놀이 기구를 좋아한다고 들었어.
③ 물론이지. 다음 주말에 너와 같이 갈게.
⑤ 아니야, 넌 집에 가서 쉬는 게 좋겠어.

3 정답 ①

남: 이 세 권의 책을 반납하고 싶어요. 제가 이틀 늦었어요.
여: 네. 연체 도서에는 연체료가 있다는 걸 아시죠?
남: 알고 있어요. 연체료는 얼만가요?
여: 하루에 50센트예요.

문제해설 | 도서 연체료가 얼마냐고 묻는 남자의 질문에 대한 여자의 응답으로는 ①번이 가장 적절하다.
② 그것을 읽다가 지겨워졌어요.
③ 그냥 다음에는 늦지 마세요.
④ 작가의 이름을 먼저 확인해 보셔야 해요.
⑤ 한 번에 다섯 권까지 대출할 수 있어요.

4 정답 ②

여: Jeremy, 이번 주말에 뭐할 계획이야?
남: 내 친구들과 함께 자선 음악회에 갈 거야.
여: 재미있겠다. 무엇을 위한 자선 행사인데?
남: 불우 아동들을 위한 기금을 모아.

문제해설 | 자선 음악회의 취지를 묻는 여자의 질문에 대한 남자의 응답으로는 ②번이 가장 적절하다.
① 난 음악회에 자주 가기 때문이야.
③ 한국 대중 가수들이 공연을 할 거야.
④ 온라인으로 주문하면 푯값은 겨우 30달러야.
⑤ 학교 음악회를 준비하는 내 친구들을 도우려고.

5 정답 ③

남: Megan, 너 어디 가니?
여: 공부하러 도서관에 가는 중이야.
남: 그거 잘됐다. 날 위해 책 한 권만 대출해 줄 수 있어?
여: 물론이지. 그 책 제목이 뭔데?

문제해설 | 도서관에서 책을 대신 대출해 줄 수 있는지를 묻는 남자의 질문에 대한 여자의 응답으로는 ③번이 가장 적절하다.
① 난 혼자 공부하는 게 더 좋아.
② 응, 난 너와 함께 가고 싶어.
④ 미안하지만, 난 그 책이 없어.
⑤ 내가 책을 좀 사주기를 원하니?

6 정답 ⑤

여: 얘, 자판기가 어디 있는지 아니?
남: 복도 끝에 있어. 하지만 지금은 고장이 났어.
여: 오, 이런. 그럼 편의점에 가야겠다.
남: 그럴 필요 없어. 로비에 또 다른 자판기가 있어.

문제해설 | 자판기가 고장이 나서 편의점에 가야겠다고 하는 여자의 말에 대한 남자의 응답으로는 ⑤번이 가장 적절하다.
① 고맙지만, 괜찮아. 난 목이 마르지 않아.
② 미안해, 하지만 동전이 없어.
③ 넌 지금 당장 그걸 수리하는 게 좋을 거야.
④ 복도에 음료수를 가져오면 안 돼.

7 정답 ④

남: 우리의 새 아파트 어때요?
여: 거실을 제외하고는 아늑하고 따뜻해 보이네요.
남: 무슨 문제가 있나요?
여: 벽 색깔이 너무 어두워요.

문제해설 | 남자가 새 아파트의 문제점을 묻고 있으므로, 이에 대한 여자의 응답으로는 ④번이 가장 적절하다.
① 여기는 너무 더워요.
② 임대 보증금이 올랐어요.
③ 기분 나쁘게 했다면 미안해요.
⑤ 기회를 놓치고 싶지 않기 때문이에요.

8 정답 ⑤

여: 캐나다에서 오는 친구와 내가 할 수 있는 좋은 게 없을까?
남: 사찰 체험 프로그램이 외국인들에게 인기가 있다고 들었어.
여: 그거 좋네! 하지만 나는 그것에 대해 잘 몰라.
남: 인터넷에서 정보를 더 찾아보는 게 어때?

문제해설 | 사찰 체험 프로그램에 대해 잘 모른다는 여자의 말에 대한 남자의 응답으로는 ⑤번이 가장 적절하다.
① 예전에 여기에 절이 하나 있었어.
② 맞아. 그것은 내게 좋은 경험이었어.
③ 넌 그 프로그램에 대해 어떻게 알았어?
④ 아마 내가 너한테 한국 전통 문화에 대해 알려줄 수 있을 거야.

9 정답 ④

남: 이 교통량 좀 봐! 정말 안 좋다.
여: 진정해. 영화는 한 시간 후에 시작하는걸.
남: 우리가 시간 맞춰 갈 수 있을 것 같니?
여: 물론이지. 우리에게 시간은 많아.

문제해설 | 제시간에 갈 수 있을 것 같냐고 묻는 남자의 질문에 대한 여자의 응답으로는 ④번이 가장 적절하다.
① 미안해. 난 시간 맞춰 가지 못했어.
② 표는 이미 매진이야.
③ 응. 7시 30분까지는 끝날 거야.
⑤ 물론이지. 아마 근처에 다른 곳이 있을 거야.

DICTATION ANSWER pp. 10-11

1. Are you free / deadline for it
2. opened last month / come with us
3. overdue books / the late fee
4. a charity concert / the charity for
5. the library / check out a book
6. the vending machine / I should go to
7. cozy and warm
8. Can you think of / popular with foreigners
9. Calm down / make it

02강 그림 일치

기출예제 p. 12

남: 안녕하세요, Miller 선생님. 저는 Joshua의 아버지입니다.
여: 안녕하세요, Smith 씨. 학부모와 교사의 모임에 와 주셔서 감사합니다.
남: 만나서 반갑습니다. 방이 멋져 보이네요. 와! 벽을 좀 보세요.
여: 아시다시피, Joshua는 사자와 판다 사이의 코끼리를 아주 좋아하죠.
남: 그 애가 천장에 달린 모빌도 좋아하나요?
여: 네, 그래요. 아이들이 함께 그것을 만들었어요.
남: 아이들이 참 잘했군요. 책꽂이 옆에 있는 저 장난감 공룡이 훌륭해 보여요.
여: 아, 아이들이 공룡에 대해 배우는 중이어서 제가 그곳에 두었습니다.
남: 그것 참 재미있겠네요. 크리스마스트리 밑에 두 개의 상자가 있어요. 그것들은 무엇에 쓰나요?
여: 반 친구들을 위한 선물입니다. 아이들을 위해 사탕을 좀 샀거든요.
남: 아하. 크리스마스트리가 매우 멋지게 장식되어 있군요. 트리 맨 위의 별은 정말 예쁘네요.
여: 감사합니다. 모임이 곧 시작되겠어요. 위층으로 올라가시죠, Smith 씨.

LISTEN & APPLY pp. 13-15

1 ③ 2 ⑤ 3 ⑤ 4 ⑤ 5 ④
6 ② 7 ④ 8 ③

1 정답 ③

여: Peter Smith의 책 사인회 준비는 어떻게 돼가고 있나요?
남: 아, 걱정하지 마세요. 제가 이미 준비를 모두 끝냈어요.
여: 그래요? 직사각형 탁자를 놓았나요?
남: 네, 행사장 앞쪽에 놓았어요.
여: 잘했네요. 그리고 그 위에 꽃장식도 놓았나요? 멋질 것 같은데.
남: 물론이죠. 그리고 탁자 위에 그의 책도 몇 권 놓아두었어요. 탁자 위에 쌓아 놓았죠.
여: 오, 훌륭해요. 의자는요?
남: 탁자 뒤에 편안한 것으로 두었어요.
여: 완벽해요. 마지막으로, 벽에 현수막 같은 것을 걸었나요?
남: 네! 'Peter Smith의 책 사인회'라고 쓴 것을 걸었어요.
여: 와! 잘했어요!

문제해설 | 책은 탁자 위에 일렬로 놓은 것이 아니라 쌓아 놓았다고 했다.

2 정답 ⑤

남: 중고 물품 세일을 위한 모든 것이 거의 준비된 것 같아요.
여: 좋아요. 그런데, 창고 문 위에 있는 것은 뭐예요?
남: 현수막을 말하는 건가요? 제가 직접 만들어서 오늘 아침에 걸었어요.
여: 오, 좋아요.
남: 그리고 탁자를 진입로 오른편에 놓았어요.
여: 보여요. 가격 표시판도 만들었네요.
남: 그래요. 탁자에 있는 모든 옷과 모자는 각각 5달러예요.
여: 진입로 왼편에는 무엇이 있나요?
남: 책이 든 상자가 있어요. 사람들의 관심을 끌려고 상자 위에 풍선을 좀 달았어요.
여: 효과가 있겠네요. 책 앞에 있는 오래된 램프들은 어디서 가져온 거예요?
남: 우리 이웃인 Fields 씨의 것이에요. 그가 제게 자기를 위해서 그것들을 좀 팔아달라고 요청했어요.
여: 오, 그렇군요.

문제해설 | 오래된 램프들은 창고 문 앞이 아니라 책 앞에 있다고 했다.

3 정답 ⑤

여: 안녕, Chris! 크리스마스를 위해 거실을 꾸몄니?
남: 응. 주말 내내 그걸 했어. 사진 볼래?
여: 물론. [*잠시 후*] 우와, 이건 바로 내가 크리스마스를 위해 우리 집을 꾸미고 싶은 모습이야. 오, 벽난로 옆에 크리스마스트리를 놓았구나.
남: 응. 그게 아늑한 분위기를 만들어 내, 그렇지 않니?
여: 정말 그래! 트리 꼭대기에 별 모양 장식을 달아서 마무리를 했고.
남: 그래, 맞아. 그리고 나와 내 가족들은 벽난로 옆 소파에서 쉬는 동안 크리스마스 장식들을 즐기는 걸 좋아해.
여: 근사하게 들리네. 벽난로 위에 걸린 이 양말들은 내 어릴 적 크리스마스의 추억을 생각나게 하네. 그런데, 이 선물 상자들 안에는 뭐가 있어?
남: 아, 그 안에는 초콜릿이 들어 있어. 트리 아래에 두면 초콜릿이 녹을 수 있어서 탁자 위에 둔거야.
여: 좋은 생각이야. 벽난로가 트리에 꽤 가까워.

문제해설 | 초콜릿이 들어 있는 상자는 나무 아래가 아니라 탁자 위에 있다고 했다.

4 정답 ⑤

여: 우리는 교실을 다시 꾸미는 것을 끝냈어요, Kwon 선생님. 어떻게 생각하세요?
남: 멋져 보인다. 오! 칠판 위에 동그란 시계를 올려 두었네.
여: 네. 그곳에 있어야 보기가 쉬워요. 그리고 우리가 게시판을 어디에 두었는지 보세요.
남: 칠판과 창문 사이인, 벽의 왼쪽 면으로 이동시켰구나.
여: 맞아요. 그리고 수업 시간표는 이제 칠판 오른쪽에 있어요.
남: 그렇네. 잘했다!
여: 우리는 또 교실을 더 밝게 하기 위해 커튼을 열어 두었어요.
남: 좋은 생각이네. 그런데 창문 아래에 어항은 어떻게 된 거야?
여: 그건 너무 깨지기 쉬워요. 우리는 그것을 옮겼고, 대신에 거기에 식물을 두었어요.
남: 좋아. 모든 것이 완벽하네. 너의 학급 친구들이 빨리 이걸 봤으면 좋겠어.

문제해설 | 창문 아래에는 깨지기 쉬운 어항 대신 식물을 두기로 했다고 했다.

5 정답 ④

남: 봐. 지난 여름에 갔던 캠핑 여행 사진을 찾았어.
여: 멋지다! 그 사진을 본 적이 없는 것 같아. 왼쪽에 있는 게 우리 텐트니?
남: 응, 저 삼각형 모양의 텐트가 우리 거야. 빗속에서 텐트를 세우는 건 힘들었어.
여: 맞아! 만약 비가 그치지 않았다면, 오른쪽의 저 개울이 넘쳤을 거야.
남: 저 모닥불도 피우지 못했을 거고.
여: 모닥불 뒤에 있는 모든 장작들을 봐. 우리가 얼마나 많이 모았는지 믿어지지가 않네.
남: 응, 우린 그게 전부 다 필요하지는 않았어. 하지만 텐트와 장작 사이에 있는 바비큐용 그릴로 요리할 때 내가 그것을 좀 썼어.
여: 맞아. 아, 텐트 앞에 있는 저 캠핑 의자들이 보이니? 그것들은 편안했어.
남: 그래. 그것들은 캠핑에 안성맞춤이었어.
여: 캠핑 또 가고 싶다.

문제해설 | 바비큐용 그릴은 모닥불 앞이 아닌 텐트와 장작더미 사이에 있다고 했다.

6 정답 ②

여: Alan, Sujin의 생일을 위한 교실을 다 꾸몄니?
남: 응. 모든 것이 준비되었어. 정말 멋져 보여.
여: 내가 만든 생일 현수막도 걸었어?
남: 응, 탁자 위의 벽에 걸려 있어.
여: 꽃들은? 너 Sujin이 꽃을 좋아하는 거 알잖아.
남: 준비 못 했어. 그렇지만 나는 꽃 모양의 풍선 두 개를 현수막 오른쪽 벽에 걸어 두었어.
여: 오, 그거 귀여운 생각이네. 우리가 산 케이크는 어디에 있어?
남: 탁자 위에 있어. 그리고 나는 선물을 포장해서 탁자 아래에 두었어.
여: 좋다! 우리가 사진 찍을 수 있도록 카메라를 가져와야겠다!
남: 걱정 마. 내 것을 가져와서 삼각대 위에 설치해 두었어.
여: 너 모든 것을 다 생각했구나! 아주 멋진 파티가 되겠다!

문제해설 | 남자는 꽃 모양의 풍선을 현수막 양쪽이 아닌 현수막 오른쪽 벽에 걸어 두었다고 하였다.

7 정답 ④

여: 안녕, Billy! 뭐 하고 있니?
남: 아, Jenny! 그냥 우리 집 사진을 보고 있었어. 난 향수병에 걸린 것 같아.
여: 그럴 만도 해. 거의 일년 동안 집에 못 갔잖아. 그 사진 좀 봐도 돼?
남: 물론이야. 여기 있어.
여: 오, 이층집이네. 정말 멋져!
남: 고마워. 2층에 창문이 세 개 있어.
여: 네가 그 창문에서 보이는 전망을 좋아한다고 내게 말했던 게 기억나.
남: 맞아. 사실, 이 커다란 나무 그늘에서 쉬던 게 가장 그리워. 내가 어렸을 때 그걸 직접 심었거든.
여: 그렇구나. 아, 마당에 큰 정사각형의 수영장이 있구나!
남: 응. 남동생이랑 거기에서 수영을 하곤 했어. 난 파라솔 아래의 의자에 누워 있는 것도 좋아했지.
여: 상상이 가. 너무 슬퍼하지 마. 이번 방학에 집에 갈 수 있잖아.
남: 그랬으면 좋겠어.

문제해설 | 마당에 원형이 아니라 정사각형의 수영장이 있다고 했다.

8 정답 ③

남: 우리 학교의 재활용 캠페인을 위한 포스터 다 만들었어?
여: 응, 했지. 여기 있어. 어떻게 생각해?
남: 마음에 들어! 흰 바탕이 눈에 잘 띄게 해주네.
여: 고마워. 그리고 'RECYCLE'이라고 크게 대문자로 맨 위에 적었어.
남: 가운데에 있는 그림도 꽤 멋지다. 그건 뭐야?
여: 그것은 양손이 지구를 들고 있는 그림이야.
남: 그리고 지구 가운데에 커다란 나무 한 그루가 자라고 있네.
여: 맞아. 나는 지구 위에 두 개의 구름도 그렸어.
남: 그것들 멋져 보인다. 그런데 포스터 아래쪽에는 뭐라고 쓴 거야?
여: '세계는 당신의 손에 있습니다'야. 캠페인의 슬로건이야.

문제해설 | 남자는 지구 가운데에 여러 그루가 아닌 하나의 큰 나무가 자라고 있다고 했다.

DICTATION ANSWER pp. 16-19

1. a rectangular desk / are stacked up / did you hang
2. made it myself / catch people's attention / in front of
3. to be decorated / a finishing touch / hanging over
4. above the blackboard / on the right side / too fragile
5. that triangular one / behind the fire / perfect for camping
6. on the wall / wrapped the present / brought mine
7. I feel homesick / three windows upstairs / used to swim
8. recycling campaign / a pair of / at the bottom of

03강 주제 · 의견

기출예제 p. 20

여: John, Anderson 선생님의 사회 수업에서 잘하고 있어?
남: 음, 선생님이 말씀하시길 토론이 많이 있을 거래. 나는 벌써 스트레스를 받고 있어.
여: 내가 그 선생님 수업을 들었을 때, 나도 그렇게 느꼈지만, 분명 너는 그게 아주 도움이 된다는 것을 알게 될 거야.
남: 토론이 어떻게 도움이 될 수 있어?
여: 토론에 참여하는 것은 너의 논리적 사고를 향상시키는 데 도움을 줄 거야.
남: 어떻게 그런지 모르겠어.
여: 토론은 네가 네 주장을 더 강하게 하기 위해 생각을 논리적으로 조직하는 것을 가르쳐 줘.
남: 이해는 되는데, 아직 어려운 것 같아.
여: 더 해보면, 더 잘하게 될 거야.
남: 알았어. 시도해 볼게.

LISTEN & APPLY pp. 21-22

1 ③	2 ②	3 ④	4 ③	5 ①
6 ⑤	7 ⑤	8 ②		

1 정답 ③

[전화벨이 울린다.]
남: 여보세요?
여: 안녕, 아빠. 저 Liz예요.
남: 안녕, Liz. 별일 없지?
여: 저, 어떤 것에 대해 아빠의 조언을 얻고 싶어요.
남: 직장에 문제라도 있니?
여: 그건 아니에요. 실은, 제 룸메이트와 잘 지내지 못하고 있어요.
남: 그거 유감이구나. 그녀와 다투었니?
여: 꼭 그렇지는 않아요. 단지 그녀가 아파트를 청소하는 걸 돕지 않아서요.
남: 아, 일주일 단위로 할 일을 나누지 그러니?
여: 그렇게 했지만, 그녀는 여전히 그것들을 하지 않아요.
남: 그럼 그녀한테 더 배려심을 가져야 한다고 말은 해 봤니?
여: 아뇨. 그녀와 싸우고 싶지는 않아요.
남: 하지만 네가 그녀에게 말하지 않으면 걔는 자신의 행동을 바꾸지 않을 거야.
여: 아빠 말씀이 맞는 것 같아요. 오늘 그녀에게 이야기할게요.

문제해설 | 여자는 룸메이트와의 갈등에 대해 말하고 있고, 남자는 그것을 해결하기 위한 방안으로 그녀에게 직접 이야기를 하라고 조언하고 있다.

2 정답 ②

여: 안녕하세요! 여기 Global Fitness 신규 회원이신가 봐요.
남: 맞아요. 어떻게 아셨어요?
여: 저는 트레이너라서 대부분의 회원들을 알죠.
남: 아, 잘됐네요! 뭐 좀 여쭤보고 싶어요. 사실 전 매일 세 시간씩 운동을 해요. 그런데 운동 후에 몸이 많이 아파요.
여: 매일 세 시간이요? 지나친 운동은 위험할 수 있어요.
남: 전 운동은 원래 아파야 하는 거라고 생각했어요.
여: 그렇지 않아요. 과도한 운동은 심각하게 몸을 손상시킬 수 있어요.
남: 정말이요?
여: 네. 쉽게 척추를 다치거나 관절에 손상을 입을 수 있어요.
남: 와. 그건 몰랐어요.
여: 그리고 심지어 근육 손상도 초래할 수 있고요.
남: 알려주셔서 감사해요. 효과적으로 운동하는 방법에 관해 조언을 좀 해 주시겠어요?
여: 물론이죠. 이쪽으로 오세요.

문제해설 | **남자는 운동 후 몸이 아픈 것에 대해 물어보고 있고, 여자는 과도한 운동이 척추, 관절, 근육에 손상을 입힐 수 있다며 그 위험성에 대해 이야기하고 있다.**

3 정답 ④

남: 뭘 보고 있니?
여: 인터넷에서 새로운 휴대전화 모델을 좀 알아보고 있어.
남: 아, 새 휴대전화를 살 계획이야?
여: 응. 이게 아주 좋아 보여.
남: 나도 방금 같은 것을 보고 있었어. 그건 후기가 아주 좋아.
여: 맞아, 하지만 인터넷에 올라온 후기는 결코 믿을 수가 없어.
남: 무슨 말이야?
여: 인터넷에 있는 정보에 대해서는 주의해야 해. 요즘 많은 기업들이 긍정적인 후기를 올리도록 블로거들에게 돈을 지급하고 있거든.
남: 그렇게 생각해?
여: 응. 뉴스에서 그게 큰 문제가 되고 있다고 들었어.
남: 그럼 인터넷에서 읽는 것을 항상 믿어서는 안 되겠구나.
여: 맞아. 난 이 휴대전화를 사기 전에 가게에서 그걸 한번 사용해 볼 거야.

문제해설 | **두 사람은 블로거들이 기업으로부터 돈을 받고 인터넷에 제품 후기를 좋게 올리는 경우가 있으므로, 인터넷 정보를 맹신해서는 안 된다고 이야기하고 있다.**

4 정답 ③

여: 안녕, Ted. 너 내일 무슨 계획 있니?
남: 아직 없어. 왜?
여: Rachel과 난 야구 경기를 보러 갈 거야. 혹시 네가 우리와 함께 가고 싶은지 궁금해서.
남: 고맙지만, 난 야구장에 가는 걸 좋아하지 않아.
여: 아, 야구를 안 좋아하니? 그건 몰랐네.
남: 야구를 안 좋아하는 게 아니야. 나는 그냥 집에서 보는 걸 선호해.
여: 아, 정말? 야구는 야구장에서 보는 게 더 신나지 않니?
남: 난 그렇게 생각하지 않아. 야구장은 너무 시끄러워서 경기에 집중할 수가 없어. 게다가, TV로 경기를 보면 아나운서들에게서 정보를 더 얻을 수 있어.
여: 네 말이 어느 정도는 맞을지 모르지만, 그래도 난 그곳에 직접 가고 싶어.

문제해설 | **남자는 야구장은 시끄러워서 경기에 집중할 수가 없기 때문에 집에서 TV로 해설을 들으며 야구 경기를 보는 것을 선호한다고 했다.**

5 정답 ①

남: 나 오늘 학교 가는 길에 트럭이 사고 내는 걸 봤어.
여: 트럭이 앞에 있는 차와 충돌했어?
남: 아니. 트럭이 방향을 너무 빠르게 틀다가 넘어졌어.
여: 오 안 돼! 어떻게 그런 일이 벌어졌지?
남: 트럭이 벽돌을 운반하고 있었어. 내 생각엔 벽돌이 너무 많았던 것 같아.
여: 그런 것 같네. 트럭 운전자들은 때론 한 번에 너무 많이 운반하려고 해. 그것은 정말 위험해.
남: 맞아. 아무도 안 다쳤으니 그 운전자는 참 운이 좋았어.
여: 벽돌을 반 정도만 운반하는 것이 더 현명했을 텐데, 그리고 다시 돌아가서 나머지를 운반하고.
남: 나도 동의해. 길에 온통 벽돌이 널려 있었어. 그것이 정말 심한 교통 체증을 일으켰어.
여: 너무 안됐다. 분명히 많은 사람들이 직장에 늦었겠지.

문제해설 | **남자는 트럭 사고를 목격하고, 사고의 원인이 벽돌을 너무 많이 실어서였다고 말하고 있다.**

6 정답 ⑤

여: 과거에는, 구입할 만한 고가구를 찾는 데 돈을 쓰는 것은 이상하게 여겨졌습니다. 하지만, 요즘에는 많은 사람들이 취미나 집안 장식용으로 골동품들을 수집하기 시작했습니다. 그 결과, 도시에 많은 골동품 상점들이 생겼지만, 그것들은 대개 상당히 비쌉니다. 만일 여러분이 정말로 특별한 골동품들을 저렴한 가격으로 구하고 싶다면, 여러분은 도시를 떠나 소도시의 상점들을 확인하셔야 합니다. 살펴볼 만한 또 다른 좋은 장소는 가정 판매입니다. 사람들은 종종 단지 쓸모없는 오래된 물건들을 치워버리려고, 그것들을 거의 헐값에 팔아도 만족합니다. '누군가의 쓰레기가 다른 사람에게는 보물이다.'라는 옛 속담을 기억하세요.

문제해설 | **여자는 특별한 골동품들을 저렴한 가격으로 구할 수 있는 방법으로, 소도시의 상점들을 확인해 보거나 가정 판매를 살펴보라고 말하고 있다.**

7 정답 ⑤

여: 안녕, Mark. 불어 퀴즈는 어떻게 봤어?
남: 망쳤어! 그렇게 많은 단어를 외우는 건 불가능해.
여: 나도 그렇게 생각했지만, 그런 다음 플래시카드를 만들기 시작했어.
남: 그게 도움이 되었니?
여: 많이 도움이 되었어. 매일 열 개의 새로운 단어만 배운다면 말이야.
남: 겨우 열 개? 난 모든 단어를 한꺼번에 공부하고 있는데.
여: 그게 실수인 것 같아.
남: 왜 그런데?
여: 네가 한꺼번에 너무 많은 단어를 배우면, 대부분의 것을 금방 잊어버리게 될 거야.
남: 그래서 넌 매일 열 개의 새로운 플래시카드를 만든다고?
여: 맞아. 내가 어떻게 만드는지 볼래?
남: 물론. 같이 만들자.

문제해설 | 여자는 많은 단어를 한꺼번에 외우려고 하지 말고, 매일 조금씩 학습하는 것이 기억하는 데 도움이 된다고 했다.

8 정답 ②

남: 와인 병을 따는 것을 본 적이 있다면, 여러분은 그것들이 탄산음료나 다른 음료들과는 다르게 밀봉된다는 것을 알 것입니다. 뚜껑 대신에, 그것은 코르크가 있습니다. 전통적으로, 코르크는 특별한 종류의 목재로 만들어집니다. 하지만 요즘에는, 많은 코르크들이 플라스틱과 같은 다른 재료들로 만들어집니다. 이러한 인공 코르크들은 공기가 병 안으로 들어가는 것을 효과적으로 막을 수 있어서, 와인의 맛을 변화시키지 않습니다. 또한, 그것들은 와인 제조업자들이 사용하기에 더 저렴합니다. 하지만, 그것들은 재활용할 수 없고 오랫동안 매립지에 남아 있기 때문에, 인공 코르크의 환경적인 영향에 대한 몇몇 우려가 있습니다.

문제해설 | 남자는 인공 코르크 마개는 밀봉 효과가 뛰어나고 저렴한 반면, 재활용이 불가능하고 잘 썩지 않아서 환경적으로 부정적인 면이 있다면서, 인공 코르크의 장단점을 설명하고 있다.

DICTATION ANSWER pp. 23-25

1. get your advice / assign weekly chores / be more considerate
2. work out every day / harm your body / how to exercise effectively
3. be careful about information / try out this phone
4. I wonder if / concentrate on / partly right
5. crash into / no one got hurt / bad traffic jam
6. collect antiques / low prices / get rid of
7. felt the same way / helped a lot / how I make them
8. are sealed / are made of / keep air out of

04강 할 일 · 부탁

기출예제 1 p. 26

여: 안녕, Jason. 그거 요리책이니?
남: 응, 이건 베스트셀러야.
여: 오, 네가 요리에 관심이 있다는 건 몰랐어.
남: 음, 건강에 더 좋은 음식을 먹고 싶어져서.
여: 좋은데. 그 책에 좋은 요리법이 있으면 나에게 알려줘.
남: 그래, 그럴게. [*잠시 후*] 근데 이 요리법들은 쉬워 보이지 않는데.
여: 그냥 요리해 봐. 넌 실수로부터 배울 수 있어.
남: 알아, 하지만 난 실험하면서 시간을 낭비하고 싶지 않아.
여: 음, 지역 주민 회관에서 요리 수업을 한다고 들었어. 확인해 보는 게 어때?
남: 이미 해 봤어. 하지만 그건 내 일정과 맞지 않아. 누군가가 나에게 요리하는 법을 보여주기만 하면 좋을 텐데.
여: 그럼 내가 몇 군데 유용한 요리 웹사이트를 알려 줄 수 있어. 넌 그 사이트들을 방문해서 온라인으로 제공되는 요리 영상들을 볼 수 있을 거야.
남: 고마워. 그렇게 해 주면 큰 도움이 될 것 같아.

기출예제 2 p. 27

여: Jim, 과학 박람회에서 발표를 할 거니?
남: 응. 내가 처음으로 대중 앞에 발표하는 거라서 정말 긴장돼.
여: 걱정 마. 넌 잘 할 거야. 주제가 뭐야?
남: 곤충을 음식으로 먹는 거야.
여: 재미있겠는데. 왜 그걸 골랐어?
남: 그게 미래의 식량 문제에 대한 가능한 해결책이기 때문이야.
여: 그래서 발표에서 뭘 하려고 하는데?
남: 곤충을 기반으로 하는 요리법 몇 가지를 소개하고 곤충을 먹는 것에 대한 사람들의 의견을 조사한 결과를 공유할 거야.
여: 빨리 보고 싶다. 이게 네가 처음으로 대중 앞에서 발표하는 것이니까 내가 네 사진을 찍어 줄게.
남: 고마워. 그런데 우리 형 Tom이 사진을 찍을 거야.
여: 그래. 내가 너를 도울 일이 있을까?
남: 물론. 청중들에게 유인물을 나눠주는 일을 도와줄 수 있니?
여: 응, 그걸 할게.
남: 고마워.

LISTEN & APPLY pp. 28-30

1 ③ 2 ③ 3 ⑤ 4 ⑤ 5 ⑤
6 ③ 7 ④ 8 ③

1 정답 ③

[*휴대전화가 울린다.*]
여: Sally입니다.
남: 안녕, 여보. 나예요.
여: 오, 안녕. 내가 나중에 다시 전화해도 될까요? 회의하러 가려던 참이었거든요.
남: 그럼, 빨리 말할게요. 난 그냥 당신이 저녁 식사 예약을 했는지 알고 싶어요.
여: 예약이요? 오늘 밤에 무슨 일 있어요?
남: 당신 부모님을 만나기로 계획하지 않았어요?
여: 아닌 것 같은데요. 다음 주로 약속을 변경했던 것 같아요.
남: 아, 내가 잘못 알았나 봐요.
여: 내가 수첩에 적어놨어요. 최대한 빨리 확인해 볼게요.
남: 알았어요. 그냥 내 휴대전화로 전화해서 나한테 알려 줘요.
여: 알겠어요. 만약 그게 오늘이면 당신이 아이들을 어린이집에서 확실히 데려올 수 있나요?
남: 물론이죠.

문제해설 | 남자가 약속 날짜에 대해 궁금해하자 여자는 수첩에 적힌 일정을 확인해 보겠다고 했다.

2 정답 ③

여: Adams 박사님, 바쁘세요?
남: 아뇨, Green 박사님. 실은, 제 오전 예약들을 막 끝냈어요.
여: 잘됐네요. 그럼, 부탁 좀 드려도 될까요?
남: 그럼요. 뭔데요?
여: 음, 이 차트 보이시죠?
남: 네. 그건 우리 암 환자들의 세부사항들을 보여주는 차트잖아요, 맞죠?
여: 맞아요. 그런데 이름이 A로 시작해서 M까지인 환자들만 나와 있어요.
남: 아. 명단의 나머지 반이 없어진 것 같군요.
여: 네. 제 발표를 위해 분실된 정보가 필요하거든요.
남: 제가 그걸 찾아봐 드릴까요?
여: 네, 부탁해요. 전 회의에 필요한 자료를 좀 복사해야 해서 지금 그걸 할 수가 없어요.
남: 문제없죠. 지금 바로 해 드릴게요.

문제해설 | 여자는 자신이 회의 자료를 복사하는 동안 남자에게 분실된 환자 차트를 찾아달라고 부탁했다.

3 정답 ⑤

여: Dwayne, 이탈리아 음식 만드는 법을 아니?
남: 이탈리아 음식? 내가 썩 좋은 요리사가 아니란 거 알잖아.
여: 그냥 네가 요리법을 알지도 모른다고 기대했어.
남: 만약 내가 안다면, 그걸 너와 공유하겠지. 유감스럽게도, 난 몰라. 왜 묻는 거니?
여: 내 친구들이 오늘 밤에 축구 경기를 보러 올 거야. 그리고 난 친구들에게 저녁을 요리해주고 싶어.
남: 그렇구나. 그래서 그들에게 이탈리아 음식을 만들어 주고 싶다고?
여: 아까는 좋은 생각인 것 같았는데, 그냥 뭔가를 시켜야 할까 봐.
남: 도서관 옆에 있는 식당에 훌륭한 이탈리아 음식이 있어.
여: 하지만 배달을 안 하는 것 같은데.
남: 걱정 마. 내가 운전해서 너에게 좀 사다 줄게.

문제해설 | 남자는 여자를 위해 식당에서 이탈리아 음식을 사 오겠다고 했다.

4 정답 ⑤

여: 얘, Robert! 어딜 그렇게 뛰어가니?
남: 안녕, Kelly. 내 고양이가 집에서 뛰쳐나갔어.
여: 저런. 집 주위는 살펴봤니?
남: 응, 근데 어디에서도 고양이를 찾을 수가 없어.
여: 오, 정말 안됐다. 내가 할 수 있는 일이라도 있니?
남: 실은, 이 포스터를 복사하려고 했어. 좀 더 필요해서 말이야.
여: 아, 포스터를 만들었구나. 그건 고양이 사진이니?
남: 응. 그리고 밑에 내 주소랑 전화번호를 넣었어.
여: 그것들을 복사하는 걸 내가 도와줄까?
남: 글쎄, 대신에 이 포스터 몇 장 좀 가져갈래? 그걸 너희 동네에 붙여줘.
여: 알겠어. 누군가가 네 고양이를 찾으면 좋겠다.
남: 고마워. 난 이제 가봐야겠다.

문제해설 | 고양이를 잃어버린 남자는 여자에게 포스터를 몇 장 가지고 가서 여자의 동네에 붙여 달라고 부탁했다.

5 정답 ⑤

여: 안녕하세요, Kent 교수님. 잠시 대화할 수 있을까요?
남: 물론이지. 들어와서 앉으렴.
여: 감사합니다. 지난주에 수업 빠진 것에 대해서 말씀드리고 싶었어요.
남: 아! 네가 작은 등산 사고가 있었다고 들었어.
여: 네, 제 발목을 아주 심하게 다쳤는데, 지금은 괜찮아요.
남: 잘됐구나. 그렇지만 우리는 네가 빠진 수업 시간에 많은 내용을 다루었단다.
여: 그래서 제가 왔어요. 제가 어떤 것을 읽어야 하는지 알려주시겠어요?
남: 글쎄, 나는 잠시 후에 학과 회의가 있거든. 하지만 수업 조교에게 전화해서 너를 도와주라고 할게.
여: 오, 정말 감사합니다. 그녀를 어디에서 찾을 수 있죠?
남: 여기에서 기다려. 그녀는 잠시 후에 잠깐 들를 거야.

문제해설 | 남자는 조교에게 전화를 걸어 여자가 빠진 수업 시간에 다룬 내용에 관해서 여자를 도와주도록 하겠다고 했다.

6 정답 ③

여: Brian, 오늘 방과 후에 무슨 계획 있니?
남: 음, 할 일이 몇 가지 있어. 왜?
여: 네가 뭐 좀 도와줬으면 해서 말이야.
남: 아, 그래? 방과 후에 바로 반 친구 아파트에 잠시 들러야 하는데.
여: 그 이후에는 한가하니? 내 침대랑 책상을 옮기는 데 도움이 좀 필요해.
남: 아, 네 방 구조를 바꿀 거니?
여: 아니. 어제 페인트칠을 했는데, 이제 모든 것을 제자리로 옮겨야 하거든.
남: 그렇구나. 음, 난 6시에 엄마가 저녁 식사를 만드시는 걸 도와드려야 해.
여: 8시쯤 오는 건 어때? 오래 걸리지 않을 거야.
남: 좋아, 문제없어.
여: 잘됐다. 보답으로, 네가 정말 좋아하는 브라우니를 좀 구워줄게.
남: 정말? 음… 빨리 먹고 싶다!

문제해설 | 여자는 남자에게 페인트칠을 하며 옮겨 놨던 가구들을 제자리로 옮기는 것을 도와 달라고 부탁했다.

7 정답 ④

[전화벨이 울린다.]
여: 음… 여보세요?
남: Ella? 너 아직도 집이니?
여: 응. 몇 시야?
남: 10시야. 산으로 가는 버스가 한 시간 후에 떠나. 서둘러야 해.
여: 이런. 늦잠을 자 버렸네. 바로 갈게.
남: 넌 제시간에 도착하지 못할 것 같아. 미리 너에게 표를 받았어야 했는데.
여: 걱정하지 마. 서두르면, 제시간에 갈 수 있을 거야.
남: 음… 기다려봐! 아마 매표소에서 표를 받을 수 있을 거야.
여: 좋은 생각이야. 그렇게 하면 정말 시간이 절약될 거야.
남: 표 정보를 알려주면, 내가 그걸 받아 적을게.
여: 그래. 난 그것들을 5월 20일에 샀고, 번호는 F20에서 F27까지야.
남: 알았어. 지금 매표소에 가볼게.

문제해설 | 남자는 늦게 올 여자를 위해 버스표 번호를 가지고 표를 미리 발급받으려고 한다.

8 정답 ③

여: 얘, Nick. 그거 Robert Ford의 새 소설이니?
남: 응, 맞아. 너도 그걸 읽고 있니?
여: 난 지난주에 다 읽었어. 훌륭한 책인 것 같아.
남: 난 오늘 밤에 다 읽을 계획이야. 내일 아침에 도서관에 반납해야 하거든.
여: 그래, 넌 그 책 어떠니?
남: 음… 정말 흥미로워. 그런데 내가 이야기를 완전히 이해한 건지 잘 모르겠어.
여: 응, 줄거리가 꽤 복잡하지. 난 사실 그걸 읽으면서 메모를 했어.
남: 나도 그걸 생각했었더라면 좋았을걸. 정말 헷갈리거든.
여: 우리 내일 만나는 게 어때? 네가 그걸 이해하는 데 도움이 되도록 이야기에 대해 얘기해볼 수 있어.
남: 그게 좋겠다. 12시에 한가하니?
여: 난 2시까지는 동아리 모임이 있는데, 그땐 괜찮아.
남: 잘됐다. 학교 식당에서 만나자.

문제해설 | 여자는 소설의 줄거리를 잘 이해하지 못하는 남자를 위해 책 내용에 대해 함께 이야기해 보자고 했다.

DICTATION ANSWER pp. 31-33

1. have plans / wrote it down / pick up the kids
2. see this chart / missing information / make copies
3. how to make / cook them dinner / get some for you
4. ran away / made some posters / put them up
5. have a seat / hurt my ankle / come by
6. give me a hand / some help moving / I can't wait
7. must have overslept / make it in time / save time
8. plan on finishing it / understand the story / talk about the story

05강 지불할 금액

기출예제

p. 34

남: 도와 드릴까요?
여: 저 치즈 케이크가 맛있어 보이네요! 얼마죠?
남: 케이크 전체에 30달러 또는 조각당 5달러입니다.
여: 좋아요. 두 조각을 살게요.
남: 케이크와 함께 아이스크림을 사시겠어요? 한 주걱에 2달러입니다.
여: 아뇨, 괜찮아요.
남: 알겠습니다. 음료도 하시겠습니까?
여: 네, 중간 크기로 커피 두 잔 주세요.
남: 중간 크기의 커피는 3달러이고 큰 것은 6달러입니다. 하지만 케이크를 구매하시므로, 크기가 큰 커피는 한 잔당 5달러만 내시면 됩니다.
여: 좋습니다! 그럼 큰 것으로 주세요.
남: 그렇다면 치즈 케이크 두 조각과 큰 커피 두 잔이네요. 또 다른 게 필요하신가요?
여: 아뇨, 근데 제게 할인 쿠폰이 있어요. 그것을 지금 써도 될까요?
남: 잠시만요. *[잠시 후]* 물론이지요. 총액에서 10%가 할인되네요.
여: 오, 잘됐네요. 여기 제 신용카드요.

LISTEN & APPLY pp. 35-36

1 ② 2 ⑤ 3 ④ 4 ③ 5 ②
6 ② 7 ② 8 ④

1 정답 ②

여: 안녕하세요. 앞줄 좌석이 아직 남아 있나요?
남: 네, 있습니다, 손님.
여: 잘됐네요. 얼마죠?
남: 어른은 40달러이고 어린이는 25달러입니다.
여: 좋아요, 세 장 살게요. 어른 두 명과 어린이 한 명이요.
남: 아, 죄송합니다. 앞줄 좌석은 두 석만 남아 있네요.
여: 아, 이런. 다음으로 가장 좋은 좌석은 어떤 거죠?
남: 발코니석입니다. 어른은 30달러이고 어린이는 15달러입니다. 그 좌석들도 아주 좋습니다.
여: 그럼 그거면 될 것 같네요. 전 무대만 잘 보이면 되거든요.
남: 그 위에서 보면 아주 잘 보일 겁니다.
여: 좋아요. 발코니석으로 세 장 주세요.

문제해설 | 여자는 발코니석으로 어른 두 명($30×2)과 어린이 한 명($15×1)의 티켓을 구입하겠다고 했으므로, 여자가 지불할 금액은 75달러이다.

2 정답 ⑤

여: 안녕하세요, 손님. 어떻게 도와 드릴까요?
남: 이 호텔에서 스쿠터를 대여해 준다고 들었어요.
여: 네, 그렇습니다. 그것은 도시의 명소들을 둘러볼 수 있는 가장 좋은 방법입니다.
남: 저도 그렇게 들었어요. 대여료가 얼마죠?
여: 이 호텔 투숙객이시라면, 시간당 10달러입니다.
남: 사실, 저는 길 아래에 있는 숙소에 묵고 있어요.
여: 그런 경우에는, 시간당 5달러가 더 듭니다. 스쿠터를 얼마 동안 빌리실 건가요?
남: 어디 보자… 지금이 오전 11시네요.
여: 실은, 손님, 10시밖에 안 됐습니다.
남: 아, 제가 시계를 한 시간 되돌려놓는 걸 깜박했네요. 오후 1시까지만 스쿠터를 빌릴게요.
여: 알겠습니다, 손님. 신분증만 보여주시면, 스쿠터를 가져다 드리겠습니다.

문제해설 | 남자는 호텔 투숙객이 아니므로 스쿠터 대여료로 시간당 15달러를 지불해야 하고, 오전 10시부터 오후 1시까지 총 3시간 동안 빌리기로 했으므로($15×3), 남자가 지불할 금액은 45달러이다.

3 정답 ④

[전화벨이 울린다.]
남: Speedy 공항 셔틀입니다. 어떻게 도와 드릴까요?
여: 안녕하세요. 제 남편과 제가 내일 아침에 공항까지 갈 교통편이 필요해서요.
남: 알겠습니다. 비행편은 몇 시이고 계신 곳이 어디죠?
여: 저희는 시내에 머물고 있고, 비행기는 오전 9시에 출발해요.
남: 알겠습니다. 1인당 35달러입니다. 두 분뿐이신가요?
여: 네. 저희 짐에 대한 추가 요금이 있나요?
남: 1인당 짐 하나는 무료로 가져올 수 있습니다. 그다음부터는, 가방 한 개당 10달러입니다.
여: 그렇군요. 음, 가격은 적당한 것 같네요.
남: 가방을 몇 개 가져오실 건가요?
여: 제 남편은 하나이고, 전 세 개예요.
남: 알겠습니다. 제게 주소를 알려주시면, 아침에 모시러 갈 사람을 보내겠습니다.
여: 좋습니다. 감사합니다.

문제해설 | 셔틀 이용료는 1인당 35달러인데 두 명이 이용하므로 70달러($35×2)이고, 추가로 지불해야 할 여자의 짐이 두 개가 있으므로 짐에 대한 추가 요금은 20달러($10×2)이다. 따라서 여자가 지불할 금액은 90달러이다.

4 정답 ③

여: 여기 다 괜찮으신가요?
남: 그럼요. 음식이 정말 맛있었어요. 이 도시에서 최고의 미트로프를 만드시는군요.
여: 손님께서 그렇게 말씀하셨다고 요리사에게 전할게요. 더 필요한 거 있으세요?
남: 아뇨, 그냥 계산서 주세요. 저희는 이만 가야 하거든요.
여: 알겠습니다. *[잠시 후]* 여기 있습니다. 총 24달러입니다.
남: 음. 그게 맞는 거 확실한가요? 좀 많은 것 같은데요.
여: 음, 접시당 8달러인 미트로프 요리 두 접시와 개당 4달러인 사과 파이가 두 조각이네요.
남: 착오가 있는 것 같네요. 전 미트로프 요리를 먹었지만, 제 아내는 샐러드 한 접시만 먹었거든요.
여: 오, 이런, 맞네요. 제 실수예요. 샐러드는 6달러밖에 안 합니다.
남: 괜찮아요. 여기 있습니다.

문제해설 | 남자는 8달러짜리 미트로프 요리를, 부인은 6달러짜리 샐러드를 먹었고, 둘 다 4달러짜리 사과 파이를 한 조각씩 먹었으므로($4×2), 남자가 지불해야 할 금액은 22달러이다.

5 정답 ②

남: 무엇을 도와 드릴까요, 손님?
여: 음, 제 시계가 멈춰서요. 배터리를 교체하려고요.
남: 네, 어디 보죠. 그게 전부인가요?
여: 아뇨, 시곗줄도 바꾸고 싶어요. 이것들은 얼마죠?
남: 금으로 된 건 40달러이고, 은으로 된 건 30달러입니다.
여: 금으로 된 게 멋지긴 한데, 이미 하나를 가지고 있어요.
남: 알겠습니다. 그럼 은으로 된 거로 하시겠어요?
여: 네. 그럼 제가 얼마를 내면 되죠?
남: 새 배터리는 20달러예요, 그리고…

여: 아, 잠시만요, 제게 할인카드가 있어요. 이거 되나요?
남: 그럼요. 이게 있으면 시곗줄에 10% 할인을 해 드리는데, 배터리에는 적용되지 않아요.
여: 괜찮아요. 여기 있어요.

문제해설 | 배터리 교체 비용은 20달러이고 은으로 된 시곗줄의 가격은 30달러인데 시곗줄은 10%의 할인을 받아 27달러이므로, 여자가 지불할 금액은 47달러이다.

6 정답 ②

[*전화벨이 울린다.*]
여: 안녕하세요. Springfield 자연사 박물관입니다. 어떻게 도와 드릴까요?
남: 안녕하세요, 이번 주에 제 아내와 두 아이를 데리고 박물관을 방문하고 싶어서요.
여: 좋은 생각이시네요. 많은 교육적인 전시들과 재미있는 가족 활동들이 있답니다.
남: 입장료는 얼마인가요?
여: 음, 입장료는 평일에 12달러입니다. 그리고 주말에는 3달러가 더 들고요.
남: 그렇군요. 꽤 비싸네요.
여: 아이들이 몇 살인가요?
남: 딸은 11살이고 아들은 8살이에요.
여: 음, 사실 10살 미만의 아이들은 박물관에 무료로 입장합니다.
남: 아, 잘됐네요. 그렇다면 이번 일요일에 들러야겠네요.

문제해설 | 남자가 방문하고자 하는 주말에는 평일 입장료인 12달러보다 3달러 더 비싸다고 했으므로 남자와 남자의 아내, 11살짜리 딸은 각각 입장료 15달러씩을 지불해야 하며($15×3), 8살짜리 아들은 무료로 입장할 수 있으므로, 남자가 지불할 금액은 45달러이다.

7 정답 ②

여: 실례합니다. 이 쿠션들은 얼마인가요?
남: 정사각형 모양의 쿠션들은 각각 10달러, 둥근 것들은 5달러예요.
여: 나쁘지 않네요. 제 소파에 둘 몇 개를 사고 싶어요.
남: 네. 둥근 것들은 지금 할인 판매 중이에요. 네 개를 사시면 10% 할인을 해 드려요.
여: 좋네요. 그걸로 네 개 살게요.
남: 네. 마음에 드시는 거로 네 개를 고르세요.
여: 알겠습니다. [*잠시 후*] 저는 이 정사각형 모양의 것도 좋아요. 그것도 할인해 주실 수 있나요?
남: 죄송하지만, 그것들은 이미 가능한 최저가로 가격을 내렸어요.
여: 네. 어쨌든 그걸 살게요. 배달을 해주시나요?
남: 그럼요. 20달러 넘게 구매하셨으니 배달은 무료입니다.
여: 아, 좋아요. 감사합니다.

문제해설 | 각각 5달러인 둥근 모양의 쿠션 네 개는 10% 할인을 받아 18달러이고, 정사각형 모양 쿠션 한 개는 가격이 10달러이므로, 여자가 지불할 금액은 28달러이다.

8 정답 ④

남: 안녕하세요. 제 딸을 위한 책상을 사고 싶은데요. 하나 추천해 주시겠어요?
여: 알겠습니다. 이게 가장 인기 있는 모델입니다.
남: 아주 좋군요. 이건 얼마죠?
여: 300달러입니다. 사시겠어요?
남: 조금 비싸네요. 가격을 낮춰주실 수 있나요?
여: 책상은 안 돼요. 그렇지만 어울리는 책장이 지금 50% 할인을 해요.
남: 책장 정가가 얼마인데요?
여: 120달러입니다.
남: 그렇군요. 그럼 책상과 책장 둘 다 사겠습니다. 배달 비용을 지불해야 합니까?
여: 네, 20달러입니다. 그런데 500달러 이상 구매하시면 무료로 배송해 드립니다.
남: 글쎄요, 더 필요한 게 없습니다. 배달료를 지불할게요.
여: 그래요. 먼저 여기에 주소를 기입해 주세요.

문제해설 | 책상이 300달러이고 책장이 120달러인데 50% 할인하고 있으므로 60달러이므로 총 360달러이다. 구매 금액이 500달러 미만이므로 배달료 20달러를 추가로 내야 하므로, 남자가 지불할 금액은 380달러이다.

DICTATION ANSWER pp. 37-39

1. two adults / $15 for children / three tickets
2. see the sights / $5 an hour / turn my watch back
3. need a ride / two of you / $10 per bag
4. just the check / two slices of / Here you are
5. change its band / a silver one / the battery
6. lots of educational exhibits / on weekends / get into the museum
7. are on sale / give me a discount / a delivery service
8. lower the price / free shipping / fill in

06강 목적

기출예제 p. 40

남: 주목해 주시겠습니까? 저는 교장 Wilson입니다. 아시다시피, 이번 금요일은 우리의 한 달 동안의 물품 기부 행사의 마지막 날입니다. 이미 참여해주신 분들께 감사드립니다. 그러나, 그 행사에 대한 우리의 참여가 아직 기대에 못 미쳐서, 우리는 더 많은

것을 해야 합니다. 우리가 아직도 구하고 있는 물품은 아동 의류, 장난감, 학용품 그리고 책입니다. 이 물품들 중 어느 것이라도 갖고 계시면, 금요일까지 학교 식당으로 가져다주세요. 어떠한 기부도, 심지어 단 한 자루의 연필도 큰 도움이 될 것입니다. 여러분의 작은 행동이 큰 차이를 만든다는 것을 잊지 마세요. 여러분이 이 행사에 참여하시기를 정말로 권장합니다. 들어주셔서 감사합니다.

LISTEN & APPLY pp. 41-42

1 ④	2 ①	3 ③	4 ③	5 ④
6 ③	7 ⑤	8 ②		

1 정답 ④

여: 아마 여러분 중 많은 분들이 이번 여름에 처음으로 해외에 가시는 것 같습니다. 많은 항공사들이 유럽(행)에 큰 할인 혜택을 제공하고 있고, 여행사들은 학생들의 관심을 끌도록 기획된 특별 상품들을 제공하고 있습니다. 좋은 경험이 될 수 있지만, 다른 나라들을 방문하는 것은 가볍게 여겨질 일이 아닙니다. 집을 떠나기 전에 숙제, 즉 여러분의 목적지의 풍습과 전통을 조사하십시오. 또한 같이 갈 사람을 현명하게 선택하십시오. 여러분이 서로 잘 맞고 여행의 목적이 같은지 확인하십시오. 그렇지 않으면, 매우 특별해야 할 시간이 결국에는 재앙이 될 수 있습니다.

문제해설 | 여자는 해외여행을 가는 사람들에게 유의해야 할 사항들에 대해 조언하고 있다.

2 정답 ①

남: 수년 동안, 〈College Days〉는 저희 방송국에서 가장 성공적인 시트콤 중의 하나였습니다. 모든 연령대의 시청자들이 이 프로그램의 재미있는 주인공들의 모험을 즐겨 왔습니다. 하지만, 이번 시즌이 이 프로그램의 마지막이 될 것입니다. 어려운 결정이었지만, 저희는 그렇게 해야만 했습니다. 몇몇 주연 배우들이 할리우드에서 자신들의 (연기) 경력을 쌓기 위해 프로그램을 그만두기로 이미 결정했습니다. 그들을 대체하려 하기보다, 저희는 프로그램을 종영하는 것이 저희가 할 수 있는 최선이라고 결정했습니다. 하지만, 저희는 지난 에피소드들을 계속 방영할 것입니다.

문제해설 | 남자는 〈College Days〉의 몇몇 주연 배우들이 시트콤에서 하차하게 되어 이번 시즌 방송이 마지막이 될 것을 공지하고 있다.

3 정답 ③

여: 한미 여성 클럽의 올해 마지막 모임에 오신 것을 환영합니다. 여러분도 아시다시피, 우리는 크리스마스와 신년 연휴 기간 동안에 휴회를 할 것입니다. 내년에는, 몇몇 요청의 결과에 따라, 우리의 정규 모임일에 변동이 있을 것입니다. 여러분 중 많은 분들이 우리의 모임을 월요일에서 수요일 저녁으로 변경하자고 요청하셨고, 그것이 이제 투표에 의해 확정되었습니다. 저는 여러분에게 그 변경 사항을 상기시켜 드리는 이메일도 보내드릴 것입니다. 1월에 우리와 함께 할 몇몇 신입 회원분들을 모시고 우리의 모임을 재개하겠습니다. 다음 모임 때까지, 모두 즐거운 성탄절을 보내시고, 새해 복 많이 받으십시오!

문제해설 | 여자는 회원들에게 내년부터 클럽 모임의 요일이 변경됨을 알리고 있다.

4 정답 ③

남: 체중을 줄이거나 건강을 개선하고자 하십니까? 많은 사람들이 식사에서 정크푸드를 없앱니다. 어떤 사람들은 자기 전에 야식 먹는 것을 끊기도 합니다. 그러나 여러분이 정말 진전을 이루고 싶다면 여러분이 먹는 방법도 바꿔 보시기를 제안드립니다. 음식을 천천히 먹고 삼키기 전에 한 입 한 입 완전히 씹는 것에 집중해 보세요. 여러분의 뇌는 위장이 다 찼다는 것을 인지하는 데 몇 분이 걸릴 수 있습니다. 천천히 먹는 것이 여러분의 뇌가 이 정보를 처리할 시간을 줄 것입니다. 그러면 여러분은 과식하기 전에 배부르다고 느낄 것입니다. 천천히 먹고 정성 들여 씹음으로써 우리는 소화도 촉진하게 됩니다. 우리의 위장이 잘 씹은 음식으로부터 비타민과 영양분을 흡수하는 것이 훨씬 더 쉬워집니다. 그러니 더 건강한 삶을 영위하기 위해 더 천천히 드십시오.

문제해설 | 남자는 음식을 천천히 먹고 완전히 씹어 삼키는 것이 건강에 어떻게 이로운지에 대해 알려주고 있다.

5 정답 ④

여: 고객 여러분께 안내 말씀드립니다! 저희의 특별 휴가 세일을 이용하시기 위해 Ferndale's를 찾아 주셔서 감사합니다. 하지만, 토요일자 신문에 실린 저희의 광고에 작은 실수가 있었다는 것을 발견했습니다. 그 광고에는, 저희의 모든 재킷이 40% 할인된다고 쓰여 있습니다. 유감스럽게도, '가죽'이라는 단어가 그 광고에서 누락되었습니다. 저희는 그 오류에 대해 진심으로 유감스럽게 생각합니다. 저희의 다른 모든 재킷들은 실제로는 10%를 할인해 드리고 있으며, 이것 역시 매우 저렴한 상품입니다. 그리고 그 광고에 있는 나머지 정보는 정확하니 안심하십시오. 즐거운 쇼핑 되시길 바랍니다!

문제해설 | 여자는 고객들에게 신문에 실린 광고 내용에 오류가 있었음을 알리며 사과하고 있다.

6 정답 ③

남: 주목해 주시겠습니까? 교장 Gomez 박사입니다. 여러분들도 알다시피, 우리 학교 현장 학습은 이번 주 금요일로 예정되어 있습니다. 그러나, 기상 예보에 따르면, 목요일 밤에 큰 눈보라가 예상됩니다. 여러분의 안전을 위해, 우리의 모든 여행들을 취소하는 것을 고려하였습니다. 하지만 우리는 대신에 여행의 일정을 다시 짜기로 결정했습니다. 그러니, 모든 1, 2학년 학생들의 여행은 다음 주 월요일에 있을 예정이며, 반면에 3학년 학생들

의 여행은 다음 주 화요일에 있을 예정입니다. 이 정보를 여러분의 부모님께 꼭 공유하기 바랍니다.

문제해설 | 남자는 예정된 현장 학습일 하루 전에 큰 눈보라가 예상되어 기존 일정을 취소하고, 새롭게 정한 날짜를 학생들에게 알리고 있다.

7 정답 ⑤

여: 안녕하십니까. 여름이 다가오면서 여러분 중 많은 사람들이 방학 동안에 돈을 벌기 위한 방법들을 찾고 있습니다. 그런데, 저는 여러분 중 몇몇이 우리 학교에서 보낸 것처럼 보이는 주소로부터 이메일을 받았다고 들었습니다. 그 이메일에는 여러분이 이번 여름에 학교를 위한 잡지 구독권을 판매함으로써 쉽게 돈을 벌 수 있다고 쓰여 있습니다. 하지만 우리는 결코 이런 종류의 이메일을 보낸 적이 없습니다. 언제든지 여러분이 '쉬운'과 '돈'이라는 말이 함께 쓰인 것을 보게 되면, 의심하셔야 합니다. 이런 이메일은 응답하지 말고 삭제하십시오. 만일 여러분이 돈을 벌 방법들을 찾고 싶다면, 방과 후에 학생 직업 안내 센터에 들르십시오. 그들은 여러분이 일자리를 찾는 것을 도와줄 것입니다.

문제해설 | 여자는 학교에서 보낸 것처럼 위조된 이메일에 속지 말라고 학생들에게 경고하고 있다.

8 정답 ②

남: 안녕하세요. 여러분도 아시다시피, 지난달에 Harold Green 씨가 회사에서 퇴임하셨습니다. 그는 열심히 일했고 훌륭한 지도자였습니다. 이 기회를 빌려 그에게 다시 한번 감사를 드리고 싶습니다. 지난주, 그의 자리에 많은 분들을 고려한 끝에, 저희는 드디어 Harold 씨의 후임을 결정했습니다. 오늘부로, Karen Johnson 씨가 고객 서비스 부서 관리직을 맡으실 것입니다. 그녀는 이전에 저희의 경쟁 업체들 중 한 곳에서 비슷한 직책으로 일하셨으며, 저희 회사에 많은 참신한 아이디어를 주실 것입니다. 그녀는 Harold 씨가 쓰시던 자리에 앉으실 것이니, 기회가 되시면 잠깐 들러서 인사를 나누십시오. 시간 내주셔서 감사드리며, 좋은 하루 보내십시오.

문제해설 | 남자는 퇴임한 Harold Green 씨의 후임으로 새로 오게 된 Karen Johnson 씨를 직원들에게 소개하고 있다.

DICTATION ANSWER pp. 43-45

1. go abroad / customs and traditions / same goals
2. the most successful / the show's last / ending the show
3. taking a break / change our meetings / remind you of
4. make progress / chewing each mouthful / improve our digestion
5. a slight mistake / regret the error / please be assured
6. large snow storm / reschedule them instead / share this information
7. magazine subscriptions / have your doubts / without responding
8. an excellent leader / a replacement for / one of our competitors

07강 이유

기출예제 p. 46

[전화벨이 울린다.]
여: 여보세요?
남: 안녕, Sarah. 나 Alex야. 너에게 물어볼 게 있어.
여: 그래. 뭔데?
남: 음, 난 다음 주 금요일에 열리는 전국 야구 선수권대회 표를 두 장 가지고 있는데, 안타깝게도 난 갈 수 없어. 너 표를 원하니?
여: 응, 물론이지, 그런데 난 표가 다 팔렸다고 생각했는데.
남: 그래. 하지만 우리 회사는 모든 경기의 표를 미리 사두어서 내가 몇 장을 구할 수 있었어.
여: 잘된 일인데, 넌 왜 못 가니?
남: 난 그날 고객과 중요한 회의가 있어서 비행기를 타고 시외로 나가야 해서 경기를 볼 수 없어. 네가 네 남동생을 데리고 함께 갈 수 있을 것 같은데.
여: 그래, 그도 가고 싶어 할 거야. 하지만 네가 일 때문에 경기에 갈 수 없다니 유감이구나.
남: 그건 걱정하지 마. 경기 즐겁게 봐.

LISTEN & APPLY pp. 47-48

1 ① 2 ⑤ 3 ④ 4 ⑤ 5 ③
6 ⑤ 7 ⑤ 8 ③

1 정답 ①

남: 안녕, Hannah. 내가 뭘 도와줄까?
여: 네, Smith 교수님. 저는 수업을 바꾸고 싶어요.
남: 이 수업을 다른 시간에 듣고 싶은 거니?
여: 아니요, 저는 비즈니스 101 수업을 교수님의 경제학 입문 수업으로 바꾸고 싶어요. 너무 늦었나요?
남: 아니, 아주 늦지는 않았어. 너의 학적 사항을 우선 확인해 볼게.
여: 네. 제 학생증 번호는 031-1178입니다.
남: 잠깐만. *[잠시 후]* 오, 미안해. 너는 어쨌든 그 수업을 수강할 수 없겠다.
여: 왜 안 되나요? 제 성적이 충분하지 않나요?

남: 그게 문제가 아니야. 나는 네가 1학년이라고 생각했어. 그 수업은 1학년에게만 제공되고 있거든.
여: 오. 다음 학기는 어떤가요?
남: 그건 괜찮을 거야. 다음 학기에는 모든 학생들에게 열릴 거야.

문제해설 | 남자는 여자가 수강하려는 경제학 입문 강의는 1학년에게만 제공되는 수업이라고 했다.

2 **정답 ⑤**

여: 안녕하세요. 무엇을 도와 드릴까요?
남: 안녕하세요. 최근에 제가 하이킹 클럽 현수막을 학교 도서관 앞에 설치했어요. 그런데 지금 그것이 사라졌어요.
여: 그렇군요. 그것을 설치하기 위한 허가는 받으셨나요?
남: 네. 이곳에 와서 알맞은 양식을 작성했어요.
여: 음, 학교에서는 일주일이 지나면 모든 현수막을 내려요. 허가받은 것들 조차도요.
남: 그렇지만 그것은 아직 설치한 지 3일밖에 안 됐어요!
여: 저희의 기록을 좀 살펴볼게요. [*잠시 후*] 음, 저희는 댄스 클럽 현수막을 철거했지만, 당신의 것은 아마 아직도 올라가 있을 거예요.
남: 그렇지 않아요. 그리고 댄스 클럽 현수막은 아직도 그곳에 있어요.
여: 직원이 그 두 현수막을 혼동했나 보네요. 제가 오류를 바로 잡도록 할게요.
남: 감사합니다! 그렇게 해주시면 좋겠습니다.

문제해설 | 여자는 직원이 남자의 현수막을 다른 현수막과 혼동하여 잘못 철거한 것 같다고 했다.

3 **정답 ④**

여: 또 늦어서 죄송합니다.
남: 조심하는 게 좋겠어요. 상사가 화를 내실 거예요.
여: 알아요. 진짜 문제가 될 거예요. 어떻게 해야 할지 저도 모르겠어요.
남: 교통 체증 때문인가요? 최근에 출퇴근 혼잡 시간대에 교통이 꽤 안 좋긴 했어요.
여: 아니요. 새 아파트로 이사한 뒤로 저는 쭉 걸어서 출근하고 있어요. 사실 저는 늦잠을 잤어요.
남: 아마도 당신은 더 믿음직한 알람 시계가 필요할 것 같네요.
여: 아니요, 그런 게 아니에요. 저는 그저 밤늦게까지 제 휴대전화로 게임을 해요.
남: 그건 좋은 이유가 아닌데요. 당신은 휴대전화를 딱 끄고 자야 해요.
여: 저도 알지만 멈출 수가 없어요!

문제해설 | 여자는 밤늦게까지 휴대전화로 게임을 하느라 늦잠을 잔다고 했다.

4 **정답 ⑤**

[*전화벨이 울린다.*]
남: Lakeside 리조트에 전화 주셔서 감사합니다. 어떻게 도와 드릴까요?
여: 안녕하세요. 7월 7일에 예약을 하려고 전화 드렸습니다.
남: 알겠습니다. 안타깝게도, 그날 유일하게 이용 가능한 객실은 호수 전망이 아닙니다.
여: 괜찮아요. 얼마인가요?
남: 1박에 170달러입니다.
여: 약간 비싸네요. 그러나 그곳의 방들이 괜찮다고 들었으니, 그걸로 하겠습니다.
남: 좋습니다. 제가 더 도와드릴 것이 있나요?
여: 네. 공항 셔틀버스를 예약하고 싶습니다.
남: 죄송하지만, 저희는 더 이상 셔틀버스를 운영하지 않습니다.
여: 아. 그러면 예약을 취소해주세요. 셔틀버스를 운영하는 다른 리조트를 아시나요?
남: 네, Golden 리조트요. 호수에서는 떨어져 있지만, 수영장이 있습니다.

문제해설 | 여자는 남자가 리조트에서 셔틀버스를 더 이상 운영하지 않는다고 하자 예약을 취소하고, 셔틀버스를 운영하는 다른 리조트를 추천해달라고 했다.

5 **정답 ③**

[*전화벨이 울린다.*]
여: Major Music 사에 전화를 해주셔서 감사합니다. 저는 Hillary입니다.
남: 안녕하세요. Felix Schwartz라고 합니다. 제가 며칠 전에 CD를 주문했어요. 주문 번호는 321654예요.
여: [*타자치는 소리*] 안녕하세요, Schwartz 씨. 어떻게 도와 드릴까요?
남: Keane 밴드의 새 앨범을 주문했는데 제 주문을 취소하고 싶어요.
여: 네. 무슨 문제가 있나요?
남: 아니요, 그런데 저는 사인이 담긴 한정판을 원해요.
여: 실은, 그건 인터넷상에서 사실 수 없어요.
남: 압니다. Birmingham가(街) 가게에서만 판매될 거라고 들었어요. 그래서 그걸 사려면 그 가게를 방문해야 한다고요.
여: 네. 주문을 취소해드릴 수 있지만, 취소 수수료가 있어요.
남: 알겠습니다. 선택의 여지가 없네요.

문제해설 | 남자는 밴드의 사인이 담긴 한정판 앨범을 구매하기 위해 온라인 주문을 취소하기를 원한다.

6 **정답 ⑤**

[*전화벨이 울린다.*]
여: 안녕, Brian. 널 만나러 공원으로 막 가려던 참이었어.
남: 안녕, Charlotte. 그럼 통화가 돼서 다행이다.
여: 어? 무슨 일이야? 길이 많이 막혀?
남: 아니, 하지만 아무래도 우리 달리기하기로 한 걸 다음으로 변경해야 할 것 같아.

여: 아. 너 또 야근해야 하는 거니?
남: 아니. 실은, 10분 전쯤에 퇴근해서 집에 왔어.
여: 그럼 무슨 일이야? 무슨 일이 생겼어?
남: 별일 없어. 근데 몸이 아파. 감기에 걸렸나 봐.
여: 저런. 넌 집에 있으면서 좀 쉬는 게 좋겠어. 나는 너 없이 갈게.
남: 고마워, Charlotte. 달리기 즐겁게 해.
여: 고마워, Brian. 몸 조심해.

문제해설 | 남자는 감기에 걸려 오늘 여자와의 달리기 약속에 나갈 수 없다고 했다.

7 정답 ⑤

남: 제가 예상했던 것보다 일찍 돌아오셨네요. 회의는 어땠어요?
여: 뭔가가 잘못되었어요, Mark. 회의가 오후 2시에 시작한다고 말하지 않았나요?
남: 네, 그랬어요. 뭐가 잘못되었나요?
여: 네. 막 회의실에서 돌아온 거예요. 거기에 아무도 없었어요.
남: 정말이요? 2번 회의실로 가셨어요? 아시다시피, 회의실이 세 개 있잖아요.
여: 네, 확실히 2번 회의실이었어요. 연기나 취소에 관한 메시지를 받았나요?
남: 아니요. 일정을 다시 확인해 볼게요.
여: 그렇게 해 주세요. 이 회의에 빠지고 싶지 않아요.
남: [*잠시 후*] 아, 죄송해요. 제가 실수를 했어요. 회의는 내일 오후에 하기로 되어 있네요.
여: 정말이요? 음, 회의에 참석할 수 있으니 다행이네요. 하지만 이런 실수를 다시 하지 않도록 주의해 주세요.

문제해설 | 여자는 남자가 회의 날짜를 잘못 알려줘서 당황했다.

8 정답 ③

남: 무슨 일이니, Lisa?
여: 배고픈데, 점심 사 먹을 돈을 집에 놓고 왔어.
남: 내 것을 나누자. 나는 점심으로 햄버거를 먹을 거야. 나랑 나눠 먹어도 돼.
여: 정말이야?
남: 응. 실은, 네가 원하면 절반보다 더 많이 먹어도 돼.
여: 고마워! 너 햄버거를 안 좋아하니?
남: 아니, 좋아해. 네 개도 먹을 수 있어. 근데 너무 많이 먹지 않으려고 노력 중이야.
여: 다이어트 중이야?
남: 아니. 오늘 밤에 가족들과 저녁을 거하게 먹을 예정이라서, 점심은 가볍게 먹고 싶어.
여: 아, 알겠다. 저녁 식사를 위해 배를 좀 비워 놓으려는 거구나.
남: 맞아! 우린 내가 가장 좋아하는 음식인 으깬 감자와 칠면조 구이를 먹을 거야.
여: 집에서 요리한 성대한 식사라니 좋겠다. 나도 가면 좋을 텐데.
남: 미안하지만, 이번엔 가족끼리만이야. 하지만 네가 원한다면 다음 주말에 저녁을 먹으러 와도 돼.
여: 정말? 고마워!

문제해설 | 남자는 집에서 가족들과 저녁을 거하게 먹을 예정이라 점심으로 햄버거를 조금만 먹으려고 한다.

DICTATION ANSWER pp. 49-51

1. change classes / check your records / you were a freshman
2. put up a banner / takes down / have our error corrected
3. because of traffic / reliable alarm clock / turn it off
4. make a reservation / available room / offer a shuttle
5. cancel my order / want the limited edition / there is a fee
6. stuck in traffic / work overtime / caught a cold
7. earlier than I expected / delays or cancellations / make any mistakes
8. Let's split mine / more than half / in your stomach

08강 관계 · 대화의 장소

기출예제 p. 52

남: 안녕하세요, 어떻게 도와 드릴까요?
여: 안녕하세요. 이 공원에서 야생 동물 투어를 예약했는데요. 표를 찾으려고요.
남: 예약 번호 있으신가요?
여: 네. 32461이고요, 투어 비용을 이미 지불했어요.
남: [*타자치는 소리*] Kate Smith 씨이시군요, 맞으시죠?
여: 네, 맞아요.
남: 1일 투어 4인을 예약하셨네요, 맞으세요?
여: 맞아요. 성인 2명과 아동 2명이요.
남: 여기 이용권이에요. 동물들에게 먹이를 주시면 안 돼요.
여: 알겠어요. 감사해요.
남: 즐거운 투어 되세요.

LISTEN & APPLY pp. 53-54

1 ⑤　2 ③　3 ④　4 ③　5 ⑤
6 ②　7 ④　8 ③

1 정답 ⑤

여: 안녕하세요. 어떤 문제가 있으신가요, 선생님?
남: 옆구리에 심한 통증이 있어요. 어젯밤에 한숨도 못 잤어요.

여: 알겠습니다. 전에 오신 적이 있나요?
남: 네, 2주 전쯤에 종합 검진을 받았어요.
여: 알겠습니다. 이 양식만 작성해 주세요. 선생님의 진료 기록을 찾아볼게요.
남: 나이? 혈액형? 이 사항들을 전부 다 작성해야 하나요?
여: 네. 의사 선생님이 진찰하시기 전에 이것들을 아셔야 하거든요.
남: 의사 선생님이 진찰하실 때 제가 그냥 말씀드리면 안 될까요? 제 진료 기록도 이미 갖고 계시잖아요.
여: 죄송하지만, 기본적인 사항에 대한 양식은 병원에 오실 때마다 작성해 주셔야 해요.
남: 알겠습니다. [*잠시 후*] 여기 있습니다.
여: 감사합니다. 의사 선생님께서 부르실 때까지 여기서 기다려 주세요.

문제해설 | 옆구리가 아파서 병원에 온 남자와 양식 작성을 요청하는 여자의 대화로 보아, 접수원과 환자 간의 대화임을 알 수 있다.

2 정답 ③

여: 세상에! 이곳은 정말 넓군요. 어디서부터 시작해야 할지 모르겠어요.
남: 여기가 처음이신가요?
여: 네. 전 어제 회원으로 막 등록했거든요.
남: 음, 좋은 곳을 고르셨네요. 전 수년간 여기에 다니고 있어요.
여: 다양한 종류의 많은 기구들이 있네요. 어떤 걸 사용해야 하나요?
남: 상황에 따라 다르죠. 근육을 키우고 싶으세요, 아니면 그냥 체중을 감량하고 싶으세요?
여: 전 그냥 전반적으로 건강을 향상시키고 싶어요. 책상에 너무 오랫동안 앉아 있거든요.
남: 무슨 말인지 알겠어요. 저기 있는 저 여자분과 얘기해 보세요.
여: 회색 운동복을 입고 있는 분 말인가요?
남: 네. 그분은 여기서 일하세요. 그분이 아마 당신한테 좋은 조언을 좀 해 주실 거예요.
여: 그럴 것 같네요.

문제해설 | 다양한 종류의 기구들이 있고, 근육을 키우고 싶은지 체중을 감량하고 싶은지를 묻는 것으로 보아, 헬스클럽에서 이루어지는 대화임을 알 수 있다.

3 정답 ④

남: 이제, 버스 정류장에서 출발하는 저 버스를 주의하세요.
여: 걱정하지 마세요. 보여요.
남: 좋아요. 길을 따라 주차된 저 택시들 보이시죠? 그것들을 지나서 좌회전하세요.
여: 알겠어요. [*잠시 후*] 이런, 사이드미러를 보는 걸 깜박했어요.
남: 괜찮아요. 나중에라도 기억했다니 다행이에요. 이제 여기는 오가는 차량이 없으니, 조금 더 빨리 가보세요.
여: 네. 이 정도면 충분한가요?
남: 음, 지금 시속 65킬로미터로 가고 있는데, 여기 제한 속도는 60이에요. 사실 속도위반을 하고 계시는 거예요.
여: 아, 죄송해요. 속도를 늦출게요.
남: 다음번에는 좀 더 주의하셔야 해요. 자, 다 끝마친 것 같군요. 속도를 줄이시고 저 주차장에 주차해 주실래요?
여: 그럴게요.

문제해설 | 두 사람이 도로 주행 연수를 하고 있는 상황으로 보아, 운전 강사와 수강생 간의 대화임을 알 수 있다.

4 정답 ③

여: 안녕하세요. 뭘 찾는 걸 도와 드릴까요?
남: 네. 요즘 제 피부가 너무 거칠어졌어요.
여: 음, 특히 겨울에는 피부를 관리하셔야 해요.
남: 그런 것 같아요. 제 얼굴이 땅기고 가려워요. 무엇을 추천해 주실 수 있나요?
여: 음. 알레르기가 있으세요?
남: 아뇨, 없어요. 전에는 이런 적이 없었어요.
여: 그럼 단순히 건성 피부여서 그럴 수 있어요. 저는 이 제품을 추천해요. 샘플을 발라 보시겠어요?
남: 네. [*잠시 후*] 음… 향이 좋네요. 얼마예요?
여: 할인해서 20달러예요. 보디로션도 필요하신가요?
남: 아뇨, 이것만요.
여: 상태가 나아지지 않으면, 의사의 진찰을 받아보셔야 할 거예요.
남: 네. 조언 고마워요.

문제해설 | 여자가 남자에게 거칠어진 피부 관리를 위한 화장품을 추천해 주고 샘플을 발라 보라고 하는 것으로 보아, 판매원과 고객 간의 대화임을 알 수 있다.

5 정답 ⑤

여: 아, 오셨군요. 왜 이렇게 오래 걸렸어요?
남: 죄송합니다. 임원분들 중 한 분의 노트북에 문제가 생겨서요.
여: 괜찮아요. 하지만 가능한 한 빨리 제 컴퓨터를 고쳐주세요.
남: 알겠습니다. 음, 지금은 인터넷에 연결이 되는 것 같네요.
여: 네, 하지만 제 이메일이 안 돼요.
남: 아, 공지사항을 못 보셨어요? 저희가 전체 회사 이메일 시스템을 업데이트하고 있거든요.
여: 아, 그걸 못 봤네요. 전 오늘 오후에 중요한 해외 고객과 연락을 해야 해요.
남: 걱정하지 마세요. 2시쯤에는 다시 될 거예요.
여: 그러면 좋겠네요. 그 고객에게 할인을 제공해 드리지 않으면, 그는 대신 우리의 경쟁사에서 자재를 구입하기로 결정할지도 몰라요.
남: 이건 그냥 정기적인 업그레이드예요. 어떤 문제도 없을 겁니다.
여: 음, 그렇다니 다행이네요.

문제해설 | 이메일이 안 돼서 남자를 부른 여자는 해외 고객에게 자재를 판매하는 직원이고 남자는 컴퓨터 문제를 해결해 주는 사람인 것으로 보아, 영업 부서 직원과 기술 지원 부서 직원 간의 대화임을 알 수 있다.

6 정답 ②

여: 아주 열심히 일해줘서 고마워요, Steven. 오늘 우리 정말 바빴네요.

남: 천만에요. 제가 해야 할 다른 일이 있나요?

여: 아뇨, 그렇지만 내일의 일정에 관해 그냥 이야기하고 싶어서요. 한 시간 일찍 올 수 있나요?

남: 그럼요. 특별한 행사라도 있나요?

여: 음, 사업가들 단체 손님 세 팀이 올 거예요. 그들은 모두 11시 30분에 점심 예약을 했어요.

남: 알겠어요. 그런데 세 팀을 위한 큰 탁자가 충분치 않아요.

여: 네. 그러니 당신이 먼저 도착하면, 단체 손님 모두가 함께 앉을 수 있도록 더 작은 탁자들을 다시 배치해 주세요.

남: 그럴게요.

여: 그리고 한 팀은 식사할 시간이 많지 않아서 도착하기 전에 우리가 그들의 음료를 준비하길 원해요.

남: 음료들을 꼭 준비해 놓을게요.

여: 그래요. 오늘은 이만 끝내죠. 내일 봐요.

문제해설 | 여자가 남자에게 일찍 출근해 손님들이 앉을 탁자들을 배치하고 음료를 미리 준비해 달라고 지시하는 것으로 보아, 식당 사장과 종업원 간의 대화임을 알 수 있다.

7 정답 ④

남: 아, 죄송해요, 선생님이 여기 계신 줄 몰랐어요.

여: 네. 오늘 밤에 좀 늦게까지 일하느라고요.

남: 나중에 다시 올까요?

여: 아뇨, 괜찮아요. 이 과제물들을 채점하는 게 거의 끝나가요.

남: 알겠습니다. 지금 이 쓰레기통들만 비울게요.

여: 네. [*잠시 후*] 뭐 좀 여쭤봐도 될까요?

남: 그럼요. 무슨 문제가 있나요?

여: 아뇨. 저희 반이 지난주에 평소보다 더 지저분했었는지 그냥 궁금해서요.

남: 지난주에요? 아뇨… 선생님 반은 항상 학교에서 가장 깨끗한 반들 중의 하나예요.

여: 다행이네요. 제가 휴가 중이어서 저희 반 학생들이 제대로 청소했는지를 몰라서요.

남: 평소처럼 깨끗했어요. 그래서 제 일이 아주 수월하죠.

여: 그렇다니 다행이네요.

문제해설 | 남자는 청소를 하고 여자는 과제물을 채점하는 것으로 보아, 청소부와 교사 간의 대화임을 알 수 있다.

8 정답 ③

[*휴대전화가 울린다.*]

여: 여보세요?

남: 여보세요, Erica? 저 David Smith예요. 우리 작년 Robert의 크리스마스 파티에서 만났었잖아요.

여: 네, 기억나요. 당신의 최근 영화를 정말 재미있게 봤어요.

남: 감사합니다. 제가 새 프로젝트를 시작하고 있는데, 당신이 주인공 역할에 적격일 것 같아서 전화했어요.

여: 어떤 내용인가요?

남: Valentina Tereshkova, 최초로 우주를 여행한 여성 우주 비행사에 관한 거예요.

여: 아, 그녀에 관한 이야기를 읽었어요! 그녀의 이야기는 굉장하죠. 그런데 왜 그 역할에 저를 생각하셨나요?

남: 음, 사실 당신은 그녀가 어렸을 때와 많이 닮았어요.

여: 그렇군요. 음, 관심은 있지만 제 스케줄이 비어 있는지 에이전트에 물어봐야 해요.

남: 좋아요, 하지만 답변이 곧 필요해요. 다음 달에 영화 촬영을 시작할 계획이거든요.

여: 알겠어요. 지금 당장 그에게 전화를 걸게요.

문제해설 | 여자가 남자에게 영화를 잘 봤다고 하고, 남자가 여자에게 영화의 주인공 역할을 제안하는 것으로 보아, 영화배우와 감독 간의 대화임을 알 수 있다.

DICTATION ANSWER pp. 55-57

1. pain in my side / general checkup / he examines me
2. signed up for / improve my health / some good advice
3. pay attention to / no traffic here / breaking the speed limit
4. tight and itchy / try a sample / see a doctor
5. fix my computer / overseas customer / a routine upgrade
6. working so hard / enough large tables / prepare their drinks
7. grading these papers / was messier / cleaned up properly
8. the lead role / travel into space / start filming

09강 도표 정보 파악

기출예제 p. 58

여: 여보. 여기에 Grandlife 놀이공원의 명소 패키지에 관한 팸플릿이 있어요. 그것들 중 하나를 고르죠.

남: 좋아요. 우리가 얼마나 써야 한다고 생각해요?

여: 음, 난 1인당 50달러 이상은 쓰고 싶지 않아요.

남: 좋아요. 3D 영화로, 'Amazing Sea'를 볼래요, 아니면 'Jungle Safari'를 볼래요?

여: 어느 쪽이든 좋은 것 같지만, 'Amazing Sea'가 3D로 보면 정말 멋질 것 같아서 그걸 더 보고 싶네요.

남: 좋아요. 그럼 그 영화를 봅시다.
여: 그래요. 수족관은 어쩌죠? 환상적인 돌고래들이 있다고 들었어요.
남: 음, 우리가 바다에 관한 영화를 본다면, 수족관을 또 갈 필요는 없을 것 같아요.
여: 네, 동감이에요. 점심 도시락 선택 사항을 포함시켜야 할까요?
남: 물론이죠. 그렇게 하면 시간을 좀 절약할 수 있어요.
여: 그럼 이 패키지가 남아 있네요.
남: 완벽해요! 그걸 선택하죠.

LISTEN & APPLY pp. 59-61

1 ③	2 ④	3 ②	4 ④	5 ③
6 ⑤	7 ③	8 ③		

1 정답 ③

남: 너 벌써 음악 수업을 신청했니, Lisa?
여: 응, 했어. 하나를 고르기가 힘들었어.
남: 내가 제안한 대로 Miller 교수님 수업을 신청했니?
여: 아니, 그 교수님은 이번 학기에 수업을 하나만 하시는데, 그게 꽉 찼어.
남: 그거 너무 안됐다. 그럼, 어떤 수업을 선택했니?
여: 음, 난 영화와 음악 수업에 관심이 있었는데, 오후 수업을 들어야 해서 말이야.
남: 아, 영화와 음악 수업은 오전에만 있니?
여: 응, 그리고 난 이미 음악의 역사를 수강했거든.
남: 기억 나. 우린 Cooper 교수님 수업에 같이 있었잖아.
여: 맞아, 그리고 난 화요일과 목요일에 일하기 때문에, 선택지가 많지 않았어.
남: 응, 네가 들을 수 있는 수업은 딱 하나구나. 그런데 듣기로는 대부분의 학생들은 그 수업이 좋대.
여: 그래? 그걸 알게 되니 좋구나.

문제해설 | **Miller 교수님 수업은 꽉 찼고, 음악의 역사 강의는 이미 수강했으며, 화요일과 목요일에는 일을 하고 오후 수업을 들어야 하므로, 여자가 신청한 수업은 ③번이다.**

2 정답 ④

남: 우리 어떤 세탁기를 살까요?
여: 그게, 우린 800달러 넘게 쓸 여유가 없어요.
남: 맞아요. 크기는 어떻게 하고 싶어요? 용량은 우리가 고려해야 할 중요한 사항이라고 생각해요.
여: 우린 세 식구니까 7킬로그램이 좋겠어요.
남: 그건 우리에게 너무 작을 것 같아요. 나는 더 큰 게 좋아요.
여: 알겠어요. 그럼 더 큰 걸 삽시다.
남: 위쪽으로 세탁물을 넣는 세탁기는 어때요?
여: 그건 아주 불편해요. 앞쪽으로 세탁물을 넣는 세탁기를 하는 게 훨씬 낫겠어요.
남: 그래요. 앞쪽으로 넣는 것이 사용하기에 더 편리하죠.
여: 스팀워시 기능이 있는 것에 대해 어떻게 생각해요? 나는 그건 필요하지 않다고 생각해요.
남: 정말요? 전 반대해요. 스팀워시는 진한 얼룩을 없애는 데 도움이 되요.
여: 알겠어요. 그럼 선택 사항 한 개만 남은 것 같네요.

문제해설 | **가격은 800달러를 넘지 않고, 용량이 7킬로그램보다 더 크고, 세탁물을 앞쪽으로 넣으며, 스팀워시 기능이 있는 세탁기는 ④번이다.**

3 정답 ②

남: 이번 주 토요일에 뭐 하고 싶어?
여: 우리 한동안 공연을 못 봤잖아. 요즘 상영하고 있는 좋은 공연들이 있나?
남: 어디 보자. 아, 이 뮤지컬이 정말 흥미진진하다고 들었어.
여: 솔직히 말하면, 나는 뮤지컬에 관심 없어.
남: 알았어. 음, 우리에겐 아직 여러 가지 선택 사항이 있는 것 같아.
여: 점심을 같이 먹고, 그 후에 3시 30분에 이 공연을 보러 가는 건 어때?
남: 토요일에는 사촌과 점심을 먹기로 했어. 우리 저녁을 같이 먹고 연극을 보러 가는 건 어때?
여: 그래. 그런데 나는 너무 늦게까지 밖에 있고 싶진 않아.
남: 우리가 이걸 보면, 9시 전에 극장에서 나올 수 있어.
여: 완벽해 보여!

문제해설 | **여자는 뮤지컬에 흥미가 없다고 했고, 남자는 저녁을 함께 먹고 공연을 보러 가자고 제안했으며, 9시 전에 끝나는 공연이라고 했으므로 두 사람이 볼 공연은 ②번이다.**

4 정답 ④

남: 안녕. 너 신입생이구나, 그렇지? 이 표가 너의 멘토가 누구인지 알려줄 거야.
여: 응, 맞아. 그런데 멘토가 뭐야?
남: 멘토는 신입생들을 첫해 동안 도와주겠다고 자원한 고학년 학생이야.
여: 아, 정말? 이 표는 어떻게 보는 거야?
남: 우선, 너는 너의 학부를 확인해야 해. 나는 철학을 전공하고, 그것은 인문대학에 속해 있어.
여: 아, 그렇구나.
남: 다음에, 네 학생증 번호의 앞 두 숫자를 확인해야 해. 나는 01이야. 그러면 내 멘토의 이름을 찾을 수 있지.
여: 한번 해볼게. 내 전공은 컴퓨터 공학이고, 내 학생증 번호는 21로 시작해.
남: 컴퓨터 공학? 그것은 이과대학부지, 맞지?
여: 사실, 컴퓨터 공학은 공과대학부의 일부야.
남: 아, 정말? 그렇다면, 여기 너의 멘토 이름이 있다.
여: 좋아! 도와줘서 고마워.

문제해설 | **여자의 전공인 컴퓨터 공학은 공과대학부이고, 학생증 번호는 21로 시작하므로, 여자의 멘토는 Austin이다.**

5 **정답 ③**

여: 오, 이 활동 일정표 좀 봐. 뭔가를 골라보자.
남: 그래. 난 하이킹이 좋다고 들었어. Grand 산은 이맘때쯤 아름다워.
여: 좋긴 한데, 난 주말에는 일찍 일어나고 싶지 않아.
남: 알았어. 그다음 활동에 맞춰서는 일어날 수 있겠니?
여: 응, 하지만 난 축구는 좋아하지 않아.
남: 알겠어. 이 미술 전시회는 뭐지?
여: 지역 예술가들이 자기들의 작품을 파는 마을로 우리를 데려가는 거야.
남: 재미있겠다. 그게 스노클링보다 확실히 더 나을 거야.
여: 왜? 넌 물속에 들어가는 게 무섭니?
남: 응, 무서워. 그리고 난 낚시에는 관심이 없어.
여: 나도 그래. 그럼 이걸로 신청하자.
남: 좋아.

문제해설 | 여자는 일찍 일어나는 것과 축구를 싫어하고, 남자는 물속에 들어가는 것을 무서워하며 낚시에 관심이 없다고 했으므로, 두 사람이 신청할 활동은 ③번이다.

6 **정답 ⑤**

여: 와, 이 식당 정말 괜찮아 보인다!
남: 정말 그래. 그리고 음식이 훌륭하다고 들었어.
여: 빨리 먹어 보고 싶어!
남: 메뉴를 한번 보자. 햄버거를 먹는 게 어때?
여: 아니, 나는 햄버거를 별로 좋아하지 않아. 그렇지만 다른 메인 요리들도 다 괜찮아 보인다.
남: 맞아, 그러면 곁들임 요리와 음료를 먼저 정하자.
여: 글쎄, 나는 음료는 필요 없어. 물이면 좋아.
남: 좋아, 그렇지만 우리는 곁들임 음식을 먹어야 해. 분명 맛있을 거야.
여: 좋은 생각이야. 두 가지 선택 사항이 있네. 못 고르겠어!
남: 그럼 그냥 더 저렴한 거로 하는 건 어때?
여: 글쎄, 더 비싼 게 더 맛있을 거야.
남: 좋아. 그걸로 주문해!

문제해설 | 두 사람은 햄버거를 제외한 메인 요리와 음료 없이 곁들일 음식이 추가된 더 비싼 메뉴를 원하므로, 두 사람이 선택할 메뉴는 ⑤번이다.

7 **정답 ③**

여: 이봐, Steve. 뭘 읽고 있어?
남: 아, 그냥 이 모집 광고를 보고 있어. 이번 학기에 아르바이트를 구하고 싶거든.
여: 네가 하고 싶은 것을 찾았니?
남: 음, 애완견 돌보는 사람이나 웨이터가 되는 건 상관없지만, 도서관 사서가 되는 것은 아주 지루할 것 같아.
여: 응, 그건 정말 지루할 것 같아. 너는 이번 학기에 수업이 언제 있어?
남: 수업은 매일 있지만, 항상 오후 3시에 끝나.
여: 그래. 너는 도시 외곽에서 일하고 싶진 않을 거야, 그렇지?
남: 응, 너무 멀어.
여: 그럼 선택 사항이 두 개 있네.
남: 여기가 시간당 돈을 더 주네. 지금 당장 전화해야겠다.

문제해설 | 남자는 애완견 돌보기나 웨이터 일은 괜찮다고 했고, 오후 3시 이후에 시내에서 일하고 싶다고 했다. 또한 시간당 돈을 더 많이 주는 일을 원하므로, 남자가 선택할 일자리는 ③번이다.

8 **정답 ③**

[전화벨이 울린다.]
남: 안녕하세요. Newtown 부동산 중개소입니다. 어떻게 도와 드릴까요?
여: 안녕하세요. 저는 Newtown 지역에서 집을 좀 빌리고 싶어요.
남: 네. 현재 임대가 가능한 지역이 몇 군데 있어요.
여: 잘됐네요. 저는 6명의 대학생이 머물 만한 공간을 찾고 있어요.
남: 알겠습니다. 각각 자신만의 방이 필요하신가요?
여: 아니요, 방 3개면 충분할 것 같아요.
남: 네. 그리고 예산은 어느 정도인가요?
여: 700달러 이상은 쓰고 싶지 않아요.
남: 알겠습니다. 도심의 동쪽이나 서쪽 중 선호하는 쪽이 있나요?
여: 서쪽에 있는 집이 더 나을 것 같네요.
남: 지하철역에 가까이 있어야 하나요?
여: 우리 모두 버스를 타고 통학해서 그건 상관없어요. 하지만 가격은 많이 신경 쓰는데, 저렴할수록 더 좋아요.
남: 그럼 고객님께 안성맞춤인 곳이 있는 것 같네요.

문제해설 | 방이 3개에 도심의 서쪽에 있는 집을 원하고, 지하철역에서 가까울 필요는 없지만, 가격은 700달러 이하이면서 저렴할수록 좋다고 했으므로, 여자가 선택할 집은 ③번이다.

DICTATION ANSWER pp. 62-65

1. sign up for / an afternoon class / since I work
2. can't afford to / would much rather / remove tough stains
3. playing these days / have several options / stay out too late
4. who your mentor is / major in philosophy / the name of your mentor
5. this time of year / in time for / being in the water
6. the food is excellent / get a side dish / might be tastier
7. be pretty boring / too far away / give them a call
8. available to rent / your budget / take the bus to school

10강 내용 일치

기출예제 p. 66

여: 안녕하세요, 저는 Global in Action의 Janet Danish입니다. 아시다시피, 점점 더 많은 사람들이 이제는 뭔가 의미 있는 일을 하고 싶어 합니다. 그러나 그들 중 많은 수가 무엇을 해야 할지 모르고 있습니다. 그래서 저는 Global in Action을 소개하고 싶습니다. Global in Action은 개발도상국 사람들을 돕는 것을 목표로 하는 비영리 기관입니다. 그것은 2000년에 전직 테니스 선수인 Sarah Hatch에 의해 설립되었습니다. Global in Action은 전국적으로 1,000명이 넘는 회원을 보유하고 있습니다. 매년 저희는 자원봉사를 위해 회원들을 라오스나 캄보디아 같은 여러 나라로 보냅니다. 저희는 집을 짓고, 우물을 파고, 아이들을 가르치고, 그리고 지역 사회를 개선하기 위한 기타의 다양한 활동을 하는 것에 도움을 줍니다. 방학을 어떻게 보낼지 확신이 서지 않는다면, 저희와 함께하는 것을 고려해 보십시오. 여러분의 삶에서 가장 값진 경험 중의 하나를 얻게 되리라 확신합니다. 시간이 없다면, 재정적 기부도 언제나 환영합니다. 더 많은 정보가 필요하시면, 1-800-555-2134로 저희에게 전화해 주시기 바랍니다. 감사합니다.

LISTEN & APPLY pp. 67-68

1 ④ 2 ④ 3 ② 4 ⑤ 5 ②
6 ④ 7 ④ 8 ③

1 정답 ④

남: 모든 청취자 여러분, 안녕하세요. 알려 드릴 특별 소식이 하나 있습니다. 아시다시피, 다음 달은 가족 감사의 달로, 저희는 이를 기념하기 위해 백일장을 열기로 했습니다. 여러분의 가족과 그들이 여러분에게 어떤 의미인지에 관한 글을 써주시면, 장원을 선발하여 5월 5일에 그분의 이야기를 방송을 통해 읽어드릴 예정입니다. 우승자는 또한 Fresh Garden 뷔페 상품권을 받게 됩니다. 여러분의 글을 familycontest@wkcp.org로 이메일로 보내주세요. 제출 기한은 4월 15일이며, 늦게 제출한 것은 고려 대상에서 제외될 것입니다. 또한, 인당 하나의 글만이 허용됩니다. 백일장에 대해 질문이 있으시면, 555-9786으로 전화 주시기 바랍니다.

문제해설 | ④ 우승작 방송일이 5월 5일이고, 제출 기한은 4월 15일까지라고 했다.

2 정답 ④

여: 안녕하십니까, 세종 고등학교의 학생 미술 전시회에 오신 걸 환영합니다. 오늘 밤에 전시되는 모든 미술품은 저희 학교 학생들이 만들었습니다. 학교 전시장을 자유롭게 다니시면서 그것을 감상하십시오. 모든 작품은 또한 판매 중이며, 가격은 각각의 작품 뒤에 표시되어 있습니다. 오늘 밤 저희가 모은 수익금은 지역 보육원에 있는 아이들을 위한 미술용품들을 구입하는 데 사용될 것입니다. 또한, 제 왼쪽에는, 여러분이 즐길 수 있도록 다양한 무료 간식과 다과가 마련되어 있습니다. 전시회는 오후 8시 30분까지 진행될 것입니다. 즐거운 시간 보내시고, 질문이 있으시면 저에게 알려주십시오.

문제해설 | ④ 기금은 작품을 판매함으로써 마련된다고 했고, 간식과 다과는 무료로 제공된다고 했다.

3 정답 ②

여: Sea Poison tree(바다독나무)는 인도양과 서태평양의 열대 해안에서 자라는 커다란 나무이다. 그것의 잎은 아름다운 구릿빛이고, 잎맥은 분홍색이다. 그것들은 오래되면 노르스름한 색으로 변한다. 나무의 꽃은 낮에는 오므라지지만, 밤에는 피어서 꿀을 먹는 박쥐와 큰 나방들을 유인한다. 나무의 열매는 등 모양이며, 물에 뜬다. 실제로, 그것은 바다에 떠다니면서 2년까지 살 수 있다. 나무의 모든 부분은 사포닌이라고 불리는 독을 함유하고 있다. 그럼에도 불구하고, 잎은 전통적으로 복통과 관절 및 근육 통증을 치료하기 위해 필리핀에서 사용되어 왔다.

문제해설 | ② 처음에 잎은 구릿빛이다가, 오래되면 노르스름한 색으로 변한다고 했다.

4 정답 ⑤

남: Sunnyvale 고등학교 학생 여러분 안녕하세요. 만화책을 읽거나 만화 영화 보는 것을 즐기나요? 그림을 그리고 재미있는 이야기를 만드는 것을 좋아하나요? 그렇다면 여러분께 새로운 Sunnyvale 만화 동아리에 가입하길 권하고 싶습니다. 우린 매주 목요일 오후에 학교 미술실에서 만날 겁니다. Williams 선생님께서 동아리를 지도하실 겁니다. 선생님은 다른 여러 가지 미술 기법에 대해 매주 발표하실 겁니다. 동아리에서 모든 사람을 환영합니다. 설사 당신이 만화 그리는 데에 전혀 경험이 없더라도 말이죠. 우리는 매달 만화 파티도 열 것입니다. 매월 마지막 주 금요일, 우리 동아리는 학교 강당에서 우리가 가장 좋아하는 만화 영화를 볼 것입니다. 오늘 Sunnyvale 만화 동아리에 가입하세요. 더 많은 정보를 원하시면 이번 주 목요일까지 미술실을 방문해 주세요.

문제해설 | ⑤ 추가 정보를 원하면 미술실을 방문해 달라고 했다.

5 정답 ②

남: 시청할 새로운 토크 쇼를 찾고 싶으신가요? 그러면 코미디언 Edgar Washington이 진행하는 새로운 TV 프로그램인 〈The Edgar Washington Show〉를 한번 보세요. Edgar가 가수 John Green과 이야기하는 첫 회를 시청하세요. John은 성공한 가수가 되기 위한 그의 개인적인 분투에 대해 이야기를

들려줄 겁니다. 그러고 나서 Edgar는 John에게 배우 Laura Samson과의 결혼 생활과 자녀들에 대해 질문합니다. 여러분은 유명한 아버지가 되는 것에 대해 John이 한 말을 결코 추측하지 못할 겁니다. 이후에, Edgar와 John은 스튜디오 방청객들과 게임을 합니다. 운이 좋은 한 방청객은 곧 있을 John의 콘서트에 갈 수 있는 백스테이지 티켓을 획득할 수 있었습니다! 게다가, John은 TV에서 최초로 신곡을 부릅니다. 〈The Edgar Washington Show〉는 바로 여기 채널 50에서 매일 오후 4시에 시청하실 수 있습니다.

문제해설 | ② 첫 회에는 가수 John Green이 출연한다고 했다. 진행자가 John의 아내이자 배우인 Laura Samson에 대해 질문한다고 했으나, 그녀가 출연한다는 언급은 없다.

6 정답 ④

여: 여러분 안녕하세요. 제 이름은 Samantha Walters이고 오늘 여러분께 박물관을 안내해 드릴 겁니다. Springfield 과학 박물관은 Albert Schwartz 교수님께서 설립하셨습니다. 그의 목표는 과학 교육을 대중이 더 이해하기 쉽게 만드는 것이었습니다. 그것이 저희 세 개의 주요 전시회 각각에 쌍방향적 요소가 있는 이유입니다. 오늘의 투어는 45분간 계속될 것이오니, 모든 방문객께서는 이러한 독특한 전시품들을 마음껏 둘러보시기 바랍니다. 카메라 촬영은 허용되지만 음식이나 음료는 박물관 전시회장 내부에서 허용되지 않음을 유념해 주세요. 투어 중에 편하게 질문해 주세요. 그리고 모든 방문객께서는 박물관 전면에 있는 기념품 가게를 거쳐 밖으로 나오시길 부탁드립니다.

문제해설 | ④ 카메라 촬영은 허용된다고 했다.

7 정답 ④

남: 전 직원을 위한 특별 공지 사항입니다. Best Beverage의 새로운 건강 음료를 시음하는 행사가 이번 주 금요일에 열립니다. 이 음료는 소화 불량으로 고생하는 사무직원들에게 도움을 주기 위한 것입니다. 오후 3시에, Best Beverage의 영업사원들이 회의실에 와서 그들의 새로운 음료 무료 샘플을 나눠줄 예정입니다. 참가자들은 음료를 시음한 후, 짧은 설문지 작성을 요청받을 겁니다. 그리고 모든 참가자들은 Best Beverage의 음료를 공짜로 마실 수 있는 쿠폰을 받게 됩니다. 행사에 참여하고 싶으시면, 금요일 전에 회사 웹사이트에서 신청해 주시기 바랍니다.

문제해설 | ④ 참가자들은 공짜 음료 쿠폰을 받게 된다고 했다.

8 정답 ③

여: 안녕하십니까. Open Campus Day에 오신 모든 고등학생 여러분을 환영합니다. 이 환영사가 끝나면, 여러분은 각자 개인 가이드로 재학생 한 명씩을 배정받게 될 것입니다. 그들은 여러분을 데리고 다니면서 저희 대학의 모든 특징들을 여러분께 보여드릴 것입니다. 두 시간 후에, 우리는 여기에 다시 모여서 점심을 먹을 것이고, 그때 여러분은 하고 싶은 어떤 질문이든지 하실 수 있을 것입니다. 점심 후, 저희 학교의 많은 교수님들이 다양한 학과와 전공에 대해 여러분과 그룹별로 이야기를 나눌 수 있을 것입니다. 마지막으로, 하루를 마감하면서, 저희 대학의 합창 동아리가 작별 인사로 여러분을 위해 공연할 것입니다. 여러분 모두 즐거운 하루가 되시길 바랍니다.

문제해설 | ③ 학생들은 점심시간에 질문을 할 수 있다고 했다.

DICTATION ANSWER pp. 69-71

1. hold an essay contest / on the air / only one submission
2. by students / on sale / art supplies / free snacks
3. When they become old / float on water / treat stomachaches
4. make up / giving a weekly presentation / Sign up for
5. Tune in to / a successful singer / a brand new song
6. accessible to the public / free to explore / are not permitted
7. suffer from indigestion / give out free samples / receive a coupon
8. assigned a current student / in groups / as a farewell

11강 언급 내용

기출예제 p. 72

여: Daniel, 잠깐 시간 있어요?

남: 네, 무슨 일이죠?

여: 제가 내일 있을 발표 준비를 하고 있는데요. 제 슬라이드에 대한 당신의 의견을 듣고 싶어서요.

남: 무엇에 대한 발표죠?

여: 신제품을 위한 마케팅 전략에 관한 거예요.

남: 알겠어요, 슬라이드를 볼게요. 음… 좋아 보이네요! 디자인이 마음에 들어요. 단순하지만 시선을 끌어요.

여: 고마워요! 글자 크기를 키워야 할까요?

남: 아뇨, 글자 크기는 이대로가 좋아 보여요.

여: 슬라이드에 음향 효과를 추가하는 것에 대해서는 어떻게 생각하세요?

남: 음, 필요 없을 것 같은데요. 그건 핵심 내용에서 사람들의 주의를 흩트릴 수 있어요.

여: 그렇군요. 정보를 보다 효과적으로 전달하기 위해 도표를 포함하는 게 좋을까요?

남: 네, 하지만 도표가 너무 많으면 도움이 안 될 거예요.
여: 음… 맞는 말인 것 같네요.

LISTEN & APPLY pp. 73-74

1 ③ 2 ⑤ 3 ⑤ 4 ① 5 ⑤
6 ③ 7 ④ 8 ②

1 정답 ③

남: 실례합니다만, 이 박물관에 대해서 몇 가지 여쭤볼게요.
여: 그러세요. 무엇을 알고 싶으세요?
남: 박물관 운영 시간을 말씀해 주실 수 있나요?
여: 물론이죠. 저희는 화요일에서 목요일은 오전 10시부터 오후 6시까지, 금요일에서 일요일은 오전 10시부터 오후 9시까지 엽니다.
남: 알겠습니다. 입장료는 얼마인가요?
여: 하루권이 15달러입니다.
남: 비싼 것 같네요!
여: 아마도요, 하지만 이 박물관은 대략 35,000점의 예술품을 소장하고 있습니다. 저희는 훌륭한 소장품으로 유명합니다.
남: 정말요? 많은 사람들이 이 박물관을 방문하나요?
여: 네. 사실 매년 3백만 명이 넘는 관람객들이 방문하시죠.
남: 오, 그렇다면 꼭 둘러보고 싶네요.
여: 탁월한 생각이에요. 즐거운 방문 되시기 바랍니다.

문제해설 | 박물관 운영 시간은 화요일부터 목요일은 오전 10시부터 오후 6시, 금요일부터 일요일은 오전 10시부터 오후 9시까지이고, 입장료는 하루권이 15달러이며, 소장품 수는 약 35,000점이라고 했다. 또한, 방문객 수는 매년 3백만 명이 넘는다고 했지만, 박물관의 설립 시기에 대해서는 언급하지 않았다.

2 정답 ⑤

남: 보스턴에서 Fenway Park를 보게 되다니 너무 신나!
여: 네가 좋아할 거라고 생각해.
남: 사실, 난 항상 이곳을 보고 싶었어. 그렇게 유명한 야구장이잖아.
여: 이곳은 다른 스포츠를 위해서도 사용되었어.
남: 정말? 그건 몰랐네.
여: 진짜야. Fenway Park는 여러 번의 축구 경기, 미식축구 경기, 그리고 아이스하키 경기도 개최했었어!
남: 와, 그건 상상이 안 된다.
여: 그건 그렇고, 이곳의 가장 유명한 점이 뭔지 알아?
남: 큰 좌측 외야 벽 말이야?
여: 응. 그건 '그린 몬스터'라고 해. 녹색이고, 보통 벽보다 훨씬 더 높아서 그런 별명을 얻게 됐어.
남: 그렇구나. 이 경기장은 언제 지어진 거야?
여: 이건 1912년에 지어졌고, 37,000명 이상의 관중을 수용할 수 있어.
남: 와. 넌 이 경기장에 대해 모르는 게 없구나!
여: 물론이지. 난 보스턴 레드삭스의 열혈 팬이거든!

문제해설 | Fenway Park는 야구 외에도 축구, 미식축구, 아이스하키 경기장으로도 이용되었고, '그린 몬스터'라고 불리는 특이한 외야 벽을 가지고 있다고 했다. 건축 연도는 1912년이고, 수용 인원은 37,000명 이상이라고 했지만, 한 해 관중 수에 대해서는 언급하지 않았다.

3 정답 ⑤

여: 당신이 이 건물에서 쭉 근무해 오신 공사 인부들 중 한 분인가요?
남: 네. 그것은 힘든 프로젝트였습니다.
여: 얼마 동안 이 건물을 위해 일하셨나요?
남: 전 1년 전에 이 팀에 합류했는데, 프로젝트는 2년이 걸렸어요.
여: 분명 비용이 꽤 많이 드는 프로젝트겠군요.
남: 네. 이 건물을 복원하는 데 거의 천만 달러가 들었어요.
여: 비용이 많이 들었네요. 훼손이 많이 있었나요?
남: 네. 이 건물은 화재로 인해 거의 파괴되었죠.
여: 애석한 일이었겠군요.
남: 네, 그렇습니다. 이 건물은 원래 거의 500년 전에 지어졌습니다. 다시 개장하게 되면 수천 명의 관광객들이 올 것입니다.
여: 그러길 바랍니다. 시간을 내주셔서 감사합니다.
남: 별말씀을요.

문제해설 | 건물 복원 기간은 2년, 복원에 든 비용은 대략 천만 달러이고, 훼손되었던 이유는 화재였으며, 최초 준공 시기는 거의 500년 전이라고 했다. 한 해 관광 수입에 대해서는 언급하지 않았다.

4 정답 ①

여: 이봐, Ted! 네가 곧 프랑스에서 공부하게 될 거라고 들었어.
남: 응. 다음 달에 파리로 떠나서 2년간 머무를 거야.
여: 축하해! 그래, 거기서 무슨 공부를 할 거야?
남: 주로 프랑스어. 하지만 제빵 수업도 들을 수 있을 것 같아.
여: 잘됐다. 넌 항상 프랑스식 제빵 기술을 배우고 싶어 했잖아.
남: 맞아. 그리고 방과 후에 집에서 배운 것을 연습할 수 있어.
여: 집에서? 너 기숙사 방 안에 오븐을 둘 거야?
남: 아니, 사실 기숙사 방에서 살지 않을 거야. 나는 호스트 가족과 함께 살 거야. 그들은 내가 부엌을 사용해도 된다고 했어.
여: 아, 잘됐네! 좋으신 분들이구나.
남: 그들을 찾게 돼서 정말 행운이야.
여: 모든 일이 잘 풀릴 것 같네. 거기서 좋은 시간을 보내길 바랄게.
남: 고마워. 네가 아주 많이 그리울 거야.

문제해설 | 남자가 체류할 국가는 프랑스이고, 유학 기간은 2년이며, 프랑스어와 제빵 기술을 배우면서 호스트 가족과 함께 살 예정이라고 했다. 유학 비용에 대해서는 언급하지 않았다.

5 정답 ⑤

남: Amazing 운전 학원에 오신 걸 환영합니다! 저희의 수업에 대

해 더 알고 싶으신가요?
여: 네. 수업은 언제 있나요?
남: 월요일을 제외하고 오전 6시부터 오후 8시까지 매일 수업이 있습니다. 매주 월요일은 휴무예요.
여: 아, 그렇군요. 수강료는 얼마인가요?
남: 저희 수강료는 10시간 수업에 30만 원입니다.
여: 알겠습니다. 주행 코스는 어디에 있나요?
남: 저희 사무실 근처에 특별한 주행 코스가 있습니다.
여: 제가 실제 도로에서 연습할 기회가 있나요?
남: 네, 저희는 시내 도로에서 강습을 몇 번 제공합니다.
여: 좋네요. 등록하고 싶어요.
남: 반가운 소리네요. 분명히 등록한 보람 있으실 거예요.
여: 감사합니다. 저도 그러면 좋겠어요.

문제해설 | 수업 시간은 오전 6시부터 오후 8시, 휴무일은 매주 월요일, 수강료는 10시간 수업에 30만 원이고, 주행 코스는 학원 사무실 근처에 있다고 했다. 환불 정책에 대해서는 언급하지 않았다.

6 정답 ③

남: 이봐, Rachel. 오늘 수업에서 널 못 봤는데. 괜찮아?
여: 안녕, Evan! 응, 오늘 아침에 좀 아팠어. 하지만 지금은 괜찮아. Kim 선생님께서 기말 과제에 대해 뭔가를 말씀하셨니?
남: 응. 그건 세 명이 한 조로 하는 조별 과제가 될 거야. 넌 Sam이랑 나와 같은 조야.
여: 알았어. 주제가 뭐야?
남: 발명품에 관해 조사해야 해. 우린 시계를 선택했어. 그런 다음 그것에 대한 보고서를 써야 해.
여: 재미있게 들리는걸.
남: 응, 하지만 2주 후에 끝내야 해.
여: 2주라고? 지금 당장 시작하는 게 좋겠어. 정보를 어디에서 찾을 수 있지?
남: 음, 우린 온라인으로 찾아볼 수도 있지만, 책도 살펴봐야 해.
여: 좋은 생각이다. 오늘 밤에 찾아보기 시작할게.

문제해설 | 참여 인원은 세 명, 과제 주제는 시계, 제출 기한은 2주, 참고 자료는 온라인과 책이라고 했다. 과제 분량에 대해서는 언급하지 않았다.

7 정답 ④

여: 당신 Mike의 생일이 2주 뒤라는 걸 알고 있죠?
남: 아, 네! 당신은 파티를 계획하는 걸 시작했나요?
여: 음, 그 애가 누구를 초대하고 싶은지 이제 막 결정했어요. 그래서, 이제 우린 계획 세우는 걸 시작할 수 있어요.
남: 그렇군요. 내가 집안을 장식할게요. 어떤 장식품이 필요하죠?
여: Mike는 풍선을 좋아해요. 우리는 풍선이 많이 필요할 거예요.
남: 알았어요. 내가 풍선을 사 올게요. 케이크는 주문했나요?
여: 아직이요, 하지만 곧 할 거예요. 간식을 좀 만드는 것도 계획하고 있어요.
남: 좋은 생각이네요. 당신은 쿠키를 좀 만들 수 있고, 난 사탕을 좀 준비할게요.
여: 고마워요. 그럼 우린 초대장만 보내면 돼요.
남: 네. 초대장을 가져왔어요?
여: 네. 당신이 그걸 작성하면, 내가 봉투를 봉할게요.
남: 알았어요.

문제해설 | 남자가 집안 장식과 초대장 작성을, 여자가 케이크 주문과 간식 준비를 하기로 했다. 생일 선물 구입에 대해서는 언급하지 않았다.

8 정답 ②

남: Valerie, 네 머리 모양 멋지다. 영화배우 같아 보여.
여: 고마워, Abe. Da Vinci 미용실에서 잘랐어.
남: 들어본 적이 없는데. 새로 생겼어?
여: 아니, 그렇지 않아. 내가 어렸을 때부터 가던 같은 미용실이야.
남: 정말? 왜 같은 곳을 계속 다니니?
여: 분위기가 평화롭고 마음을 편안하게 해 줘.
남: 좋은 것 같네. 가격은 어때?
여: 가격도 적당해. 게다가 미용사의 실력이 뛰어나.
남: 네게 딱 맞는 미용실 같네.
여: 근데 한 가지 문제가 있어. 미용실이 두 마을 떨어져 있는 Land 백화점에 있어.
남: 아, 여기서 꽤 머네. 네가 머리를 자주 자르면 정말 힘들겠다.
여: 다행히, 석 달에 한 번씩만 가.
남: 그럼 그렇게 나쁘진 않을 것 같네.

문제해설 | 미용실의 분위기는 평화롭고 안락하고, 적당한 가격에, 미용사의 실력이 뛰어나고, 위치는 Land 백화점이라고 했다. 영업 시간에 대해서는 언급하지 않았다.

DICTATION ANSWER pp. 75-77

1. cost to get in / are famous for / to take a look around
2. several soccer matches / big left field wall / it can hold
3. working on the building / to restore the building / was originally built
4. take a baking class / in your dorm room / everything will work out
5. except on Mondays / do offer some lessons / worth your while
6. What is the topic / due in two weeks / start looking tonight
7. decided who he wants / ordered a cake / send the invitations
8. peaceful and relaxing / perfect salon for you / once every three months

12강 긴 대화 응답

기출예제 p. 78

남: 이봐요, Susan. 새로 맡은 직책은 어때요?
여: 매우 바빠요. 저는 직원 연수 프로그램을 준비하고 있어요.
남: 이해해요. 그건 작년에 제가 했던 일이거든요.
여: 당신도 그 당시에 준비할 일이 그렇게 많았나요?
남: 물론, 그랬죠.
여: 당신이 어떻게 그 모든 일을 혼자서 처리했는지 궁금할 뿐이네요.
남: 네, 힘들었어요. 하지만 가장 어려웠던 부분은 자격을 갖춘 강사를 섭외하는 일이었어요. 그런 분을 찾았나요?
여: 노력은 하고 있는데, 아직 못 찾았어요. 음, 저희가 작년과 같은 분을 고용하는 것이 괜찮을 거라고 생각하나요?
남: 왜 안 되겠어요? 그분은 일을 아주 잘 해냈어요.
여: 그런 말을 듣게 되어 다행이네요. 아직 그 강사의 연락처를 가지고 있나요?
남: 네. 그분의 전화번호와 이메일 주소를 가지고 있어요.
여: 그럼 그것들을 제게 문자메시지로 보내줄 수 있나요?

LISTEN & APPLY pp. 79-80

1 ④ 2 ① 3 ③ 4 ③ 5 ⑤
6 ⑤ 7 ③ 8 ④

1 정답 ④

남: 오, 안 돼! 왜 이렇게 길이 막히는 거지?
여: 모르겠어. 보통은 이렇지 않은데.
남: 내 스마트폰으로 교통 정보를 확인해 줄래? 그건 실시간으로 업데이트 돼.
여: 알았어. 근데 그걸 어떻게 해?
남: 두 번째 페이지에 아이콘이 있어. 그냥 그걸 터치해서 정보를 갱신해줘.
여: 알겠어. [*잠시 후*] 아, 5번가까지 계속 교통량이 많아.
남: 정말? 덜 막히는 길이 있니?
여: 아니. 지도에 있는 모든 길이 꽉 막혀 있어.
남: 우리가 5번가에 도착할 때까지 교통 체증에 꼼짝없이 앉아 있어야 한다는 거야? 너무 피곤한데.
여: 그럼 자리를 바꾸자. 네가 쉴 동안 내가 운전할게.

문제해설 | 남자가 계속된 교통 체증 상황에서 운전해 피곤하다고 말했으므로, 이에 대한 여자의 응답으로 ④번이 가장 적절하다.
① 아, 나에게 도심 지역 지도가 있어.
② 우리는 버스를 탔어야 했어.
③ 골치 아픈 일은 잊고 대신 한숨 자.
⑤ 걱정하지 마. 오늘 이 도로는 교통이 원활해.

2 정답 ①

여: Kevin, 무슨 일이 있었니? 어쩌다 그렇게 심하게 긁힌 거야?
남: 아, 아무것도 아니에요, 엄마. Lisa의 고양이랑 놀다가 그런 것뿐이에요.
여: 어머나, 세상에. 왜 그 고양이가 널 할퀸 거니?
남: 모르겠어요. 그냥 고양이랑 놀고 있었는데 갑자기 저를 할퀴었어요.
여: Lisa의 고양이가 평소에 사람들을 할퀴니?
남: 아뇨. 평소에는 귀엽고 온순해요.
여: 네가 뭔가 잘못을 한 모양이구나.
남: 음, 제가 고양이를 좀 괴롭힌 것 같아요.
여: '괴롭혔다'는 게 무슨 말이니?
남: 음, 고양이를 두 발로 서서 춤을 추게 하려고 했거든요.
여: 세상에! 고양이를 그런 식으로 괴롭히면 절대 안 되지.
남: 음, 전 이번 일로 교훈을 얻었어요.

문제해설 | 고양이를 괴롭히다가 상처를 입은 아들을 엄마가 꾸짖는 상황이므로, 이에 대한 남자의 응답으로 ①번이 가장 적절하다.
② 그게 제가 고양이보다 개를 더 좋아하는 이유예요.
③ 전 제 고양이들과 노는 게 정말 좋아요.
④ 고양이가 왜 그랬는지 모르겠어요.
⑤ Lisa의 집에 언제든지 가셔도 돼요.

3 정답 ③

남: 와, 난 포스터를 만드는 게 이렇게 힘든 일인 줄 몰랐어.
여: 그러게. 자발적으로 도와줘서 고마워.
남: 괜찮아. 널 도울 수 있어서 기뻐.
여: 좋아. 이 모금 행사에서 우리 학교를 위해 많은 돈을 모을 거야.
남: 응. 난 벌써 네 개나 끝냈어.
여: 네 개라고? 그게 다야? 하지만 넌 두 시간 동안이나 작업했잖아.
남: 응, 근데 난 그것들을 근사하게 만들고 싶어. 이것 좀 봐.
여: 아주 멋지네. 하지만 이 포스터들을 붙이려면 우리는 정오까지 그것들이 필요해.
남: 한 시간밖에 안 남았네. 몇 개가 필요한데?
여: 여덟 개. 넌 한 시간 안에 네 개를 더 만들어야 할 거야.
남: 서두르고 싶지 않은데. 근사해 보이지 않을 거야.
여: 그렇지만 이 경우에는, 질보다 양이 더 우선이야.

문제해설 | 근사한 포스터를 만들고 싶어 하는 남자의 마음과는 달리 여자에게는 제한된 시간 안에 더 많은 포스터가 필요한 상황이므로, 남자의 마지막 말에 대한 여자의 응답으로 ③번이 가장 적절하다.
① 난 자원봉사를 좀 하고 싶어.
② 너한테 기금 모금 행사에 대해 말하는 걸 깜박했어.
④ 걱정하지 마. 네가 끝낼 시간은 충분해.
⑤ 좀 쉬고 나서 오늘 저녁에 나머지를 만들자.

4 정답 ③

여: 집에 초대해 줘서 고마워. 오늘 내가 구운 케이크를 가져왔어.

남: 와, 맛있어 보인다. 고마워.
여: 네 새집 구경 좀 해도 되니?
남: 물론이지. 날 따라와. 구경시켜줄게.
여: 정말 흥미로운 조각품이네! 이건 뭐니?
남: 아, 내가 스페인에서 가져온 거야. 이 조각품이 주인에게 행운을 가져다준대.
여: 와. 여기에 정말 다양한 장식품들이 있구나.
남: 난 집안에 흥미로운 것들을 모아놓는 걸 좋아하거든.
여: 음, 우리 집이랑 정말 다르다.
남: 응. 너희 집은 항상 아주 깔끔하고 단정하잖아.
여: 응, 난 집안에다 물건을 많이 두는 걸 좋아하지 않아서 말이야.
남: 누구나 각자의 취향이 있잖아.

문제해설 | 여자가 남자의 새집에 초대를 받아 간 상황에서, 두 사람은 집에 대한 취향이 서로 어떻게 다른지 말하고 있으므로, 여자의 마지막 말에 대한 남자의 응답으로 ③번이 가장 적절하다.
① 스페인 여행은 어땠니?
② 나도 너처럼 이사 가고 싶어.
④ 집 청소를 하는 게 어때?
⑤ 너도 알다시피, 우린 둘 다 화려한 장식을 좋아하잖아.

5 정답 ⑤

남: 내일 정말 출근하기 싫어.
여: 왜 싫은데? 난 네가 새 일을 즐기고 있다고 생각했는데.
남: 맞아. 일은 맘에 드는데, 우린 월요일마다 부서 회의를 하거든.
여: 뭐 때문에 회의하는 게 그렇게 싫은데?
남: 내 동료 중 한 명 때문이야. 그 사람은 그냥 거기에 앉아서 모든 사람을 비판하기만 해.
여: 아, 모든 회의에는 그런 사람이 있더라. 그냥 그를 무시해.
남: 나도 처음에는 그렇게 하려고 했었어. 하지만 지난주에는 더 이상 참을 수가 없었어.
여: 저런. 무슨 일이 있었니?
남: 아, 내가 그 사람한테 소리를 질렀는데, 그랬더니 그 사람도 나한테 소리를 질렀어. 상황이 정말 안 좋았어.
여: 있잖아, 상대방이 나쁜 짓을 했다고 해서 너도 똑같이 해서는 안 돼.

문제해설 | 남자가 남을 비판하기만 하는 동료와 심하게 싸운 일에 대해 여자에게 말하고 있는 상황이므로, 이에 대한 여자의 응답으로 ⑤번이 가장 적절하다.
① 난 네가 그를 무시해선 안 된다고 생각해.
② 회의 시간에 늦지 않는 게 중요해.
③ 넌 다른 사람들을 비난하는 걸 그만둬야 해.
④ 난 네가 왜 나한테 소리를 질렀는지 이해가 안 돼.

6 정답 ⑤

남: 오늘 밤에 나랑 공포 영화 볼래?
여: 아, 난 공포 영화는 싫어. 공포 영화를 보고 나면 악몽을 꾸거든. 그밖에 또 뭐가 상영 중인데?
남: 어디 보자. 그 극장에는 세 편의 다른 영화가 상영 중이야.
여: 그 새로 나온 프랑스 로맨틱 코미디 영화는 상영 중이니?
남: 아니 아직. 그건 내일 개봉할 거야. 대신 일본 영화는 어때?
여: 난 보통 일본 영화는 안 좋아해. 아, 난 이거 보고 싶어!
남: 〈Terry의 이야기〉? 그건 밤 10시 15분이 돼야 시작하는데.
여: 아, 그건 너무 늦네.
남: 음… 남은 건 다큐멘터리뿐이야.
여: 너도 알다시피, 다큐멘터리는 너무 지루하잖아.
남: 아무래도 우리 영화는 다음에 보러 가야겠다.

문제해설 | 두 사람은 함께 볼 영화를 고르지 못한 상황이므로, 여자의 마지막 말에 대한 남자의 응답으로 ⑤번이 가장 적절하다.
① 난 그 멜로 영화를 재미있게 봤어.
② 그건 내 생애 최고의 영화야.
③ 난 영화를 보고 싶지 않다고 너한테 말했어.
④ 그건 다큐멘터리가 아니라 사극이야.

7 정답 ③

남: 안녕, Heather.
여: 안녕, Clark. 무슨 일 있어? 너 정말 기운이 없어 보여.
남: 맞아. 방금 역사 선생님께 보고서를 제출했거든.
여: 그거 어제까지 아니었니?
남: 응. 그래서 내가 걱정하는 거야. 너도 알다시피, 역사 선생님은 점수를 짜게 주시는 거로 악명이 높잖아.
여: 그렇지만 내가 알기로 넌 그 보고서에 온갖 노력을 다 기울였잖아. 분명히 선생님께서 그 보고서에 만족하실 거야.
남: 설령 그 보고서가 완벽할지라도, 늦었기 때문에 난 B보다 더 높은 점수는 받지 못할 거야.
여: 음, 넌 항상 수업 시간에 잘했잖니. 네 최종 성적은 틀림없이 좋을 거야.
남: 모르겠어. 난 이 수업에서 꼭 A를 받아야 하는데, 남은 건 기말고사뿐이야.
여: 기말고사를 위해 각별히 더 열심히 공부하면 돼.

문제해설 | 보고서를 늦게 내서 좋은 성적을 받지 못할까 봐 걱정하고 있는 남자가 이제 남은 건 기말고사뿐이라고 말하는 상황이므로, 이에 대한 여자의 응답으로 ③번이 가장 적절하다.
① 내 걱정은 하지 말아줘.
② 넌 보고서 준비를 하는 게 좋겠어.
④ 난 제시간에 그걸 끝내기 위해 서둘렀어야 했는데.
⑤ 선생님께 시간을 좀 더 달라고 부탁하는 게 어때?

8 정답 ④

[*휴대전화가 울린다.*]
남: 여보세요. Mike입니다.
여: 안녕, Mike. 나 Wendy야.
남: 안녕, Wendy. 내 아파트는 이상 없니?
여: 음, 네가 부탁한 대로 화분에 물을 주고 고양이하고 놀아주고 있는 중이야.

남: 좋아. 우편물을 가져오는 걸 잊지 않았지, 그렇지?
여: 그럼, 그건 전부 부엌 조리대 위에 있어. 그런데…
남: 이런. 무슨 일 있었어?
여: 음, 네 고양이랑 시간을 보내고 있다가, TV를 켜려고 했거든.
남: 아, 알았다.
여: 그런데 갑자기 TV가 번쩍하더니 꺼져버렸어! 내가 뭘 한 건지 모르겠어. 미안해.
남: 아냐, 아냐. 한동안 그 TV에 문제가 있었어.
여: 아, 정말? 난 내가 그걸 고장 낸 줄 알았어!
남: 내가 떠나기 전에 그것에 대해 너한테 말했어야 했는데.

문제해설 | 여자는 자신이 남자의 TV를 고장 냈다고 생각했는데, 남자가 원래 TV에 문제가 있었다고 여자를 안심시키고 있는 상황이므로, 여자의 마지막 말에 대한 남자의 응답으로 ④번이 가장 적절하다.
① 걱정하지 마. 지금은 잘 작동하고 있어.
② 넌 내 고양이를 좀 더 조심히 보살펴야 해.
③ 내가 너한테 내 물건 중에 어떤 것에도 손대지 말라고 하지 않았니?
⑤ 내가 돌아가면 너에게 새 걸로 하나 사준다고 약속할게.

DICTATION ANSWER pp. 81-83

1. the road so jammed / refresh the information / are blocked
2. awful scratch / sweet and gentle / tease a cat
3. Thanks for volunteering / put them up / don't want to hurry
4. interesting sculpture / lots of interesting decorations / neat and simple
5. a department meeting / criticizes everyone / yelled at him
6. have nightmares / be released / pretty boring
7. handed in my report / a strict grader / final exam left
8. watering your plants / flashed and went off / had broken it

13강 상황에 적절한 말

기출예제 p. 84

남: Peter와 Sandra는 반 친구이다. 그들은 문학 수업을 위해 책을 읽으며 주말을 도서관에서 보내고 있다. Sandra는 집중할 수가 없고 지쳐 있다. 하지만, 그녀는 Peter가 집중해 있고 활력이 넘쳐 보이는 것을 알아챘다. 사실, Peter에게는 집중력을 유지하는 비결이 있다. 집중력을 잃을 때마다, 그는 소지품을 챙겨 다른 장소로 이동한다. 그에게, 새로운 장소는 새로운 시작처럼 느껴진다. 다른 책상, 의자, 그리고 시야는 그가 생기를 되찾고 한두 시간 더 지속할 수 있게 준비되도록 도와준다. Sandra가 Peter에게 어떻게 집중력을 잃지 않을 수 있는지 물을 때, 그는 그녀에게 학습 공간을 바꿔 보라고 조언하고자 한다. 이런 상황에서, Peter가 Sandra에게 할 말로 가장 적절한 것은 무엇인가?
Peter: Sandra, 난 네가 공부하는 장소를 바꾸는 걸 권하고 싶어.

LISTEN & APPLY pp. 85-86

1 ③ 2 ① 3 ⑤ 4 ③ 5 ⑤
6 ② 7 ③ 8 ⑤

1 정답 ③

남: Trevor와 Jacob은 함께 산다. 돈을 절약하기 위해, 그들은 많은 것들을 같이 쓴다. 예를 들어, 그들은 둘 다 Trevor의 TV와 커피 메이커를 사용한다. 그들은 또한 Jacob의 컴퓨터를 같이 쓴다. 그런데, 그 컴퓨터는 Trevor에게 생소한 모델이기 때문에, 그는 프린터를 어떻게 사용하는지 모른다. 처음에 그가 뭔가를 인쇄해야 했을 때, Jacob이 그를 대신해서 해 주었다. 다음 번에, Trevor가 그것을 어떻게 사용하는지 물어봤지만, Jacob은 그냥 자신이 대신해 주는 게 더 쉬울 거라고 말했다. 요즘, Trevor는 인쇄할 것들이 많아서, 자신의 부탁으로 Jacob을 귀찮게 할까 봐 걱정이다. 이런 상황에서, Trevor가 Jacob에게 할 말로 가장 적절한 것은 무엇인가?
Trevor: 프린터 사용하는 법을 나에게 알려줄래?

문제해설 | 프린터를 사용할 때마다 Jacob에게 부탁하는 것이 그를 귀찮게 할까 봐 걱정하는 상황이므로, Trevor가 Jacob에게 할 말로 ③번이 가장 적절하다.
① 제발 날 귀찮게 하지 마.
② 네 프린터를 고장 내서 미안해.
④ 우리가 모든 것을 같이 써도 괜찮겠니?
⑤ 넌 네 컴퓨터를 사는 게 낫겠다.

2 정답 ①

여: Lucy는 시내의 한 아파트에서 산다. 어느 날 아침, 그녀는 고양이 한 마리가 크게 우는 소리에 잠을 깼다. 처음에 그녀는 그것을 무시하려고 했지만, 결국에는 일어나서 무슨 일이 일어나고 있는지 보려고 창밖을 내다보았다. 그녀는 다리를 다친 것 같은 작은 새끼 고양이 한 마리를 보았다. 그녀는 그것이 그녀의 이웃인 Jerry의 고양이일지도 모른다고 생각했고, 전날 아파트 로비에서 잃어버린 고양이를 찾는다는 전단지를 본 것을 기억했다. 그녀는 아래층으로 내려가서 그 새끼 고양이를 데려왔다. 그런 다음 그녀는 고양이를 Jerry의 아파트로 데리고 갔다. 이런 상황에서, Lucy가 Jerry에게 할 말로 가장 적절한 것은 무엇인가?
Lucy: 이게 당신의 잃어버린 고양이죠, 그렇지 않나요?

문제해설 | 다리를 다쳐 울고 있는 새끼 고양이를 이웃인 Jerry가 잃어버린 고양이라고 생각하여 그에게 데리고 간 상황이므로, Lucy가 Jerry에게 할 말로 ①번이 가장 적절하다.
② 제 새끼 고양이가 다리를 다친 것 같아요.
③ 제 새끼 고양이를 보면 저에게 전화해 주세요.
④ 아침에는 좀 더 조용히 해 주세요.
⑤ 며칠 동안 제 새끼 고양이 좀 돌봐주실 수 있나요?

3 정답 ⑤

남: Ben은 아침 식사로 커피와 베이글을 먹는 것을 좋아한다. 어느 날, 그는 출근길에 그가 가장 좋아하는 커피숍에 들른다. 그는 점원과 인사하다가, 그녀가 새로 온 직원이라는 것을 알아차린다. 그는 평소처럼 라떼 한 잔과 플레인 크림치즈 베이글 하나를 주문한다. 그가 계산하려고 할 때, 그녀는 금액이 12달러라고 말한다. 그는 그 가게의 단골이기 때문에, 금액이 10달러가 되어야 한다는 것을 알고 있다. 그는 그녀에게 가격이 올랐는지를 묻지만, 그녀는 아니라고 말한다. 이런 상황에서, Ben이 직원에게 할 말로 가장 적절한 것은 무엇인가?
Ben: 실수로 금액이 더 나온 것 같아요.

문제해설 | 새로 온 직원의 실수로 주문한 메뉴의 금액이 평소보다 더 많이 나온 것을 알아챈 Ben이 직원에게 할 말로 ⑤번이 가장 적절하다.
① 저는 여기 10% 할인 쿠폰을 가지고 있어요.
② 이건 제가 주문한 게 아니에요.
③ 베이글 좀 데워 주실래요?
④ 여기는 제가 예상했던 것보다 가격이 훨씬 더 저렴하군요.

4 정답 ③

여: 어느 날, Vincent는 백화점에서 새 바지를 쇼핑하고 있다. 그는 입어보고 싶은 청바지 한 벌을 발견한다. 그러나, 누군가가 이미 탈의실에 있어서, 그는 기다려야 한다. 그 남자가 떠난 뒤, Vincent는 안으로 들어간다. 그런데 청바지를 입어보려는 동안 그는 바닥에 휴대전화가 떨어져 있는 것을 알아챈다. 그는 옷을 다 입고 난 뒤, 그 휴대전화를 집어서 그 남자를 찾으러 나간다. 몇 분 뒤, 그는 계산대에 줄을 서서 기다리고 있는 남자를 본다. 이런 상황에서, Vincent가 그 남자에게 할 말로 가장 적절한 것은 무엇인가?
Vincent: 탈의실에 뭔가를 두고 가신 것 같은데요.

문제해설 | 휴대전화를 탈의실에 두고 나간 남자를 발견한 Vincent가 그에게 할 말로 ③번이 가장 적절하다.
① 더 큰 사이즈로 비슷한 청바지가 있나요?
② 죄송하지만, 당신이 실수로 제 휴대전화를 가져가신 것 같아요.
④ 실례합니다만, 제 휴대전화를 못 보셨나요?
⑤ 탈의실을 다 썼으니, 이제 사용하셔도 됩니다.

5 정답 ⑤

남: Gail은 도시의 한 아파트에서 산다. 그녀는 체중이 늘고 있어서, 몸매를 관리하기로 했다. 그녀는 매일 아침 공원에서 조깅을 하기 시작했다. 하지만, 지난주에 날씨가 매우 추워졌다. 그래서 Gail은 TV 앞에서 제자리 달리기를 하기로 결심했다. 어느 날 오후, Gail은 아래층 이웃이 그녀의 집 문에 부디 이른 아침에 너무 시끄럽게 하지 말아 달라고 붙여 놓은 쪽지를 하나 발견했다. Gail은 그에게 가서 얘기하기로 결심했다. 이런 상황에서, Gail이 그녀의 이웃에게 할 말로 가장 적절한 것은 무엇인가?
Gail: 죄송해요, 제 운동이 당신에게 폐를 끼치는 줄 몰랐어요.

문제해설 | 집안에서 운동하는 Gail에게 아래층 이웃이 조용히 해 달라는 쪽지를 남긴 상황이므로, Gail이 이웃에게 할 말로 ⑤번이 가장 적절하다.
① 전 이런 날씨에는 집에 있는 게 더 좋아요.
② 괜찮아요. 전 아침에 일찍 일어나요.
③ 이 근처에 가격이 적당한 헬스장이 있어요.
④ 음, 전 다른 사람이랑 같이 하느니 차라리 혼자 조깅할래요.

6 정답 ②

여: Brandy는 중국어 수업을 듣고 있다. 그녀는 항상 숙제를 제때 제출하는 모범생이다. 하지만 그녀의 선생님은 그녀가 수업 시간에 말하기를 꺼린다는 것을 알아챘다. 그녀는 무언가 잘못 말할 때마다, 부끄러워하는 것 같다. 이 때문에, 그녀는 선생님의 질문에 그녀가 (말하기) 편한 단어들을 사용해서, 간단한 대답만 할 뿐이다. 그녀의 선생님은 Brandy가 그녀의 태도를 바꾸지 않는 한 그녀의 말하기 실력이 향상되지 않을 것을 걱정해서, 그는 그녀에게 방과 후에 남을 것을 요청한다. 이런 상황에서, Brandy의 선생님이 그녀에게 할 말로 가장 적절한 것은 무엇인가?
선생님: 실수하는 걸 두려워해서는 안 된단다.

문제해설 | 선생님은 Brandy가 수업 시간에 말하는 데 대한 실수를 두려워하여 질문에 대답하기를 꺼린다는 것을 알고 걱정하고 있는 상황이므로, 선생님이 Brandy에게 할 말로 ②번이 가장 적절하다.
① 난 네가 이룬 실력 향상이 정말 자랑스럽단다.
③ 외국어를 좀 배워 보는 게 어떠니?
④ 내가 수업하는 동안에 친구들에게 말 걸지 마라.
⑤ 모든 숙제를 제때 끝마치는 것이 중요하단다.

7 정답 ③

남: 대학을 졸업한 후에, Amy는 직장을 구하는 데 어려움을 겪었다. 어느 날, 그녀의 친구가 더 큰 도시에서 일자리를 구해보려고 고향을 떠났다. 나중에, 그녀는 Amy에게 전화를 걸어 마침내 대기업에서 보수가 좋은 일자리를 구했다고 말했다. Amy는 그녀의 친구를 부러워하며, 자신의 고향에서보다 취업 기회가 더 많기 때문에 도시로 이사를 갈까 생각하고 있다. Amy는 이것에 대해 그녀의 아버지와 상의하기로 결심했다. 그날 저녁, 아버지가 돌아오시자, Amy는 아버지에게 얘기를 좀 할 수 있는지 여쭈었다. 이런 상황에서, Amy가 그녀의 아버지에게 할 말로 가장 적절한 것은 무엇인가?

Amy: 전 직장을 구하기 위해 도시로 이사를 갈까 생각 중이에요.

문제해설 I Amy는 취업 기회가 더 많은 도시로 이사를 가고 싶어 하는 상황이므로, Amy가 아버지에게 할 말로 ③번이 가장 적절하다.
① 왜 제가 직장을 구하는 걸 도와주지 않으셨어요?
② 전 지금 당장 아버지를 찾아뵐 여유가 없어요.
④ 전 가족들이 그리워서 여기에 머물고 싶지 않아요.
⑤ 제 전공이 보수가 좋은 직업을 구하는 데 도움이 될 거예요.

8 정답 ⑤

여: Andrew는 같은 회사에서 3년째 일하고 있다. 그가 처음 그 회사에 일하기 시작했을 때, 그는 끝마쳐야 하는 일의 양에 벅찼다. 그는 항상 여러 개의 프로젝트를 동시에 작업했다. 그러나 몇 달 후 Andrew는 그의 새로운 직무에 적응하였고 회사의 지원을 아끼지 않는 업무 환경에 감사하기 시작했다. 최근에 Melissa라는 신입사원이 그 회사에 일하기 시작했다. 어느 날 Melissa는 울기 시작했고 Andrew에게 자신이 회사의 부담스러운 작업량을 잘 감당할 수 있을지 모르겠다고 말했다. Andrew는 그녀를 진정시키고 용기를 주고 싶어 했다. 이런 상황에서 Andrew는 Melissa에게 할 말로 가장 적절한 것은 무엇인가?
Andrew: 포기하지 말아요. 당신은 곧 여기서 일하는 것에 익숙해질 거예요.

문제해설 I Andrew는 자신이 입사 초반에 겪었던 어려움을 이겨내고 새 환경에 적응한 것처럼 Melissa도 시간이 지나면 잘 해낼 수 있을 것이라고 용기를 주고 싶어 하는 상황이므로, Andrew가 Melissa에게 할 말로 ⑤번이 가장 적절하다.
① 당신은 새로운 일자리를 찾아봐야겠어요.
② 당신이 제 충고를 생각해 봤으면 해요.
③ 그 일은 마치기가 그렇게 어렵지 않아요.
④ 당신은 모든 프로젝트를 완료하지 않아도 돼요.

DICTATION ANSWER pp. 87-89

1. share many things / how to use / with his requests
2. a cat crying loudly / hurt its leg / brought it
3. a new employee / regular customer / have been increased
4. wants to try on / lying on the floor / waiting in line
5. get in shape / jog in place / so much noise
6. avoids speaking / seems ashamed / not improve
7. finding a job / moving to the city / decided to talk
8. was overwhelmed with / adjusted to / calm her down

14강 세트 문항

기출예제

p. 90

남: 깔끔한 사람이 되고자 합니까? 정돈하는 것은 정말로 어렵습니다, 그렇지 않나요? 정돈을 하는 간단한 방법은 여러분 주변에 있는 불필요한 것들을 없애는 것입니다. 예를 들어, 종이로 뒤덮인 책상을 마주하고 있다면, 필요 없는 것들을 버리십시오. 여러분의 자녀가 더 이상 사용하지 않는 오래된 장난감들을 갖고 있다면, 그것들을 자선 단체에 기부하는 것이 좋은 생각입니다. 망가진 램프를 6개월 넘게 갖고 있었나요? 그것이 수리되었나요? 그렇지 않다면, 그냥 버리세요. 여러분의 거실에 있는 그 꽃병도 마찬가지입니다. 수개월 동안 꽃을 꽂아놓은 적이 없다면, 그것을 (다른 사람에게) 주십시오. 여러분이 모든 것을 다 버려야 한다고 말하는 것은 아닙니다. 어떤 물건들은 오래된 추억 때문에 간직하고 싶을 것입니다. 하지만 그런 물건들을 신중하게 선택해야 합니다. 그러니, 주변을 둘러보고 여러분에게 필요하지 않은 물건이 있는지 확인해 보는 것이 어떨까요? 이런 불필요한 것들을 없앰으로써, 여러분의 물건을 정돈된 상태로 유지할 수 있습니다.

LISTEN & APPLY pp. 91-93

1 ④	2 ③	3 ②	4 ①	5 ③
6 ④	7 ①	8 ⑤	9 ③	10 ④

1 정답 ④ 2 정답 ③

여: 안녕하세요, 여러분. 제 이름은 Emily이고, One Green Earth라는 환경 단체에서 왔습니다. 우리는 깨끗하고 건강한 환경이 우리 지역 사회에 중요하다고 믿으므로, 여러분이 세상을 바꿀 수 있는 몇 가지 방법에 관해 잠시 이야기하고자 합니다. 첫 번째로, 여러분이 필요한 만큼만 사용함으로써 물을 절약할 것을 기억해주세요. 또한, 여러분은 외출할 때 항상 불을 끄고 사용하지 않는 가전제품의 플러그를 뽑아둠으로써 전기를 절약할 수 있습니다. 여러분이 다른 사람들과 함께 무언가를 하길 원한다면, One Green Earth와 같은 환경 단체에 가입하는 것이 좋은 선택이 될 수 있습니다. 우리와 같은 단체들은 대개 자원봉사자들이 거리의 쓰레기를 줍거나 숲에 나무를 심을 수 있는 행사를 엽니다. 또한 환경 단체들은 종종 (환경에 대한) 인식 제고를 위한 캠페인을 도와줄 자원봉사자를 모집합니다. 이것들은 모두 더 환경친화적인 지역 사회를 지원하는 데 도움이 되는 좋은 방법들입니다! 들어주셔서 감사합니다.

문제해설 I 1. 여자는 환경 보호에 일조하는 다양한 방법으로 물과 전기를 절약하는 것과 환경 단체에 가입하는 것에 대해 말하고 있다.
① 자원봉사의 이점

② 전기세를 줄이는 요령들
③ 지역 사회에 동참하는 방법
④ 환경에 도움이 되는 다양한 방법들
⑤ 지역 환경 단체의 역할들
2. 여자는 ③ 포스터 만들기에 대해서는 언급하지 않았다.
① 물 절약하기 ② 전기 절약하기
④ 쓰레기 줍기 ⑤ 캠페인에 참여하기

3 정답 ② 4 정답 ①

남: 안녕하세요, 학생 여러분. 오늘 저는 몸의 가장 중요한 기관 중 하나인 심장에 대해서 여러분에게 이야기할 예정입니다. 여러분은 몸의 자세가 심장 박동수에 사소하지만 영향을 끼친다는 걸 알고 있었나요? 앉은 자세에서 일어나는 자세를 취하면, 여러분의 맥박은 실제로 약간 높아집니다. 그러나, 그것은 보통 얼마 후에 정상으로 돌아옵니다. 날씨가 아주 따뜻하면, 여러분의 심장은 평상시보다 좀 더 많은 혈액을 내보내서, 기온이 높아질 때 여러분의 맥박도 올라가게 되지만, 분당 5에서 10정도일 뿐입니다. 심장 박동수는 여러분의 감정에 의해서 상당한 영향을 받기 때문에, 만약 여러분이 스트레스를 받거나 초조하면 심장 박동수가 올라갈 겁니다. 그것은 특정 약물에 의해 영향을 받을 수도 있습니다. 예를 들어, 아드레날린을 억제하는 약물은 또한 여러분의 맥박을 느리게 할 겁니다.

문제해설 | 3. 남자는 몸의 자세, 기온, 감정, 약물 등 심장 박동수에 영향을 미치는 요인들에 관해 이야기하고 있다.
① 심장의 주요 기능들
② 심장 박동수에 영향을 미치는 요인들
③ 건강한 심장을 유지하는 방법
④ 심장 박동수를 느리게 하는 방법들
⑤ 심장 질환 검진의 중요성
4. 심장 박동수에 영향을 미치는 요인으로 ① 운동은 언급되지 않았다.
② 몸의 자세 ③ 기온 ④ 감정 ⑤ 약물

5 정답 ③ 6 정답 ④

남: 건강 센터 월례 회의에 오신 여러분을 환영합니다. 우리는 아플 때 보통 의사를 찾아가고 약국에서 약을 받습니다. 이런 약물은 분명히 효과가 있는 반면, 종종 원치 않는 부작용을 갖고 있습니다. 그래서 저는 여러분이 흔한 질병을 다루기 위해 몇 가지 민간요법을 선택하는 것을 고려했으면 좋겠습니다. 예를 들어, 계피는 당뇨병 환자의 혈당 수치를 낮추는 데 도움이 되는 것으로 밝혀졌습니다. 그리고 정향유는 아픈 이를 진정시키는 데 오랫동안 사용되어 왔습니다. 많은 사람들이 딱총나무 열매 시럽이 두통을 완화하는 데 아스피린만큼 효과적이라는 것을 알고 있습니다. 그리고 말린 생강이나 신선한 생강은 메스꺼움을 치유할 수 있는 아주 훌륭한 방법입니다. 이러한 민간요법은 처방된 약보다 우리 몸에 훨씬 더 순합니다. 많은 것들이 몇 백 년 동안 안전하고 효과적으로 사용되어 왔습니다. 다음 번에 당신이 약을 먹으려고 생각할 때, 대신해볼 수 있는 자연적인 대안이 있는지 확인해 보십시오.

문제해설 | 5. 남자는 흔한 질병에 사용할 수 있는 몇 가지 민간요법을 소개하고 있다.
① 전통 의학의 역사
② 면역체계를 강화하는 방법
③ 질병에 대한 민간요법 사용
④ 처방된 약의 위험성
⑤ 의사를 고를 때 고려해야 할 것
6. 민간요법에 사용되는 것으로 ④ 꿀은 언급되지 않았다.
① 계피 ② 정향유 ③ 딱총나무 열매 ⑤ 생강

7 정답 ① 8 정답 ⑤

여: 여러분이 어디를 가든 독특한 전통을 발견하게 되는데, 가장 흥미로운 것들 중 몇몇은 음식과 관련이 있습니다. 많은 나라들이 사람들이 먹을 수 있는 것에 대한 놀라운 법과 사회적 제약을 가지고 있습니다. 예를 들어, 파푸아뉴기니의 한 부족에서는 나이 든 여자가 임신하면 생선 알을 먹을 수 없습니다. 인도에서는, 인구의 대다수가 힌두교 신자이기 때문에 소고기를 먹는 것이 일반적으로 터부시됩니다. 힌두교에서 소는 신성한 동물이므로, 죽여서는 안 됩니다. 자메이카에서, 사람들은 말을 배우기 전에 닭고기를 먹는 아이는 결코 말을 할 수 없다고 믿습니다. 나이지리아에서는, 코코넛 우유를 마시는 아이는 자라서 우둔해진다고 여겨집니다. 여러분은 이 전통 중 일부가 이상하다고 여길지 모르지만, 모든 문화에는 외부인들이 이상하거나 놀랍다고 생각하는 것이 있습니다.

문제해설 | 7. 여자는 여러 나라에서 터부시되는 음식에 관해 이야기하고 있다.
① 세계의 금기 식품
② 종교가 어떻게 사람들의 식단에 영향을 미치는가
③ 독특한 전통을 이해하는 방법
④ 여러 나라에서 가장 몸에 좋은 음식들
⑤ 세계에서 가장 흥미로운 몇 가지 요리
8. 금기 식품으로 ⑤ 돼지고기는 언급되지 않았다.
① 생선 알 ② 소고기 ③ 닭고기 ④ 코코넛 우유

9 정답 ③ 10 정답 ④

남: 안녕하세요. 오늘 밤에 대규모 단체가 올 거라서, 저는 모든 것이 잘 되어 있는지 확인하고자 합니다. 방문객들이 즐거운 경험을 하게 되면, 그들이 친구들에게 Luxury 캠핑장에서 얼마나 즐거웠는지 이야기할 거라는 것을 명심하세요. 그리고 만약 그들의 친구들이 오길 원한다면, 우리의 사업은 앞으로 더욱 늘어날 것입니다. 그러니 오늘 밤 방문객들이 가능한 한 최고의 경험을 갖도록 하기 위해, 여러분이 다음 사항들을 점검했으면 합니다. 4시에 손님들이 도착하기 전에 탁자와 의자를 꼭 배치해 놓으세요. 또한 장작을 많이 준비하고 캠프파이어 장소 옆에 깔끔하게 쌓아 두세요. 숯불 석쇠가 닦여져 있고 사용할 숯이 많은지 확인하세요. 마지막으로 가장 중요한 일은 손님들이 여기

오기 전에 텐트가 완벽하게 설치되어야 한다는 겁니다. 그러니 이 사항들을 각각 즉시 재확인해 주세요. 저는 우리의 손님들이 Luxury 캠핑장에 좋은 후기를 남겨주길 바랍니다.

문제해설 | 9. 남자는 직원들에게 캠핑 준비 사항을 점검하라고 말하고 있다.
① 새로운 캠핑장을 홍보하려고
② 고객들에게 피드백을 제공할 것을 요청하려고
③ 준비 사항을 확인하려고
④ 다양한 캠핑 활동을 소개하려고
⑤ 안전한 캠핑을 위해 유의사항을 알리려고
10. 남자는 점검할 사항으로 ④ 음식에 대해서는 언급하지 않았다.
① 탁자 ② 장작 ③ 숯불 석쇠 ⑤ 텐트

DICTATION ANSWER pp. 94-95

1-2. make a difference / turning off the lights / pick up trash
3-4. a minor effect / the temperature goes up / slow down your pulse
5-6. unwanted side effects / far gentler / thinking of taking medicine
7-8. social limitations / not allowed to eat / strange or surprising
9-10. everything is just right / the best possible experience / please double check

15강 MINI TEST pp. 98-99

1 ⑤	2 ④	3 ①	4 ⑤	5 ④
6 ④	7 ⑤	8 ①	9 ③	10 ④

1 정답 ⑤

W: I need to submit a resident registration form.
M: You have to do that at the community service center.
W: Yeah. It's across from the fitness club on Second Avenue, right?
M: (No, it moved next to City Hall last month.)

여: 난 주민등록등본을 제출해야 해.
남: 넌 주민 센터에 가서 해야 해.
여: 응. 2번가에 있는 헬스클럽 맞은 편에 있는 거 맞지?
남: 아니, 그건 지난달에 시청 옆으로 이전했어.

어휘 | submit 제출하다 resident registration form 주민등록등본 community service center 동사무소, 지역 주민 센터 |문제| register (…에) 등록하다 demanding 힘든, 부담이 큰

문제해설 | 여자가 주민 센터의 위치를 확인하고 있으므로, 이에 대한 남자의 응답으로 ⑤번이 가장 적절하다.
① 미안해. 우리 길을 잃은 것 같아.
② 사실, 난 아직 등록 못 했어.
③ 응, 난 벌써 그걸 신청했어.
④ 그런 종류의 일은 꽤 힘들어.

2 정답 ④

M: That looks great. Is it fun to paint pictures for little kids?
W: It's a lot of fun. It will look even better when it's finished.
M: Why did you paint a lake with two trees beside it?
W: I wanted to show animals playing there. The kids like seeing elephants swimming.
M: Is that why you painted a snake climbing a tree, too?
W: Yes, and isn't the sleeping monkey cute?
M: It is. It looks comfortable in the branches of the tree.
W: I think so, too. And did you see the frogs by the bottom of the banana tree on the right?
M: Oh, I see them. They're sitting together under the tree.
W: Yes. I'm glad you like it.

남: 그거 좋아 보이네요. 어린이들을 위해 그림을 그리는 게 재미있나요?
여: 매우 재미있어요. 완성되고 나면 훨씬 더 좋아 보일 거예요.
남: 왜 옆에 나무 두 그루가 있는 호수를 그리신 거예요?
여: 동물들이 거기에서 노는 것을 보여주고 싶었어요. 아이들은 코끼리들이 수영하는 모습을 보는 것을 좋아하거든요.
남: 나무에 기어올라가는 뱀을 그리신 이유도 그것인가요?
여: 네, 그리고 이 잠자고 있는 원숭이가 귀엽지 않나요?
남: 그렇네요. 나뭇가지 속에서 편안해 보여요.
여: 저도 그렇게 생각해요. 그리고 오른쪽 바나나 나무 아래에 있는 개구리들을 보셨나요?
남: 아, 보이네요. 개구리들이 나무 아래에 함께 앉아 있네요.
여: 네. 당신이 그걸 좋아하니 기쁘네요.

어휘 | climb 오르다, 올라가다 branch 나뭇가지

문제해설 | 원숭이는 자고 있는 것이 아니라 나무에 매달려 바나나를 들고 있다.

3 정답 ①

M: Is that your cat?
W: Yes. My family adopted her from an animal shelter.
M: That's great. Why does she keep rubbing against my leg?
W: She's marking you as someone she knows. Then she can recognize you later.

M: I don't understand.

W: Cats don't rely on their eyesight as much as we do. Smells are more important to them.

M: So she's becoming familiar with my smell?

W: No. She's actually leaving her own smell on you.

M: Oh, I see!

W: She's spent the past week rubbing up against everything in our house.

M: So she'll feel at home?

W: Yes. What's more, if she gets lost, she can search for her own scent.

M: Wow, then she can find her way back! That's pretty interesting.

W: Yes, cats are amazing animals.

남: 그거 네 고양이니?

여: 응. 우리 가족이 동물 보호소에서 입양했어.

남: 그거 멋지다. 그런데 고양이가 왜 내 다리에 몸을 계속 비비지?

여: 고양이가 너를 아는 사람으로 표시하는 거야. 그럼 나중에 고양이가 너를 알아볼 수 있어.

남: 이해가 안 되는데.

여: 고양이는 우리만큼 시력에 의존하지 않아. 그들에게는 후각이 더 중요하거든.

남: 그럼 고양이가 내 냄새에 익숙해진다는 거야?

여: 아니. 사실은 고양이가 자기 냄새를 너에게 남기는 거야.

남: 아, 이제 알겠다!

여: 고양이는 지난주 내내 우리 집에 있는 모든 물건에 몸을 비볐어.

남: 그래서 고양이가 편하다고 느끼는 거야?

여: 맞아. 게다가 길을 잃으면, 고양이는 자기 자신의 냄새를 찾을 수 있지.

남: 와, 그러면 고양이가 다시 돌아올 수 있구나! 그거 정말 흥미로운데.

여: 응, 고양이는 대단한 동물이야.

어휘 | adopt 입양하다 shelter 보호소 rub 문지르다 mark 표시하다 recognize 알아보다 rely on …에 의존하다 eyesight 시력 feel at home 마음이 편안하다 search for …을 찾다 scent 냄새

문제해설 | 두 사람은 고양이가 사람과 물건에 몸을 비비는 이유에 관해 이야기하고 있다.

4 정답 ⑤

W: Wow! The midterms are finally over.

M: Yes, finally. What do you feel like doing this weekend?

W: Hmm… I'd like to do something new and fun. What about you?

M: I think we should go to the movies or go skateboarding. Or we could go on a nice picnic.

W: Well, going on a picnic would be nice, but I want to do something more exciting. Look at this magazine advertisement.

M: Hip-hop dance classes? You want to learn hip-hop dancing?

W: Why not? Come on. Let's try it!

M: But I think it will be expensive.

W: These classes are free. They are held by volunteers, some of whom are famous dancers.

M: I don't know. I've never even watched a hip-hop performance.

W: Don't worry. I'll show you some video clips of performances on the Internet.

M: Hmm… Okay. I'll decide after watching them.

여: 와! 드디어 중간고사가 끝났어.

남: 응, 드디어. 넌 이번 주말에 뭘 하고 싶어?

여: 음… 난 새롭고 재미있는 것을 하고 싶어. 넌 어때?

남: 영화를 보러 가거나 스케이트보드를 타러 가는 게 좋겠어. 아니면 멋진 소풍을 갈 수도 있고.

여: 글쎄, 소풍을 가는 게 좋을 것 같지만, 난 더 신나는 걸 하고 싶어. 이 잡지 광고를 봐.

남: 힙합 춤 강좌? 너 힙합 춤을 배우고 싶어?

여: 왜 안 돼? 하자. 해 보자!

남: 하지만 그건 비쌀 것 같은데.

여: 이 강좌는 무료야. 자원봉사자들이 하는 건데, 그들 중 몇몇은 유명한 춤꾼들이야.

남: 모르겠어. 심지어 난 힙합 공연을 본 적도 없는걸.

여: 걱정하지 마. 인터넷에서 공연 비디오 동영상을 좀 보여줄게.

남: 음… 알았어. 그것들을 보고 나서 결정할게.

어휘 | midterms 중간고사 be over 끝나다 advertisement 광고 performance 공연 video clip 비디오 동영상

문제해설 | 여자는 남자를 위해 힙합 공연 비디오 동영상을 찾아서 보여 줄 것이다.

5 정답 ④

M: Excuse me. How much are your sandwiches?

W: It depends. Cheese sandwiches are $5 on white bread or $5.50 on whole-grain bread.

M: I see. I'll get one on white bread. And how much are the chicken sandwiches?

W: They're a dollar more.

M: So, $6 on white bread and $6.50 on whole-grain bread?

W: Right. So how many do you want?

M: Well, I'm buying them for my friends, but I don't know which kind of bread they like.

W: How about buying one of each?

M: Okay. I'll have one of the chicken sandwiches on white and one on whole-grain. Oh, and don't forget the cheese sandwich.

W: I won't. I'll have them ready in just a few minutes.

남: 실례합니다. 이 샌드위치들은 얼마인가요?
여: 각각 다릅니다. 치즈 샌드위치는 흰 빵으로 된 것이 5달러이고, 통밀빵으로 된 것이 5달러 50센트입니다.
남: 그렇군요. 흰 빵으로 하나 주세요. 그리고 치킨 샌드위치는 얼마죠?
여: 그것들은 1달러 더 비쌉니다.
남: 그럼, 흰 빵으로 된 건 6달러이고, 통밀빵으로 된 건 6달러 50센트인가요?
여: 맞습니다. 그럼 몇 개나 드릴까요?
남: 음, 제 친구들에게 사주려고 하는데, 그 애들이 어떤 종류의 빵을 좋아하는지 몰라서요.
여: 각각 하나씩 사는 건 어떠세요?
남: 좋아요. 흰 빵 치킨 샌드위치 하나랑 통밀빵 치킨 샌드위치 하나 주세요. 아, 그리고 치즈 샌드위치를 잊지 마세요.
여: 그럴게요. 그것들을 곧 준비해 드리겠습니다.

어휘 | whole-grain 통밀로 만든 in a few minutes 곧, 즉시

문제해설 | 남자는 흰 빵 치즈 샌드위치 하나($5)와 흰 빵 치킨 샌드위치 하나($6), 그리고 통밀빵 치킨 샌드위치 하나($6.50)를 주문했으므로, 남자가 지불할 금액은 17달러 50센트이다.

6 정답 ④

W: Hey, what on earth happened to your leg?
M: I rode my bicycle to the library yesterday. On my way home, a dog ran out into the road, and I tried to avoid it.
W: Oh, dear. Is there anything I can do for you?
M: Well, I want something good to eat. I'm tired of eating the meals served by the hospital cafeteria.
W: Oh, what do you want? Actually, I bought some fruit for you.
M: Well, I had enough fruit this morning. Now I'm in the mood for pizza.
W: Are there any pizza restaurants nearby?
M: Yes. One is very close. I have their phone number, but they don't offer a delivery service.
W: Do you want me to pick it up for you?
M: Yes. Can you do that for me?
W: No problem! Call them now.
M: Thank you. That's so nice of you!

여: 얘, 도대체 네 다리는 어쩌다 그랬니?
남: 어제 자전거를 타고 도서관에 갔었거든. 집에 오는 길에, 개 한 마리가 길로 뛰어들어서, 그걸 피하려다 그랬지.
여: 오, 저런. 내가 도와줄 일이라도 있니?
남: 음, 맛있는 게 먹고 싶어. 병원 식당에서 나오는 밥을 먹는 게 지겨워.
여: 아, 뭐가 먹고 싶은데? 실은, 널 위해 과일을 좀 사 왔어.
남: 음, 과일은 오늘 아침에 충분히 먹었어. 지금은 피자가 먹고 싶어.
여: 근처에 피자 가게가 있니?
남: 응. 한 곳이 아주 가까워. 내가 그 가게 전화번호를 갖고 있긴 한데, 거긴 배달을 안 해 줘.
여: 너를 위해 내가 가서 가져 올까?
남: 응. 날 위해 해 줄 수 있니?
여: 문제없어! 지금 당장 전화해.
남: 고마워. 넌 정말 친절하구나!

어휘 | on earth 도대체 avoid 피하다 be tired of …에 싫증이 나다 meal 식사 serve 제공하다 cafeteria 식당 in the mood for …할 기분이 나서 nearby 가까이에

문제해설 | 남자는 여자에게 피자를 가져다 달라고 부탁했다.

7 정답 ⑤

M: Who sings this song, Holly? It goes well with this rainy day.
W: It's by the band The Heavy Jackets.
M: Wow! I thought they sounded familiar. Is it a new song?
W: Yeah, it is the title track of their tenth album.
M: I used to love their music. I bought all of their albums before they broke up.
W: Do you know why they broke up? The bandmates were arguing, right?
M: Yes, but that is not why they split up. They wanted some time off to start families.
W: I see. I believe their new album will be popular.
M: I bet you're right. I wonder if they will go on tour.
W: I think they will, since they released a song.
M: If they do, I will go to their concert!
W: Count me in, too!

남: Holly, 이 노래 누가 부르는 거야? 이런 비 오는 날에 잘 어울리네.
여: The Heavy Jackets 밴드 노래야.
남: 와! 익숙하게 들린다고 생각했어. 신곡이야?
여: 응, 10번째 앨범의 타이틀 곡이야.
남: 난 그들의 음악을 정말 좋아했었어. 그들이 해체하기 전에 앨범을 모두 샀었어.
여: 너 그들이 왜 해체했는지 알아? 밴드 멤버들이 싸운 거지, 맞지?
남: 응, 하지만 그게 그들이 해체한 이유는 아니야. 그들은 가정을 꾸릴 시간을 좀 원했어.
여: 그렇구나. 그들의 새 앨범이 인기가 있을 거라고 생각해.
남: 틀림없이 네 말이 맞을 거야. 난 그들이 투어를 할지 궁금해.
여: 그럴 것 같아, 노래를 발표했으니까.
남: 만약 그러면, 난 그들의 콘서트에 갈 거야!

여: 나도 끼워 줘!

어휘 | go well with …와 잘 어울리다 break up …와 헤어지다, (관계를) 끝내다 argue 다투다 split up 분열되다, 헤어지다 time off 일시적 중단, 휴식 release 출시하다, 공개하다 count in …을 포함시키다[끼우다]

문제해설 | 두 사람은 밴드 이름이 The Heavy Jackets이고, 10개의 앨범을 발매했으며, 가정을 꾸리기 위해 잠시 해체했고, 신곡 발표와 관련한 공연 계획에 대해 언급했지만, 수상 경력에 대해서는 언급하지 않았다.

8 정답 ①

M: Good morning. I'd like to take a moment to announce a job opening in the editorial department. Our company will be hiring someone to work with the writing team as a proofreader and editor. This position does not require previous experience, but all applicants will be asked to take a proofreading test. You must have a deep understanding of grammar and good writing skills. The position will begin on March 1st, with an annual salary of $36,000. If you are interested, please send an email to the Human Resources department with your résumé and a cover letter attached.

남: 안녕하세요. 잠시 편집부의 공석에 대해 알려 드리고자 합니다. 저희 회사는 교정자와 편집자로서 집필팀과 함께 일할 분을 채용하고자 합니다. 이 직책은 경력을 요구하지는 않습니다만, 모든 지원자들은 교정 시험을 보게 될 것입니다. 여러분은 문법에 대한 풍부한 지식과 훌륭한 작문 실력을 갖추고 있어야 합니다. 이 직책은 3월 1일부터 (일이) 시작될 것이고, 연봉은 36,000달러입니다. 관심이 있으시다면, 여러분의 이력서와 자기소개서를 첨부하여 인사과로 이메일을 보내주시기 바랍니다.

어휘 | job opening (직장의) 빈 자리, 공석 editorial 편집의 hire 고용하다 proofreader 교정자 editor 편집자 previous 이전의 applicant 지원자 annual salary 연봉 human resources department (회사의) 인사부 résumé 이력서 cover letter 자기소개서 attach 붙이다, 첨부하다

문제해설 | ① 경력을 요구하지는 않는다고 했다.

9 정답 ③

M: I printed out the flight schedule to Madrid for you.
W: Oh, thank you. Let me take a look.
M: Unfortunately, there are no morning flights. The earliest one leaves at 1:30 p.m.
W: That's okay. I just don't want to arrive late at night or early in the morning.
M: What's the earliest you'd be willing to arrive?
W: Anything earlier than 9 a.m. would be a problem.
M: All right. And does it have to be a nonstop flight?
W: I'd prefer nonstop, but a single stop would be acceptable.
M: Okay. And Monday isn't possible because of the board meeting.
W: That's right. But any other day is fine.
M: All right. And you said that you couldn't get a business class seat?
W: Yes. As you know, we're tightening our travel budget. So book me a ticket on this flight.

남: 제가 당신을 위해서 마드리드행 비행기 일정표를 출력했어요.
여: 아, 고마워요. 한번 볼게요.
남: 유감스럽게도, 오전 비행기는 없어요. 가장 빠른 게 오후 1시 30분에 출발해요.
여: 괜찮아요. 전 밤늦게나 아침 일찍 도착하지만 않으면 돼요.
남: 당신이 도착하고 싶은 가장 이른 시간은 언제죠?
여: 오전 9시 이전이라면 문제가 될 거예요.
남: 알겠어요. 그리고 직항편이어야 하나요?
여: 직항편이 더 좋긴 하지만, 한 번 경유하는 거라면 괜찮아요.
남: 알겠어요. 그리고 월요일은 이사회 회의 때문에 불가능해요.
여: 맞아요. 하지만 다른 날은 괜찮아요.
남: 좋아요. 그리고 비즈니스석은 구할 수 없다고 하셨죠?
여: 네. 당신도 알다시피, 우리는 여행 경비를 긴축하고 있잖아요. 그러니 이 비행편으로 한 장 예약해 주세요.

어휘 | print out …을 출력하다 be willing to-v 기꺼이 …하다 nonstop flight 직항편 acceptable 받아들일 수 있는 board meeting 이사회 (회의) business class seat 비즈니스석 tighten 조이다; *더 엄격하게 하다 budget 예산 book 예약하다 |문제| depart 출발하다

문제해설 | 여자는 밤늦게나 오전 9시 이전 시간을 피해 도착하고, 비즈니스석이 아니며, 월요일을 제외하고, 직항편이나 한 번 경유하는 비행편을 원하므로, 여자가 비행할 요일은 수요일이다.

10 정답 ④

W: Why are you packing, Bill?
M: I'm going camping.
W: Going camping? Didn't you try the same thing last summer?
M: Yes, I did. Camping makes me feel closer to nature.
W: But if I remember correctly, you had a terrible time last year.
M: That's true. It rained the whole time, and my tent kept falling down.
W: Yes, and you came back home after only three days.
M: I know, I remember. All my clothes were wet, and I was covered in mosquito bites.
W: I felt so bad for you.

M: Well, this year I'm taking a better tent, and I checked the weather forecast.
W: Still, I can't believe you're going to try again.
M: (Don't worry. I won't make the same mistakes.)

여: 너 왜 짐을 싸고 있니, Bill?
남: 캠핑을 가거든.
여: 캠핑을 간다고? 지난 여름에도 가지 않았니?
남: 응, 그랬지. 캠핑은 내가 자연을 더 가깝게 느끼도록 해주거든.
여: 하지만 내 기억이 정확하다면, 넌 작년에 엄청 고생했었잖아.
남: 맞아. 내내 비가 왔었고, 내 텐트가 계속 무너졌지.
여: 그래, 그래서 넌 불과 사흘 만에 집에 돌아왔잖아.
남: 알아, 기억나. 내 옷은 전부 다 젖었고, 온몸이 모기한테 물린 상처투성이였지.
여: 너 정말 안됐었어.
남: 음, 올해에는 더 좋은 텐트를 가져갈 거고, 일기 예보도 확인했어.
여: 그래도, 난 네가 다시 가려고 한다는 게 믿어지지 않아.
남: 걱정하지 마. 난 똑같은 실수를 하지는 않을 거야.

어휘 | pack (짐을) 싸다, 꾸리다 correctly 정확하게 the whole time 내내 fall down 쓰러지다, 넘어지다 wet 젖은 mosquito 모기 bite *물린 상처; 물기 weather forecast 일기 예보

문제해설 | 작년에 캠핑을 갔다가 무척 고생했던 남자가 올해 또다시 캠핑을 간다고 하자 여자가 걱정하고 있는 상황이므로, 이에 대한 남자의 응답으로 ④번이 가장 적절하다.
① 그래서 난 혼자 가기로 한 거야.
② 네가 나와 함께할 수 있어서 너무 행복해.
③ 내가 떠나기 전에 그것을 확인했어야 했는데 말이야.
⑤ 내가 언제 집으로 돌아올지 정확히 모르겠어.

16강 MINI TEST pp. 100-101

1 ⑤	2 ②	3 ②	4 ⑤	5 ⑤
6 ③	7 ④	8 ④	9 ③	10 ①

1 정답 ⑤

M: Hey, Annie! I'm surprised to see you here.
W: Hi, Jordan. I take private dance lessons with Ms. Murphy.
M: But it is 11:00 a.m. Don't her classes start at three o'clock?
W: (Well, our class was moved to the morning just for today.)

남: 이봐, Annie! 널 여기서 보다니 뜻밖이야.
여: 안녕, Jordan. 나 Murphy 선생님께 댄스 과외를 받거든.
남: 그런데 (지금은) 오전 11시잖아. 그 선생님 수업은 3시에 시작하는 거 아니야?
여: 음, 수업이 오늘만 아침으로 변경되었어.

어휘 | private 개인적인 |문제| not ... anymore 더 이상 … 아닌 prefer 선호하다

문제해설 | Murphy 선생님의 수업이 3시에 있지 않냐고 묻는 남자의 질문에 대한 여자의 응답으로 ⑤번이 가장 적절하다.
① 유감스럽게도, 난 늦었어.
② 아니, 난 더 이상 댄스 수업은 듣지 않아.
③ 응, 그분은 3년 동안 나의 선생님이셨어.
④ 실은, 난 오후 수업을 듣는 것을 선호해.

2 정답 ②

M: Here's a helpful tip for everyone looking forward to the upcoming holiday season. Shopping for the perfect gift for your friends and family can be a great way to show that you care. But you won't be helping anyone if you spend more on gifts than you can really afford. Ads on television show people happily buying cars, jewelry, and expensive watches to give as Christmas gifts, but they don't show them struggling to pay their credit card bills for the rest of the year. Just because you have a card doesn't mean you should spend more money than you have. Shop wisely and you can find affordable gifts your loved ones will adore.

남: 여기 다가오는 연휴를 고대하고 계신 모든 분들에게 도움이 되는 정보가 하나 있습니다. 여러분의 친구들과 가족들을 위한 완벽한 선물을 사는 것은 여러분들이 관심을 가지고 있다는 것을 표현하는 아주 좋은 방법이 될 수 있습니다. 하지만 여러분이 실제로 살 여유가 있는 것보다 더 많은 돈을 선물에 소비한다면 어느 누구에게도 도움이 되지 않을 겁니다. TV 광고에서는 사람들이 행복한 모습으로 크리스마스 선물로 줄 자동차, 보석 그리고 비싼 시계들을 사는 것을 보여주지만, 그 해의 나머지 기간 동안 그들이 신용카드 대금을 갚기 위해 애쓰는 모습은 보여주지 않습니다. 단지 카드를 소유하고 있다는 것이 당신이 가진 돈보다 더 많은 돈을 소비해야 한다는 것을 의미하지는 않습니다. 현명하게 쇼핑한다면 당신이 사랑하는 사람들이 좋아할 적당한 가격의 선물을 발견할 수 있습니다.

어휘 | look forward to …을 고대하다 upcoming 다가오는 shop 물건을 사다 care 관심을 가지다 afford (…을) 살 여유가 되다 jewelry 보석 struggle to-v …하려고 애쓰다[분투하다] wisely 현명하게 affordable (가격이) 적당한 adore 흠모하다; *아주 좋아하다

문제해설 | 남자는 연휴를 맞이해서 자신의 재정적 여유를 고려하지 않은 채 지나치게 비싼 선물을 사는 것에 대해 주의해야 한다고 당부하고 있다.

3 정답 ②

W: Thank you for coming to my office on a Sunday.
M: No problem. So, you don't have any patients today?
W: Yes. I didn't schedule any appointments.
M: That's good. So, where would you like me to start?
W: In this room. It's usually full of sick people waiting to see me.
M: I see. Hmm, the color of the walls isn't very good. The new color you chose is much better.
W: I think so, too.
M: All right, I'll get started right away.
W: How long do you think it will take?
M: Well, I should be finished in a couple of hours. But you'll have to wait overnight for the paint to dry.
W: Okay. But will it be ready in the morning?
M: Yes, you can open your office again tomorrow.

여: 일요일에 제 사무실에 와주셔서 고마워요.
남: 괜찮아요. 그런데, 오늘은 환자가 없나요?
여: 네. 어떤 예약도 잡지 않았거든요.
남: 잘됐네요. 그럼, 어디서부터 시작할까요?
여: 이 방부터요. 이곳은 주로 제게 진찰을 받기 위해 기다리는 환자들로 가득 차죠.
남: 그렇군요. 음, 벽 색깔이 별로 좋지 않네요. 당신이 선택한 새로운 색이 훨씬 더 좋아요.
여: 저도 그렇게 생각해요.
남: 좋아요, 지금 바로 시작할게요.
여: 얼마나 걸릴 것 같아요?
남: 글쎄요, 몇 시간 후에 끝날 거예요. 하지만 페인트가 마르려면 밤새 기다려야 할 거예요.
여: 좋아요. 그래도 아침이면 다 되는 거죠?
남: 네, 당신은 내일 다시 진료를 시작할 수 있어요.

어휘 | patient 환자 schedule 일정을 잡다 appointment 약속, 예약 a couple of 두서너 개의, 몇 개의 overnight 밤새

문제해설 | patients, appointments, sick people waiting to see me 등으로 보아 여자는 의사이고, color of the walls, paint 등으로 보아 남자는 페인트공임을 알 수 있다.

4 정답 ⑤

W: Justin, I need to ask you a favor.
M: Sure, Mom. What is it?
W: Ray tells me you won't let him read your new comic books.
M: Yes, because they're mine. I bought them with the money I earned by babysitting.
W: I understand. And I'm proud of you for working so hard.
M: Thanks, Mom. But you know, he doesn't let me play with his model airplanes.
W: How old are you now, Justin?
M: I'm twelve. [*Pause*] I guess you're saying I should grow up.
W: That's right. Your brother is still a child, but you're nearly a teenager.
M: I guess you're right. I suppose it's okay if he's careful with them.
W: I'll talk with him and make sure he's very careful.
M: Okay, Mom. I'm sorry I acted like a little kid.

여: Justin, 부탁이 하나 있단다.
남: 네, 엄마. 그게 뭔데요?
여: Ray가 그러는데 네가 네 새 만화책을 그 애가 못 읽게 한다더구나.
남: 네, 그건 제 거잖아요. 제가 아이를 봐주고 번 돈으로 샀단 말이에요.
여: 알고 있단다. 그리고 난 네가 그렇게 열심히 일하는 게 자랑스럽단다.
남: 고마워요, 엄마. 하지만 엄마도 아시다시피, 그 애는 자기 모형 비행기를 제가 갖고 놀지 못하게 하잖아요.
여: 너 지금 몇 살이니, Justin?
남: 열두 살이요. [*잠시 후*] 저보고 철이 들어야 한다고 말씀하시려는 거죠.
여: 맞아. 네 동생은 아직 어린이지만, 넌 거의 십 대잖니.
남: 엄마 말씀이 맞는 것 같아요. 그 애가 그 책들을 조심히 다룬다면 괜찮을 것 같아요.
여: 내가 그 애에게 말해서 각별히 주의하게 하마.
남: 알겠어요, 엄마. 어린애처럼 행동해서 죄송해요.

어휘 | ask a favor 부탁하다 comic book 만화책 babysit 아기를 봐주다 model airplane 모형 비행기 grow up 성장하다; *철이 들다 teenager 십 대(나이가 13~19세인 사람)

문제해설 | 여자는 남자의 동생에게 만화책을 빌려주라고 남자에게 부탁했다.

5 정답 ⑤

M: So, did you reserve our hotel rooms for Miami?
W: Yes, I did. We'll be right across the hall from each other.
M: Great. How much were they?
W: Well, your room was $60 per night, and mine was $15 more.
M: What do you mean? Why was your room more expensive than mine?
W: Well, you said you didn't need a view, right?
M: Sure. I don't plan to spend a lot of time in my room.
W: Well, I want to see the ocean when I wake up. So I

paid extra for a room with a view.
M: I see. And you already paid for both rooms, right?
W: Yes. Two rooms for two nights each. You can pay me back later.
M: Great. I can't wait to go.

남: 그나저나, 마이애미에서 우리가 묵을 호텔 방을 예약했나요?
여: 네, 했어요. 우린 복도를 사이에 두고 서로 마주 보고 묵을 거예요.
남: 잘됐네요. 방값은 얼마던가요?
여: 음, 당신 방은 하룻밤에 60달러였고, 제 방은 15달러 더 비쌌어요.
남: 무슨 말이에요? 왜 당신 방이 제 방보다 더 비싼 거죠?
여: 음, 당신은 전망이 있는 방은 필요 없다고 했잖아요, 맞죠?
남: 물론이에요. 전 방에서 많은 시간을 보내진 않을 계획이에요.
여: 음, 전 잠에서 깼을 때 바다가 보였으면 좋겠어요. 그래서 전망이 좋은 방으로 해서 추가 요금을 냈어요.
남: 그랬군요. 그럼 이미 두 방에 대한 요금을 지불한 거죠, 그렇죠?
여: 네. 방 두 개 각각 2박으로요. 요금은 나중에 주시면 돼요.
남: 좋아요. 빨리 가고 싶네요.

어휘 | reserve 예약하다 view 경치, 전망 extra 추가로; *추가 요금 can't wait to-v 빨리 …하고 싶다

문제해설 | 여자는 호텔 방 두 개를 각각 이틀씩 예약했는데, 방 하나는 하룻밤에 60달러이고 다른 하나는 하룻밤에 15달러가 더 비싼 75달러이다. 따라서 여자가 지불한 금액은 270달러($\$60\times2+\$75\times2$)이다.

6 정답 ③

W: What are you doing, Peter?
M: I'm arranging my schedule for next semester. We need to sign up for classes by this week.
W: Oh, right. I need to arrange my schedule, too.
M: Will you take Dr. Campbell's class on Mondays?
W: Introduction to Design? Well... It is hard for me to attend morning classes.
M: It's a requirement for several classes we need next year, Natasha!
W: Oh, that completely slipped my mind.
M: Don't worry. There is an evening class on Wednesdays, too.
W: Really? Then I want to sign up for that class. How many credits is it worth?
M: It's worth three credits. And instead of a midterm, we can hand in a report.
W: Wow, it sounds great. Let's take it together on Wednesdays.

여: 뭐 하고 있니, Peter?
남: 다음 학기 시간표를 짜고 있어. 우리 이번 주말까지 수강 신청을 해야 하잖아.
여: 아, 맞아. 나도 시간표를 짜야 해.
남: 너 월요일에 있는 Campbell 박사님의 수업을 들을 거니?
여: 디자인 개론? 음… 난 아침 수업은 듣기가 힘들어.
남: 그건 우리가 내년에 들어야 할 몇몇 과목을 위한 필수 조건이야, Natasha!
여: 아, 그걸 완전히 잊고 있었어.
남: 걱정하지 마. 수요일 저녁 수업도 있어.
여: 정말? 그럼 그 수업을 신청하고 싶어. 그건 몇 학점짜리 수업이야?
남: 3학점. 그리고 중간고사 대신에 보고서를 제출해도 돼.
여: 와, 그거 좋네. 수요일에 그걸 함께 듣자.

어휘 | arrange 계획하다 attend 참석하다 requirement 필수 조건 slip one's mind 깜빡 잊다 credit 학점

문제해설 | 신청 기한은 이번 주말까지, 담당 교수는 Campbell 박사님이며, 수요일 저녁 3학점짜리 수업이라고 했다. 하지만 최대 수강 인원에 대한 언급은 하지 않았다.

7 정답 ④

W: Attention runners! Mark your calendars for the upcoming Hamarton Marathon on Saturday, May 30, at 8:30 a.m. Get set for three exciting races: a 10K, half marathon, and full marathon. The registration fee is $20 and includes a race shirt customized with your ID number from the race. Every runner must be at least 16 years old. Each race will begin and end at Hamarton City Park. And after the awards ceremony, stick around for live music in Hamarton City Square, featuring The Running Men. So if you want to join a race, register online at hamartonmarathon.com, where you can also download course maps, view the event schedule, and more! See you at the finish line!

여: (마라톤) 주자 여러분 주목해 주세요! 다가오는 5월 30일 토요일 오전 8시 30분에 있을 Hamarton 마라톤 대회를 달력에 표시하세요. 10킬로미터, 하프 마라톤, 그리고 풀 마라톤, 이렇게 세 개의 신나는 경주를 위해 준비하세요. 등록비는 20달러이고, 여기에는 경주를 위한 ID 번호로 맞춤 제작된 대회 티셔츠가 포함됩니다. 모든 주자는 16세 이상이어야 합니다. 각 경주는 Hamarton City 공원에서 시작하고 끝나게 됩니다. 그리고 시상식 후에는, Hamarton 시 광장에서 The Running Men이 출연하는 라이브 음악이 있으니 가지 마시고 머물러 주세요. 만약 경주에 참여하고 싶으시면, hamartonmarathon.com으로 온라인에서 등록하시면 되는데, 이 사이트에서 여러분은 코스 지도를 내려받고, 행사 스케줄 등도 보실 수 있습니다! 결승선에서 봅시다!

어휘 | get set for …을 위한 준비를 갖추다 registration fee 등록비

customized 맞춤 제작한 awards ceremony 시상식 stick around 가지 않고 있다, 머무르다 feature 출연시키다

문제해설 | ④ 세 가지 경주 모두 Hamarton City 공원에서 시작하여 끝난다고 했다.

8 정답 ④

W: Many good things happened to Susan this month, starting with her dad's promotion. Then, last week, she found out that she got a perfect score on her physics exam. Plus, her fitness plan has really paid off; she has lost eight kilograms. Several people, including Mike, the cutest guy in Susan's classes, noticed that she looks much happier. In fact, Susan went on a fun date last weekend with Mike. She knows she should be happy about all these things, but she's worried her happiness won't last. She remembers her grandfather saying, "Life is like a box of chocolates. If you eat all the sweets first, you have to eat all the bitters next." So Susan talks to her mother about her worries. In this situation, what is Susan's mother most likely to say to Susan?

Susan's mother: Susan, (the best is yet to come. Just enjoy what you have now.)

여: 아버지의 승진부터 시작해서, 이번 달에 Susan에게 좋은 일이 많이 생겼다. 그러고 나서, 지난주에 그녀는 물리 시험에서 만점을 받은 것을 알았다. 게다가, 그녀의 운동 계획은 정말 성과가 있었는데, 그녀는 8kg을 감량했다. Susan의 반에서 가장 귀여운 남학생인 Mike를 포함해서 여러 사람들이 그녀가 훨씬 더 행복해 보인다는 것을 알아챘다. 사실, Susan은 Mike와 지난 주말에 재미있는 데이트를 했다. 그녀는 이런 모든 일들에 행복해해야 한다는 것을 알지만, 자신의 행복이 지속되지 않을까 봐 걱정이다. 그녀는 할아버지가 '인생은 초콜릿 상자와 같단다. 먼저 단 것을 모두 먹으면, 다음에는 계속 쓴 것만을 먹어야 한단다.'라고 말씀하신 것을 기억한다. 그래서 Susan은 엄마에게 그녀의 걱정에 관해 이야기한다. 이런 상황에서, Susan의 어머니가 Susan에게 할 말로 가장 적절한 것은 무엇인가?

Susan의 어머니: Susan, 최고의 순간은 아직 오지 않았어. 그냥 현재 네가 가진 걸 누리렴.

어휘 | promotion 승진 physics 물리학 fitness 건강, 운동 pay off 성과를 내다 notice 눈치채다 bitter 맛이 쓴 |문제| be yet to-v 아직 …하지 않고 있다

문제해설 | Susan이 할아버지의 말씀대로 행복한 상황이 곧 끝나버릴까 봐 걱정하고 있으므로 어머니가 할 말로 ④번이 가장 적절하다.

① 조심하지 않으면, 넌 모든 것을 잃을지도 모른단다.
② 실망하지 않도록 최악의 상황을 대비하렴.
③ 그건 피할 수 없어. 그 문제는 그냥 내버려 둬.
⑤ 네 모든 노력이 성과를 거두지 못한 건 유감이야. 다음번에는 더 잘 할 거야.

9 정답 ③ 10 정답 ①

M: Good morning, everyone. Thank you for attending today's leadership workshop. We all have experience speaking in front of coworkers. But to be a truly effective leader, you must first be an effective communicator. Whenever you speak in front of a group, have a clear message in mind. That means that you should have specific information that you want to discuss, and you should not stray from that topic. Also, if you have time, preparing visual aids such as pictures, graphs, or lists can be very beneficial. But don't display too much information at once. This could distract the audience and make it harder for them to understand your message. Finally, you should include the audience in your presentation by asking questions and letting them share their ideas. People will pay closer attention to what you are saying if they feel they are part of the conversation. So keep these tips in mind before making your next presentation.

남: 여러분 안녕하세요. 오늘의 리더십 워크숍에 참석해 주셔서 감사합니다. 우리는 모두 동료들 앞에서 발표해 본 경험이 있습니다. 그러나 진정 유능한 리더가 되기 위해서는 당신은 먼저 유능한 의사 전달자가 되어야 합니다. 당신이 여러 사람들 앞에서 이야기할 때마다, 명확한 메시지를 생각하십시오. 그 말인즉 당신은 논의하고자 하는 구체적인 정보를 갖고 있어야 하고, 그 주제에서 벗어나면 안 된다는 말입니다. 또한, 여유가 있다면 그림, 도표나 목록과 같은 시각 자료를 준비하는 것이 매우 이로울 수 있습니다. 하지만 너무 많은 정보를 한 번에 보여주진 마세요. 이는 청중을 방해할 수 있고 당신의 메시지를 이해하기 어렵게 만들 수 있습니다. 마지막으로, 당신은 질문을 하고 청중이 자기 생각을 공유하게 함으로써 그들을 당신의 발표에 참여시켜야 합니다. 사람들은 그들이 대화의 일부라고 느끼면 당신이 말하는 것에 더 관심을 기울이게 될 것입니다. 그러니 당신이 다음에 발표를 하기 전에 이 조언들을 유념하십시오.

어휘 | coworker 동료 effective 효과적인; *유능한 communicator 의사를 전달하는 사람 specific 구체적인 stray 벗어나다, 옆길로 새다 visual aid 시각 자료 beneficial 이로운 display 보이다, 드러내다 distract 방해하다 audience 청중, 관중 share 공유하다 pay closer attention to …에 더 관심을 기울이다 keep ... in mind …을 명심하다[유념하다] |문제| capture 잡다, 사로잡다 stick to …에 달라붙다; …을 고수하다; *…에 집중하다

문제해설 | 9. 남자는 발표 시 메시지를 효과적으로 전달하는 방법을 소개하고 있다.

① 직장에서의 리더십 유형
② 사람들의 주의를 끄는 방법

③ 집단에게 효과적으로 의사전달을 하는 방법
④ 시각 정보를 보여주는 최상의 방법
⑤ 발표하는 동안 저지르는 흔한 실수
10. 남자는 ① 몸짓 언어 사용하기에 대해서는 언급하지 않았다.
② 명확한 메시지 전달하기 ③ 주제에 집중하기
④ 시각 자료 보여주기 ⑤ 질문하기

MEMO

MEMO